Portsmouth-Built
Submarines of the
Portsmouth Naval Shipyard

Published in cooperation with the
Portsmouth Submarine
Memorial Association

Portsmouth-Built
Submarines of the
Portsmouth Naval Shipyard
by
Richard E. Winslow III

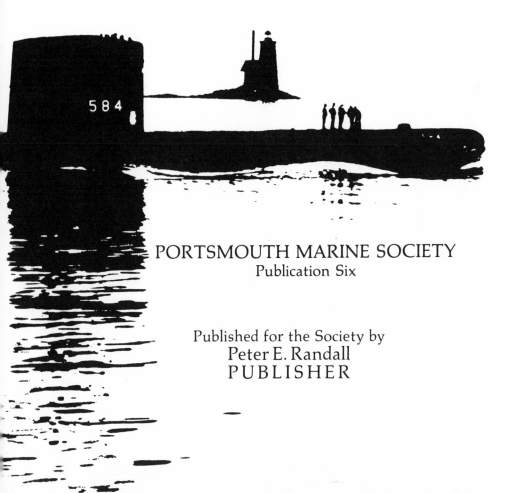

PORTSMOUTH MARINE SOCIETY
Publication Six

Published for the Society by
Peter E. Randall
PUBLISHER

© 1985 by the Portsmouth Marine Society
Paper edition published June 2000

Printed in the United States of America
Designed and Produced by Peter E. Randall
    Box 4726,Portsmouth, NH 03802

Cover: The colorful emblems are official launching party tags issued to naval personnel and civilian employees authorized to launch boats from the shipways. Perhaps as few as 300 were issued during wartime launches. Joseph P Copley Collection.

Chapter opening art: logo, courtesy Portsmouth Naval Shipyard.

Frontispiece: Seadragon on sea trials in October 1959 passing Whale's Back Light in Portsmouth's outer harbor. UNH.

A publication of
  The Portsmouth Marine Society
  Box 147, Portsmouth, NH 03802

Winslow, Richard Elliott, 1934
    Portsmouth-Built: Submarines of the Portsmouth Naval
Shipyard.
    (Publication / Portsmouth Marine Society; 6)
    Bibliography: p.
    Includes index.
    1. Submarine boats - New Hampshire -Portsmouth - History.
    2. Shipbuilding - New Hampshire - Portsmouth - History.
    3. Portsmouth (N.H.) -History, Naval. I. Title. II. Series:
    Publication (Portsmouth Marine Society); 6.
    V858-W56 1985 623.8'257'097426 84-18127
ISBN 0-915819-28-7

Contents

For Philip and Katherine Young with thoughts of exhilarating research, the joy of writing, Amherst, the United States Navy, haddock chowder, New England lakes and streams, fishing in coves and pools, blueberries, pine grove campsites and a fresh approach to seemingly old and already solved things.

Jenkin's Gut was once a natural channel between two Navy Yard islands. In 1904 site became Dry Dock #2. UNH.

Preface

FOR MORE THAN 350 years, from the days of oak and hemp and wind to those of nuclear power, Portsmouth has meant shipbuilding. Indeed, the term "Portsmouth-built" has come to signify superior quality to ship designers and engineers the world over. The Portsmouth Naval Shipyard's most momentous era occurred between 1914 and 1971, when the Shipyard built 134 submarines. The proud tradition of Portsmouth-built submarines is the subject of this book.[1]

This study began at Thomas C. Wilson's well-stocked private library in Portsmouth, New Hampshire, which I visited on many occasions. Wilson, the founder of the Piscataqua History Club and an authority on the Russo-Japanese Peace Convention of 1905, was a great collector of Portsmouth lore.

"Here is a collection of submarine photographs," he once said, opening up one of his many scrapbooks and photo albums. "A history of Portsmouth subs is needed, and such a book would be well received in this community." Wilson hoped to write such a book, as he commented twenty years ago, but he did not do so. He died in 1980, at the age of 73. During the last months of his life, Wilson donated his vast collection to the Portsmouth Athenaeum, which has preserved this valuable legacy.[2]

In one sense, I have been researching this book all my life. As the son of a career naval officer, I spent my early years at submarine bases at Pearl Harbor, New London, and Portsmouth. Living around the sons and daughters of many World War II submarine skippers, I saw these officers when they would drop off their children at the base pool or appear at a Navy picnic in aloha shirts. Such memories have returned during the writing of this book.

Living in the Portsmouth area for some years has also helped. Around coastal New Hampshire, southern Maine, and northeastern Massachusetts, the Shipyard has a reputation as an excellent place to work. Many employees spend their entire careers here, continuing the tradition as the second, third, or even the fourth generation of their families in Shipyard service. Many submariners who retire from the navy begin a second career at the Shipyard. Learning from many of these people has influenced my conclusions.

The American novelist Thomas Wolfe once wrote, "It'd take a guy a lifetime to know Brooklyn t'roo and t'roo. An' even den, yuh wouldn't know it all." The same is true of the Shipyard. Any one person can know or research only a fraction of the stories of the 134 Portsmouth-built submarines. The thousands who have worked at the Shipyard and the thousands more who have served aboard Portsmouth subs could fill many volumes with their recollections. This book can only highlight the Shipyard's history.[3]

This study focuses on the fifty-seven-year period between the 1914 government contract to build the *L-8* and the 1971 commissioning of the *Sand Lance*, the last Portsmouth-built sub. This era comprises two world wars, the advent of the nuclear age, and the shifting moods of American politics. Each greatly affected the Shipyard.

I have selected about a dozen submarines with extraordinary histories for extended development. Concentrating on the major points of selected ships and events will avoid needless duplication. The sagas of the *Squalus, Thresher, Seadragon, Sea Wolf, Bowfin,* and *Batfish* have already appeared as full-length books.

"A sub is just a piece of iron without the men behind it," Shipyarder John Shea told me. I readily concur. In addition to the history of the Shipyard and its subs, this book also tells the story of the people who worked on and lived in these pieces of iron.[4]

The interviews I conducted with dozens of people who actually lived through these events added a dimension which the printed or handwritten pages may fail to convey. All who talked to me displayed pride in their relationship to the U. S. Navy or to the Shipyard. This attitude is contagious.

As a whole, the history of the Shipyard's 134 submarines represents an exciting era of achievement and innovation. Unquestionably, Portsmouth-built submarines have written one of the most positive pages of accomplishment in the annals of the United States Navy.

"Stand by for diving!" a submarine skipper orders. Klaxons shriek out, preparatory to the descent. These pages offer in part a cumulative half-century log of the voyages of the Portsmouth-built boats.

Acknowledgments

SUBMARINES are tremendously complicated machines," and "No one person builds a sub. One is only part of a team." These were two of many comments I heard while gathering materials for this study. After vicariously donning shipwright's clothes and protective gear, I quickly realized that writing a book about submarines is similarly a complicated endeavor, requiring the time and effort of many people. Both processes involve scale-model outline projections, design changes, experimentation with new parts, sea trials, shakedown cruises, and the elimination of "bugs" to commission the best boat and to produce the best book. With such a helpful crew and after two years of research and writing construction, I am now launching this book.

I thank, first of all, Captain Joseph F. Yurso, USN, Shipyard Commander of the Portsmouth Naval Shipyard, who granted access to materials inside the Shipyard. Commander James V. Connor, USN, Administrative Officer; Robert Johnston and John Wheeler, Public Affairs Specialists; Ruth Dow, *Periscope* Editor and Margery Jennings, Editorial Clerk; Josephine Rafferty, Shipyard Librarian and Constance Barberi, Security Clerk, also aided my efforts.

I have learned much from the works of submarine writers John D. Alden, Clay Blair, Jr., and Norman Polmar, who have explored these ocean depths before me.

Many librarians, archivists and photographers have cheerfully responded to my numerous requests. I have visited every pertinent library and depository — public, academic, federal, state and private — along coastal New England as far north as Bath, Maine, south to Boston and west to Concord, New Hampshire.

During a week of research at the Submarine Force Library and

Museum, Naval Submarine Base, Groton, Connecticut, Director Gary R. Moulton and his staff made vast resources available to me.

At his Lowell, Massachusetts home, Chester L. Somers shared his collection of submarine materials, a collection requiring twenty years to gather and an entire room to house. Somers plans eventually to donate this treasure to the Nimitz Library, United States Naval Academy, Annapolis, Maryland.

I thank those who granted me interviews for talking at length about their experiences aboard submarines and at the Shipyard. Many also lent scrapbooks, newspaper clippings, and documents relating to their careers for incorporation into this text. I hope I have faithfully presented their eyewitness accounts of historic events.

Many people who helped with my earlier Portsmouth Marine Society publication, *The Piscataqua Gundalow: Workhorse for a Tidal Basin Empire*, came forward a second time to assist the research, writing, revisions and photography. I again extend my gratitude to Peter E. Randall, Fred D. Crawford, Nancy A. Hunt, and to Joseph G. Sawtelle, President, and Joseph P. Copley, Secretary, of the Portsmouth Marine Society. Michael Pagano also provided important material.

Chester L. Wolford of North East, Pennsylvania, helped straighten out my early drafts. At the offices of the *Portsmouth Herald*, librarian Christine Ross facilitated my research with the newspaper's microfilm reels of back issues. Larry Cody of the Portsmouth Naval Shipyard handled many details concerning reproduction of Shipyard photographs.

From University and other collections John Bardwell, Director of Media Services, University of New Hampshire, Durham, provided many of the excellent photo reproductions which grace these pages.

Responding to my inquiries, two people went out of their way to assemble thick packets of information. Virginia Conn, Public Affairs Officer of the David W. Taylor Naval Ship Research and Development Center, Bethesda, Maryland, searched the archives of that institution and sent photocopies of pertinent articles and documents. In a similar effort, Richard T. Speer, Naval Historical Center, Washington, D.C., reviewed his files for unpublished materials.

Richard E. Winslow, Jr., Arthur H. Castelazo, Philip Hoyt, Eugene Allmendinger, Russell Van Billiard and Joseph P. Copley, all Shipyard veterans, read the manuscript for accuracy.

Finally I thank the officers, members and friends of the Portsmouth Marine Society and the Portsmouth Submarine Memorial Association who envisioned the need for this book and arranged for the return of the *USS Albacore* to the banks of the Piscataqua.

Little Harbor
Rye, New Hampshire
Independence Day, 1984.

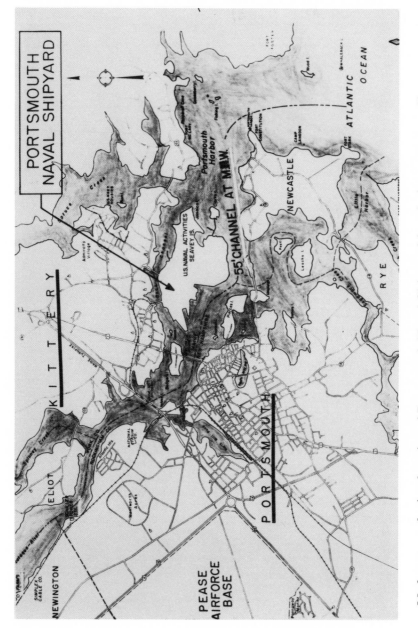

Modern map depicts location of Portsmouth Naval Shipyard in relation to surrounding Portsmouth-Kittery area. Note Yard is protected by outer harbor defenses while still adjacent to open sea. UNH.

I Building the First Portsmouth Subs, 1914-1918

Before Submarines

BY 1914, when Secretary of the Navy Josephus Daniels awarded the Portsmouth Navy Yard a government contract to build a submarine, there had long been an evolving tradition of shipbuilding in the Piscataqua area. Since the official founding of the Yard in 1800, more than a century of work and experience had established a first-rate facility equipped to meet the complex demands of submarine construction. A new age of the Yard had arrived. American submarines had been built in private yards since 1900; the Portsmouth Navy Yard was chosen to construct the first sub in a government facility.

The Yard's legacy dated from 1603, when Martin Pring, an Englishman, sailed up the Piscataqua River. In 1622, Sir Ferdinando Gorges and John Mason received much of present-day Maine and New Hampshire as a land grant from England. Settlement began the following year. In 1629 the two landowners divided their holdings at the Piscataqua River, Mason keeping New Hampshire and Gorges retaining Maine.[1]

Separated from the mainland by the Back Channel, the two islands which eventually became the site of the Yard were originally called Puddington's Islands. Both were on the Maine side. John Puddington, the original owner, dried fish and repaired boats there in the 1640s. Ownership of the islands changed hands through the years. Later known as Fernald's Island and Seavey's Island, they were separated by a narrow channel, Jenkin's Gut, which ran between them. In the early 1900s, when Jenkin's Gut was filled in, the two islands became the single island which exists today.

Blessed by an abundance of raw materials, the early colonists in the Piscataqua region engaged in shipbuilding. Langdon's (later Badger's) Island, another Maine island upstream and opposite Portsmouth,

New Hampshire, became the favored site of the early shipwrights. In 1690 the British government built the *Falkland*, a fifty-four gun frigate of the Royal Navy, which was the first authenticated warship built in the Piscataqua area.

During the American Revolution, Badger's Island remained the headquarters for shipbuilding as its location fell within Portsmouth's harbor defenses. John Langdon, the patriot leader, owned Badger's Island at this time. When the war began, he immediately offered its use for the American war effort. The *America* and the *Ranger* among others were built there. The shipyards on the island were less active after the war's end in 1783; although they were never owned or designated as such by the new government, they served as America's unofficial navy yard until 1800.

In 1798 Benjamin Stoddard, the secretary of the navy, sought to establish a government yard on the eastern seacoast. Basing his choice on a report prepared by Joshua Humphries, the chief naval constructor, Stoddard recommended the purchase of Fernald's Island as the site for a navy yard. Owner John Langdon wanted $25,000 for Langdon's Island, which consisted of about eighteen to twenty acres. Sidestepping Langdon's stubbornness, Stoddard paid $5500 for the fifty-eight acres of Fernald's Island. The date of acquisition was June 12, 1800, marking the Yard's official beginning. Even at this lower price, the American government could not avoid the machinations of land speculators; the island had turned over twice since 1794 for quick profit.

Fernald's Island quickly became known as Navy Yard Island. A two-story dwelling, later moved to higher ground, became the commandant's quarters. Until 1812 the Yard was little more than a few sheds and workshops, together with a marine barracks.

Although the Yard was actually across the Piscataqua on the Maine side, it was known from its inception as the Portsmouth Navy Yard. Official mail sent to this fledgling yard was addressed to the Portsmouth Navy Yard, Portsmouth, New Hampshire, the location of the nearest post office. Maine was then a district of Massachusetts under whose jurisdiction Navy Yard Island belonged, and the village of Kittery had no postal service. The name and its address stuck.

The War of 1812 generated much activity at the Yard with the repairing of the *Wasp, Rattlesnake* and *Enterprise*. In 1815 the first ship of the new Yard, the *Washington*, a seventy-four-gun-ship-of-the-line, was launched. After the war ended in 1814, the Yard slumped in a typical boom-and-bust cycle, to be often repeated in the future.

Post-war decline brought forth rumors that the Yard was going to be closed. A nine-page petition, signed by Portsmouth's most prominent citizens, opposed this action. With John Langdon's signature heading the list, the petition, directed to Secretary of the Navy Benjamin W. Crowninshield in March 1816, summarizes the Yard's accomplishments and potential:

> ... recent reports say that the Navy Bureau approbate the abolition of the Navy Yard at this place ... permit us to state such facts ...
>
> This harbour combines advantages superior to any other in the Union. Its vicinity to the ocean, the great depth of water (sufficient at low tides for first-rate ships)—ever free from ice and its natural situation so favorable that at no great expence, it may be rendered almost impregnable ...
>
> The Navy Yard is on an Island containing about fifty Acres, the property of the United States. It is half a mile from town, and one and a half from the ocean. The improvements are, two spacious Timber docks, Mast house, Sail loft, Store, Blacksmiths shop, Gunners store, Boatswain's Store, Mould loft, Barracks, Commanders house, Officers quarters, Office, Hospital, Magazine, and permanent slip and ways, covered by a substantial ship house, sufficiently large to build within a 100 Gun Ship, also a wharf at which a ship of the line can lay with every thing on board, get under way and have from six to ten fathoms to sea at low water. The Country bordering on this river and Winnipisiokee Lake, furnishes excellent White oak, Norway pine, Spruce and every species of Timber that grows in New England. Mechanics in all branches of ship building, can be commanded in any number and at any time. The Washington bears incontestible evidence of their excellent workmanship, and the records of the Accountants Office will prove at much less wages than in any part of the United States ...

After citing many economic and military advantages of the Portsmouth facility compared to those at Boston and at Norfolk, these New Hampshire businessmen concluded:

> We have too much confidence in the wisdom and justice of our rulers to believe they will give up this Yard without particular enquiry into the advantages it possesses, which we think will furnish such facts as will ensure their fostering care instead of abandoning so valuable an establishment.[2]

Whether or not Crowninshield responded to this petition is not known. However, the alarm of the Piscataqua region was stilled as the Yard was not closed. To insure its future development, representatives and senators from New Hampshire (and shortly thereafter, those from

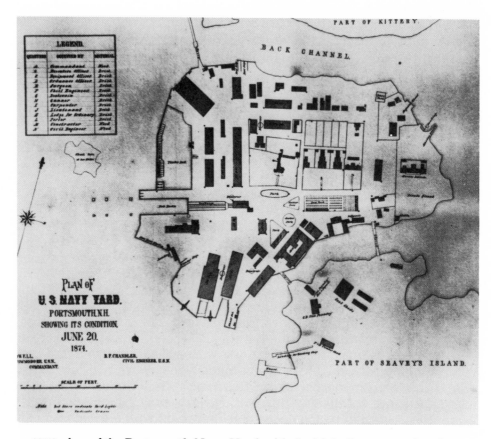

1874 plan of the Portsmouth Navy Yard with Jenkin's Gut separating the two islands. Channel would later be filled in to form site of Dry Dock #2. UNH.

the state of Maine) sent to Washington staunchly promoted the Yard's interests. This kind of support duly became expected of these delegations regardless of party affiliation. The First Congressional District of New Hampshire was known as, and remains, "the Navy Yard District."

Maine entered the Union in 1820. The following year Maine ceded any right to jurisdiction held over Navy Yard Island, which was legally a federal reservation. The next forty years of peace saw the erection of many new buildings and facilities. In 1838 a shiphouse was begun, and the structure was extended in 1854 to accommodate the building of the steam frigate *Franklin*. This building then became known as the Franklin Shiphouse, one of the largest buildings of its kind in the United States.

During these years, one tradition started at the Yard regarding an eccentric character. Jacob Mull was a sailing master until 1831 and then

*Flanked on either side by forest of ship masts, Franklin Shiphouse domi-
nates Navy Yard waterfront in 1883. SB.*

a Yard employee from 1833-1847. He died in 1851. In 1840, after losing a
bet of a glass of rum to Charley McIntire, another Yard worker, Mull
became the subject of a humorous (and premature) epitaph, and McIntire's lines became part of the Yard's lore, passed from one generation to
another.

> Here lies the rigging, spars, and hull
> Of Sailing Master Jacob Mull.
> Where he has gone, no one can tell,
> But all suppose he has gone to hell.
> And if he cannot curse and swear
> He'll take no peace or comfort there.[3]

The Civil War triggered a great shipbuilding boom from 1861 to
1865. Twenty-six ships slid down the ways. The most famous was the
Kearsarge, a steam sloop with nine guns launched in 1861. She sank the
Confederate raider *Alabama* off the coast of France in 1864. To meet the
sudden increase in construction and repair, the American government
purchased Seavey's Island (about 105 acres). In 1866, the deal was
finally closed for $105,000, with twenty-eight partial owners.

After the end of the war, the Yard lapsed into a peacetime lull and
reduced its work force. In 1876 Congress actually debated the question of

closing the Yard. An appointed board looked into the matter, made recommendations, and advised against such action.

To protect the Yard, during this long period of peace, two New Hampshire politicians came to the fore in Washington. Frank Jones, Portsmouth's wealthy capitalist, was the representative from the Navy Yard District from 1875 to 1879. He was assigned to the Committee of Naval Affairs and worked diligently to promote his district's interests. He introduced appropriate bills in Congress and fought for their passage. In 1877, for example, Jones wanted to install a Dafoll trumpet signal on Whale's Back Light, an island at the entrance to Portsmouth Harbor. A year later Congress appropriated $15,000 for the signal and repairs to the lighthouse.

During the administration of President Chester A. Arthur (1881-1885), William E. Chandler of Concord served as secretary of the navy. Nicknamed the "stormy petrel" of New Hampshire politics, Chandler did not forget his native state. He and Arthur visited the Yard in 1882. Chandler advised Congress in 1883 that the Yard should be retained if for no other reason than as a supply station and arsenal.[4]

Although few vessels were built, the Yard now became a major repair facility for existing ships. Throughout this time Yard employees from Portsmouth, by far the largest contingent, commuted to work from the Navy Yard Landing at the foot of Daniel Street. Various Navy Yard ferry boats carried them across the Piscataqua. Among the well-known private ferries of that era were *Skedaddle*, *Joe Hooker* and *Ku-Klux*. Other workers used wherries, dories, whaleboats, yawls, seine boats and even condemned government boats.

As the Yard entered the twentieth century, modernization became more evident with each passing day. During the 1890s, New Hampshire senators William E. Chandler and Jacob H. Gallinger introduced bills for a modern dry dock for the Yard. Congress finally authorized its construction. The contract was awarded to John Pierce of New York for over $1 million in 1899. The site of this huge project was the channel of Jenkin's Gut between Navy Yard and Seavey's Islands. Filling the rest of the channel with excavated material made the two islands into one. The dry dock was completed in 1904. During the summer of 1905, Henderson's Point, extending off Seavey's Island and long a hindrance to navigation on the Piscataqua, was blasted away.[5]

An even more significant event that year brought the attention of the world to the Portsmouth Navy Yard. At the invitation of President Theodore Roosevelt the plenipotentiaries of the empires of Russia and Japan arrived at the Yard to negotiate the end of the Russo-Japanese War. Holding their sessions throughout the summer on the second floor of the new Supply Building (now known as Building 86), the delegates signed the Treaty of Portsmouth on September 5, 1905, to end the war.

The establishment of a prison at the Yard followed a protracted sequence of events. During the Spanish-American War, a tent colony on Seavey's Island served as a detention camp for over 1600 Spanish prisoners of war. The prison ship, the *USS Southery*, came to the Yard in 1903 and was anchored at a pier in the Back Channel. Housing American naval prisoners on board, she remained in service as a prison ship until the 1920s. In 1906, a paper battle ensued between the Yard commandant and the Board of Health of Kittery over the Yard piggery administered by the *Southery*. The former pronounced it "sweet and clean," while the latter insisted the piggery was to be a menace to the health of Kittery. In 1908 the navy built a prison, ultimately called the U. S. Naval Disciplinary Command. The "Castle" or the "Rock" was an eight story building and one of thirty buildings eventually built for this penal colony.[6]

Expansion continued. In 1910 a contract was let for construction of a new 134-bed hospital on Seavey's Island. It was needed, in part, to handle a serious problem. Just the year before, a cocaine ring had been exposed. A number of inmates at the prison and on the *Southery* were discovered to be using the drug. The navy's campaign against the states of New Hampshire and Massachusetts, the pharmacists of Portsmouth and an individual smuggler was successful. New Hampshire established anti-cocaine laws, the pharmacists of Portsmouth combined in an agreement not to sell the drug to enlisted men, and the smuggler was apprehended and punished.[7]

This era of expansion was highlighted by a visit to the Yard on October 23, 1912, by President William H. Taft and Secretary of the Navy Philander C. Knox.

The present steel bridge to Kittery (Gate No. 1) was completed in 1914, and included a railroad bridge. The hospital and access road had been completed in 1913. From locomotive cranes to the building of new shops and the expansion of old ones, the Yard was both a self-sufficient community and a self-contained industrial operation by 1914. It was ready for any task it might be assigned.[8]

Evolution of the American Submarine

The growth of the Yard paralleled the increasing importance of the submarine's part in the fleet of the United States Navy. Submarines and their torpedoes were vilified by early contemporaries. "The history of the adoption of the torpedo as a recognized implement of warfare," wrote American journalist Allan D. Brown in 1882, "is not unlike that of

USS Holland *in dry dock. Note bulbous whale-like hull, later incorpo-rated in* Albacore, *for optimum undersea speed and maneuverability. PM.*

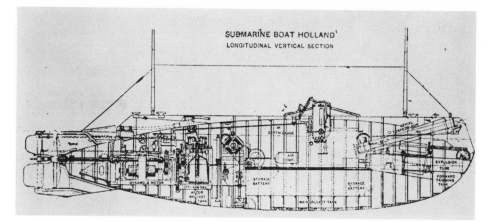

1896 plan of John Holland's submarine. Sold to the United States Navy, the boat was commissioned into service as Holland (SS-1) *in 1900. Navy's first submarine was 65 feet long and carried one torpedo tube in the center bow. PM.*

gunpowder or of shells. Each in its turn was met by the cry, 'Inhuman, barbarous, and unchivalrous.'" To landlocked civilians, a submarine suggested a frightening and sinister weapon, shrouded in oily mystery, threatening friend and foe alike. Yet naval inventors and militarists have long recognized its two advantages: surprise and the ability to withdraw with relative safety from counterattack.[9]

Submarines, or torpedo boats as they were first called, have always fired Yankee imagination. In 1776 David Bushnell built the *Turtle*, the first submersible used in combat. This submarine prototype attempted to break the British blockade of New York harbor. Later, in 1801, Robert Fulton built the *Nautilus*, which submerged using ballast tanks and a horizontal rudder, the world's first use of a diving plane. During the Civil War the Confederate *Hunley* became the first submarine to sink a ship in combat. In 1864 she attacked the Federal warship *Housatonic* off Charleston harbor. The explosion of the torpedo and the *Housatonic*'s magazine sank both ships. The Union in turn sponsored the construction of the metal submarine *Intelligent Whale* from 1864 to 1872. This experiment was finally abandoned.[10]

Three widely separated developments soon spurred interest in the submarine's potential. The novel *Twenty Thousand Leagues Under the Sea* (1870) by the French author Jules Verne, elicited international attention. The fictional *Nautilus*, commanded by Captain Nemo, revealed the submarine as a feasible combat weapon. In the 1860s various inventors, led by Robert Whitehead of England, perfected the first self-propelled torpedo. By 1870 the problem of propulsion was solved. The electric storage battery, long under development, became efficient enough to power a propeller shaft. The battery required no surface air and could operate below the surface as well as on it.

As European countries, especially France, encouraged private submarine builders for national defense, the United States Navy became interested in obtaining a sub for coastal defense. In 1888, after successfully competing against six other bidders, John P. Holland began work on the *Plunger*. The Navy Department and Congress frustrated his efforts by interfering in the financing and design. After wrangling over the *Plunger*'s design, Holland exclaimed, "What will the navy require next? That my boat should be able to climb a tree?"[11]

Finally Holland abandoned the unfinished *Plunger* and began another submarine at his own expense. This craft was launched in 1897 and was powered on the surface by a gasoline engine and, while submerged, by battery-fed electric motors. The navy purchased this submarine on April 11, 1900, now observed as the official birthday of the Submarine Service. On October 12, 1900, the navy commissioned the sub as *USS Holland*, or *SS-1* (as the first submarine, the *Holland* was assigned hull number SS-1, or Submarine-1, and later subs received hull numbers in order of their appearance).

The Electric Boat company, which had absorbed the major Holland patents by 1904, enjoyed a brief monopoly in submarine production. Known more familiarly as Electric Boat or EB, this company first built subs at a subsidiary plant, the Fore River Ship Building Corporation, in Quincy, Massachusetts.

Simon Lake, another pioneer inventor, entered the field with boats that were also powered by a gasoline engine and electric batteries. After competitive trials between Holland's *Octopus* and Simon Lake's experimental sub, the *Lake*, in 1907, the navy decided to accept subs built to the designs of both men. In 1908 Simon Lake founded his own organization, the Lake Torpedo Company on the Pequannock River, Bridgeport, Connecticut.[12]

An intense rivalry developed between the two companies. By 1912 both of these competitors abandoned gasoline engines, which made so much noise that they were called "rock crushers." The gasoline engine furthermore was subject to leaking gas vapor and exhaust fumes, resulting in many disastrous or near-disastrous explosions. The development and adoption of a "heavy oil" or diesel engine, named after its inventor, Rudolph Diesel of Germany, solved this problem.[13]

During these early days the submarine branch was hardly a sought-after billet in the Navy. Sailors on submarines did not receive increased pay because of hazardous duty. Submarines were nicknamed "pigboats," because before the use of periscopes they bobbed up and down like porpoises or "sea pigs" in order to attack.[14]

Many American naval officers were dissatisfied with the Electric Boat and Lake submarines. They felt the Navy Department should exercise some control over submarine design and construction in order to build subs equal or superior to those being built by foreign nations. The time was ripe for the United States Navy to break the monopoly of private companies by building submarines to their own specifications within their own navy yards.

Portsmouth's First Submarine Contract

Strong lobbying in Washington during early 1914 secured the first submarine contract for the Portsmouth Navy Yard, which then constructed the *L-8*, the first government-built submarine.

The national and state elections of 1912 saw the Democratic Party, led by Woodrow Wilson, taking advantage of the split between the regular

Republicans under President Taft and Theodore Roosevelt's "Bull Moose" Progressives. After Wilson's victory in which he carried New Hampshire by exactly fifty-six votes, the president-elect selected Josephus Daniels of North Carolina to be secretary of the navy. New Hampshire reflected this national tide. The state legislature sent a Democrat to the Senate, while voters of the First District elected a Democrat to the House. These two men joined Senator Jacob H. Gallinger in Washington. Gallinger, a Concord physician, had been a Republican fixture in the Senate since 1891. These men, regardless of party affiliation, were united on the issue of more work for the Yard.

A fortuitous situation was developing in Washington on this very question. Although he had been a newspaperman, and lacked experience in naval matters, Secretary of the Navy Daniels tackled his job with energy. He chose Franklin D. Roosevelt of New York as the assistant secretary of the navy. They began to institute many reforms in their department as well as touring the government yards in 1913.

The old method of having the Navy purchase submarines alarmed Daniels. "I thought that the only way to compel the two private submarine builders to make the best submarines at a reasonable price," Daniels wrote, "was to demonstrate that they could be built in a Navy Yard."[15]

In addition to Portsmouth, the government yards on the east coast at that time included Boston, New York, Philadelphia, Norfolk and Charleston.

The Lake Torpedo Company, headed by Simon Lake, was in financial straits. Knowing the difficulties of Lake's company, Electric Boat wanted an exclusive contract for building submarines for the navy.

"[I told him] we had enough contracts to keep both yards busy," Daniels said to the persistent Electric Boat lobbyist, "and . . . the company he represented had been almost as unsatisfactory as the Lake Torpedo Company." Despite continual pressure, Daniels refused to give Electric Boat a monopoly and in fact gave every encouragement to the Lake Torpedo Company to assure its survival.[16]

In Washington during the spring of 1913, Daniels became acquainted with William E. Chandler, the stalwart of New Hampshire Republicanism and former navy secretary, living there in retirement. The two men met at a party. "He had many anecdotes and incidents," Daniels wrote in his diary. Although differing politically, Chandler took a keen interest in Daniels' administration of the navy, and occasionally gave him public support.[17]

During the second session of the 63rd Congress in early 1914, the expectations of the Portsmouth Yard were dashed. "Only $10,000 allowed for this Navy Yard," exclaimed one headline in the *Portsmouth Herald*, the town's leading newspaper which was owned and edited by Fernando Wood Hartford.

Born in upstate New York in 1872, F. W. Hartford had long been a booster and promoter for his adopted city, ultimately becoming mayor of Portsmouth in 1920, and serving seven terms. Through his various political and business ventures, Hartford fell heir to the powerful role in Portsmouth's affairs once held by Frank Jones. Hartford also knew the Yard well and the political setting in which it worked. As a young man he had worked in the Yard for several years, becoming the chief bookkeeper there at the age of twenty-one. He also served as the chief clerk of the purchasing department and installed the Labor Board Employment bureau. Maintaining a lifelong interest in the navy and the Yard, broken only by his death in 1938, Hartford employed his newspaper to push for various projects. While naval appropriations bills were in committee, Hartford's editorials vigorously supported the Yard.

Learning that Daniels was about to award a $525,000 contract for the building of a submarine to one of the government yards, Hartford headlined his front page story for February 26 "HERE IS OUR CHANCE ON SHIPWORK." "It can be safely said that Portsmouth has the advantage over the other stations," the *Herald* declared, "as the building can be carried out with extreme secrecy and the work really done under lock and key in the Franklin shiphouse."[18]

On March 5, a meeting of the Portsmouth Board of Trade at the Rockingham Hotel in Portsmouth was well attended. President Thomas F. Flanagan of the Navy Yard Improvement Association spoke before the board and called attention to the Association's effort to bring the sub contract to Portsmouth. The Franklin Shiphouse, he maintained, was large enough to build three subs at the same time if necessary and at reduced cost. A delegation was formed, and Commander Laurence S. Adams, the industrial manager of the Yard, who was experienced with such construction, supplied the necessary data. On Monday, March 9, the lobbyists left for Washington, armed with satchels of papers, to present their case.

In Washington they met first with the New Hampshire congressional delegation, and undoubtedly with the Maine one as well, for a two state congressional bloc. Then the lobbyists met with Daniels and officials of his department to assure them that "there would be practically no outlay to get ready for this work" and that the "yard had the lowest overhead charges of any yard in the country." Daniels gave his approval.

"SUBMARINE TO BE BUILT HERE" headlined the *Herald*'s front page on Wednesday, March 11, 1914 and continued, "Good News for the Navy Yard Employees." A telegram was reprinted:

F. W. Hartford
Portsmouth, N.H.
        Navy Department has decided to
        build the submarine at Portsmouth.

                                                    G[19]

Gallinger, a veteran of many naval appropriation bill battles, had
won the day. The *Herald* claimed credit for its publicity and editorials,
but Hartford was not satisfied. "The next goal to be reached is the
making of this yard a battleship base," the paper commented, "and the
wiping out of the crime committed when the yard was robbed of its
battleship division."

On March 16, Daniels officially announced that submarine No. 48
(*L-8*) was to be constructed "by the Government" at Portsmouth. The sub
was to follow plans approved for submarines *L-5*, *L-6* and *L-7* built by the
Lake Torpedo Company, with the necessary plans furnished on June 29.[20]

Building the L-8

The awarding of the contract for the *L-8* signaled a new era for the Yard.
On June 30, 1914, the Statutes at Large passed by the second session of the
Sixty-third Congress included legislation against any further dealings
by the private yards. One provision established the Yard's bargaining
power in the future, declaring:

> Except where otherwise directed, the Secretary of the Navy
> shall build any of the vessels herein authorized in such navy yards
> as he may designate, should it reasonably appear that the persons,
> firms, or corporations, or the agents thereof, bidding for con-
> struction of any of said vessels have entered into any combination,
> agreement, or understanding the effect, object, or purpose of
> which is to deprive the Government of fair, open, and unrestricted
> competition in letting contracts for the construction of any of said
> vessels.[21]

With the outbreak of war in Europe during the summer of 1914,
the pace of the Yard quickened. The Franklin Shiphouse was selected as
the site for the sub's construction. Before the keel could be laid, much
preliminary work had to be done. Materials had to be ordered, received
and assembled. The molds of the sub's hull took time to prepare. During
December 1914 the hull division laid down the molds and began bending
the keel.[22]

The year of 1915 found 1150 employees at the Yard. On February
1, the Navy Department extended the industrial management system to

Navy Yard scene on May 2, 1914, just three months before outbreak of the
Great War. Admiral's flag flying from Building #13, administrative
headquaraters of the Yard. Men (left foreground) firing a salute with Mall
and Commandant's Quarters A in center background. KHNM.

the Portsmouth Navy Yard. This action separated strictly military
aspects from the industrial functions. The commandant, a line officer,
was in charge of the station and directed all military features. The
industrial manager, either a naval constructor or an experienced engineering officer, assumed direct charge of the industrial work. In building
the *L-8* and subsequent subs, Commander Laurence S. Adams, the
industrial manager, was free to devote his full energies to this purpose.[23]

Adams's responsibility was crucial to the United States government.
The *L-8* was one of eleven of the L-class submarines built by the Navy
during 1915-1917. These boats were 165-foot, 456-ton submarines with
diesel engines for surface propulsion. For armament, the L-boats had
four torpedo tubes in the bow. A single 3-inch, 23-caliber gun was
mounted on deck for attacking small surface ships. The speed of the
L-boats was relatively high, cruising at 14 knots on the surface with
diesels and operating on electric motors at 10½ knots while submerged.

Her crew complement was twenty-eight men.

Even before the keel laying, Adams received some welcome news. The navy decided to install a set of Edison batteries, developed by the famed inventor Thomas Edison. Rigorously tested by the Navy Department, the batteries eliminated a number of unsatisfactory features of lead batteries. The chief advantage was the avoidance of chlorine gas, one of the most dreaded risks inherent in submarine service. Secretary Daniels also arranged for Rear Admiral David W. Taylor, the highly talented chief constructor of the Navy and Chief of the Bureau of Construction and Repair, to visit Portsmouth. There Taylor and Adams would personally confer on the progress of the new submarine.[24]

At 10:00 A.M. on Wednesday, February 24, 1915, the keel was laid for the *L-8*. A multitude of military and civilian officials, as well as visitors, attended the ceremony. They witnessed Captain Thomas Snowden, the head of the military department and Adams drive the first rivet into the midship frame. The two men handled the riveting instruments "like veterans."[25]

Work continued on the *L-8* during 1915 and 1916. In the Franklin Shiphouse, the *L-8* shared space with other subs under construction as well as with a dirigible balloon.[26]

The Yard work force swelled to 5100 in 1917. Secretaries Daniels and Roosevelt visited the Yard periodically on their inspection tours. "The Riveter," an eleven-stanza poem by Rose Villar, published in *Life Buoy*, the Yard newspaper, captures the frenetic atmosphere during the building of the *L-8*: one verse reads:

> Rat-a-tat-rat-a-tat-rat-a-tat-tat,
>   You can hear it from morn till night.
> 'Tis the sound of the riveter's hammer; at work
>   For the cause of right against might.[27]

The *L-8* was ready for her machinery within eleven months but delay in its manufacture elsewhere postponed hope for her early launching. When the machinery finally arrived in March of 1917, the Yard workers installed it in record time. By building this submarine at Portsmouth the Navy Department saved $52,000 in patterns and plans as well as $80,000 more in general construction costs. The *L-8*, appropriated for $535,000, cost only $403,000.

The United States entered the Great War on April 6, 1917 as crews were in the last stages of readying the submarine for launching. That evening the Coast Guard stations and crews in the Portsmouth district automatically transfered from the Treasury Department to navy control. In the turmoil of these wartime developments, the launching was set for Monday, April 23, 1917.[28]

Launching of L-8 from Franklin Shiphouse in 1917. JPCC.

Launching of L-8, Portsmouth's first submarine, decorated with flags and pennants, on April 23, 1917. Deck gun would be mounted later. PA.

Heading the launching party of about one hundred people was the sub's sponsor, Miss Nancy Guill, granddaughter of Commandant Howard. At 1:00 P.M. the party marched to a reviewing stand. The program included selections by the navy band and a prayer by the base chaplain. At 1:20 P.M. Miss Guill smashed a bottle, (probably of champagne) against the pointed bow, exclaiming, "I christen thee *L-8*."

The sub slid down the ways from the Franklin Shiphouse into the waters of the Piscataqua to the cheers of the crowd. The *L-8* veered and brushed by the side of the old steam tug *Penacook*. The tug immediately sprang a leak and sailors stashed mattresses against the puncture while other crew members shifted the weight of the moveable gear and equipment to the undamaged side to raise the height of the waterline above the break. The tug survived to pull another day, and the launching of the *L-8* was now history.[29]

In an editorial the *Portsmouth Herald* noted the significance of the event:

> On Monday the men of the Portsmouth Navy Yard witnessed the actual advancement of our great naval station from a mere repair yard to a place among the construction yards in every sense of the word. The launching of the *L-8* marks a new epoch in the life of this community.[30]

"U.S.S. U-Boat L-8," a poem by R.J. Gilker, offered a tribute to the Yard's first submarine. One stanza reads:

> First U-boat built in a navy yard,
>   Of matchless strength and beauty great,
> To find an equal would be hard
>   Of the submarine L-Eight.[31]

Sea Trials and Completion of the L-8

Before commissioning, additional work had to be done on the *L-8*. On May 26, after two days spent testing the sub's equipment at berth in the Yard, the *L-8* sailed on her sea trials.[32]

Evers Burtner, a civilian from the Massachusetts Institute of Technology, conducted metal strain tests of the *L-8* during her submergence. The hulls of early American submarines were riveted; welding technology was not developed enough to assure hull strength. "I was in the boat off the Isles of Shoals to make measurements," Burtner said, "indicating the structure was strong enough for naval requirements." The *L-8* made a 200-foot dive in about 250 feet of water and lowered a 500-pound mushroom anchor. "The torpedo hatch over the battery compartment leaked salt water a little," Burtner said. "With further lowering, the gasket over the hatch sealed and there was no more leaking." For half an hour Burtner made measurements with his gauges to collect data for a written report. The riveted hull withstood the strain. Satisfied, Burtner gave his findings to the captain. The sub then blew her ballast tanks, weighed anchor, and returned to the Navy Yard.[33]

On August 30, 1917, the *L-8* was commissioned with Lieutenant James Parker, Jr., in command. The *L-8* began training operations along the east coast. Once she started to enter an Atlantic port (the name was not disclosed due to wartime security measures). Stopped by a patrol boat, the *L-8* did not respond to various signals relating to nationality and other information. Without the proper code and signal flags, the *L-8* risked being treated as any enemy vessel. The patrol boat then fired a shot, as the men on the deck of the *L-8* made a lively scurry and waved flags. There was a tense moment before she was finally recognized.[34]

On October 20, 1918, the *L-8*, part of the four-boat contingent of Submarine Division 6, left Charleston, South Carolina, for patrol duty in the Azores. The division arrived there on November 7. At sea when the war ended, the *L-8* reached Bermuda on November 13, and was then ordered to return to the United States. The *L-8* was Portsmouth's only sub involved in active combat service during the Great War.[35]

A Submarine Yard

The shift in emphasis in the Yard's role from a repair facility for surface ships to full-fledged submarine yard increased as the war continued. Four extra building ways for submarines, together with cranes, were constructed. During the period of 1917-1918, workers laid the keels of six more submarines. By the war's end, this trend could not be reversed. In 1923 the Navy Department, designating officially what had been a reality for years, named Portsmouth a submarine yard.

From fewer than 2000 employees before the war began, the Yard peaked at 5722 in October of 1918; about 1000 of the workers were women. During the war period some fifty-one new buildings were erected and additions put onto existing structures. On August 26, 1916, $6 million was appropriated for equipping the Yard for construction work. Women served in the navy in a new capacity. The first detachment of lady "yeomen" arrived in April 1917. These business school graduates joined the Naval Reserve as stenographers, replacing men required for duty in other branches of the service.

For the building of submarines, security and secrecy around the

One of many women who joined the Yard's work force during World War I, a carpenter swings a mallet. UNH.

Yard were absolutely essential. Large signs saying "BEWARE OF SPIES" were posted in the various shops. Below this warning, each sign read, "Don't talk about what you are doing or are going to," "The enemy has ears everywhere," and so forth.[36]

The Yard relied heavily on civilians for technical assistance. Evers Burtner left his teaching duties at M.I.T. to work as a draftsman on the second floor of one of the new building ways structures. "There was an intense special course during the war period at M.I.T.," Burtner said, "to train electrical, civil, mechanical and agricultural engineers in the marine fundamentals. After completion of this special course, they were hired at the Yard as inspectors and draftsmen. If one were qualified, an ensignship was offered." Under the direction of Robert J. Boyd, the chief draftsman, these recent college graduates were engaged in the drafting of plans for submarines.[37]

Many left their drafting tables during the noon hour to eat a bag lunch they had carried with them to work. After lunch one draftsman returned to discover an overturned ink bottle and a large black blot on the plans he had been meticulously laboring over. "Scared the chap," Burtner said. On closer inspection, the anguished man found a dry bottle with a black piece of paper cut to imitate a blot. He had fallen for an old draftsman's trick.[38]

Washington officials visited the Yard throughout this war period. On Sunday, September 2, 1917, Assistant Secretary Roosevelt arrived for an informal visit with Commandant Howard. "The war has shown that the Portsmouth and Boston navy yards," Roosevelt said upon his return to Washington, "must be maintained as they are absolutely necessary to our naval defense."[39]

Secretary Daniels appeared a number of times. The popularity he had gained in Portsmouth naval circles for awarding the *L-8* contract had waned. By General Order 99 on June 30, 1914, Daniels abolished officers' wine messes aboard all vessels. The navy brass felt insulted. As a song of that day put it:

> Bryan he drinks grape juice,
> And Daniels likes it well.
> They'll make the Navy drink it —
> They will like hell![40]

After the first resentment wore off, the new order was actually a relief; alcoholism never became a serious problem in the navy. With sophisticated submarines using increasingly intricate machinery and equipment requiring the most sober and expert handling, alcohol had no place in the life of officers and seamen, whether they were at sea or in port.

On October 31, 1918, Daniels appeared in a surprise visit and addressed more than 5000 employees from the steps of the commandant's quarters. He was enthusiastically received and applause interrupted his remarks repeatedly. Daniels said:

> Some people are asking the question — if this war is over soon...They ask whether the Navy will go back to a little small concern and whether the great Naval work will continue? The answer I can make to that question is this: Last week the President of the United States...sent to Congress recommendations for a three year building program which will be the biggest building program any nation ever entered upon, and we are going to build it boys, whether the war ends or the war does not end.[41]

After hearing this good news, the Yard employees gave Daniels three rousing cheers.[41]

The progress of the *O-1*, the Yard's second submarine, exemplified this wartime spirit. Launched from the Franklin Shiphouse on July 9, 1918, this submarine "will soon be out doing her bit against the Huns," in the words of *Life Buoy*. The submarine went on her sea trials on November 5, considerably ahead of schedule.[42]

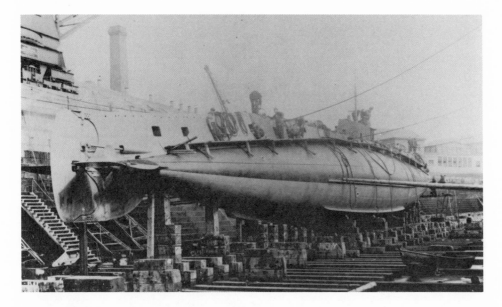

O-1, *Portsmouth's second submarine, in dry dock. Note workers on scaffolding. UNH.*

The news of the Armistice on November 11, 1918, arrived in Portsmouth about 3:00 A.M., about ten minutes after the State Department made the official announcement in Washington. The war was over! Workmen at the Yard quickly received the news.

"The place went crazy. Impromptu parades started up," said Wilma "Bill" Letch, a machinist's helper. "The Yard got a half day off. No work could have been done anyway under such conditions of excitement."[43]

Officers and crew of S-7 assemble on deck for typical group pose. Total of 32 men made up complement for 1920s era boat. SB.

S-3, Portsmouth's third boat, sliding down greased skids from Franklin Shiphouse during December 1918 launch. PA.

II   *Developing More Sophisticated Submarines, 1919-1941*

The Unreliable S-Boats

THE TWO DECADES between the world wars represented a period of transition and adjustment for the Yard, her submarines, and the United States Navy. The number of civilian employees at the Yard dipped from its wartime high of 5500 to 1750 by 1923. The Great Depression thwarted growth until the threat of war in the late 1930s and early 1940s generated renewed activity at the Yard.[1]

The end of the Great War in 1918 ushered in a spirit of pacifism among the victorious Allied powers. These governments stopped appropriating funds to maintain large navies and slashed their military budgets.

In 1918 Secretary of the Navy Josephus Daniels, committed to a three-year building program, found that public support for this policy vanished at war's end both within the United States and abroad. In 1919 he cancelled the program. The naval appropriation bill of July 11, 1919, was more concerned with war memorials than with military preparedness. One appropriation authorized $500,000 toward the construction of the War Memorial Bridge across the Piscataqua, connecting Portsmouth with the Navy Yard by way of Kittery. The states of Maine and New Hampshire were each required to appropriate $500,000. The War Memorial Bridge was opened in August 1923 and eliminated the need for ferries. Money for submarines, however, was scarce. Many peace groups sought to ban submarine warfare entirely, while professional navy men around the world fought for the submarine's survival. The S-boats, the mainstays of the American naval submarine force between the wars, suffered the effects of limited funds and prevailing lassitude.[2]

Each S-boat cost only two million dollars. Of the fifty-one S-class

Superstructure of the S-3, Portsmouth's third boat, breaking water on sea trials. PM.

Starboard side of S-1, a Fore River boat, under repair at the Portsmouth Navy Yard on December 30, 1922. Two workmen at left standing around riveting pot to keep warm. Airplane storage tank (center right) housed a small collapsible seaplane, which could be rolled out and quickly assembled. KHNM.

(left) Miss Eleanor V.D. Adams, daughter of Naval Constructor Laurence S. Adams and sponsor of S-6, poses at boat's bow at December 1919 launching. PA.
(below) Riveting party gathers at the Franklin Shiphouse on January 20, 1919 to drive first rivet into keel of S-9. Two civilians in center foreground are rivet passer and rivet heater.

Launching of USS Snapper (S-4), *August 1937. PNSY.*

subs completed through 1925, the Yard built eleven. This number would
have been even lower had not several of their keels been laid before the
war ended. Minor accidents involving the *S-3*, the Yard's first S-boat,
provided ominous portents of the S-boats' failings. On December 12, 1918,
a small fire broke out aboard the *S-3* on Franklin Shiphouse building
ways. At her scheduled launching on December 17, the *S-3* stuck after
moving three feet. The grease had frozen. Finally on December 21, a
successful launch took place.[3]

On August 27, 1919, the *S-4*, the first sub from this shed, was
launched from Building #115. After her christening the submarine
"bedecked with Flags and with Old Glory snapping in the wind,"
as reported by *Life Buoy*, "made a beautiful sight as she took the water."

A new development entered into the planning and construction of
subsequent S-boats. During the spring and summer of 1919, six
ex-German U-boats, assigned to the United States in post-armistice
negotiations, arrived at New York City. The U.S. Navy sent the *U-111* to
Portsmouth. After tests and sea trials Yard engineers and designers
dismantled the boat's engines, motors and other machinery. They
discovered that the German compressor for blowing ballast was more
advanced and efficient than the American version. During the early
1920s Yard engineers redesigned the German model, added modifications, and developed the superior "Portsmouth compressor." Details

German-manufactured four-stage air compressor, a ballast blowing device, taken from U-88. After testing, modifications and improvements at the Yard, this machine evolved into the "Portsmouth Compressor," standard equipment on American subs until World War II. KHNM.

about the compressor are few, but this Portsmouth-first invention became standard equipment on all American submarines until World War II. The Yard also lifted other features from the *U-111* to produce the best submarines possible.

Despite these improvements, the S-class submarines were still plagued with many problems. Designed during the war to attack enemy warships, they could not do so. More than 200 feet in length, the S-boats carried four torpedo tubes and averaged fifteen knots on the surface and eleven knots submerged. They were too slow and fragile for extended fleet operations. Several sank during the 1920s, including two built at the Yard.[4]

Bow of S-6 (SS-111) in center foreground with stern of S-8 at left. PA.

Five submarines, including Portsmouth's S-3, S-4 and S-6 undergoing repairs at the Yard. Note temporary wooden decks, scaffolding and tarpaulin. PA.

S-7 participating in manuevers with fleet in Juan de Fuca Strait off Port Angeles, Washington. Hull camouflaged with light and dark paint. Note deck gun. PA.

S-8 in dry dock. PA.

Portsmouth boats S-4, S-6 *and other S boats at their berthings in Navy Yard. PM.*

S-12 *leaving Navy Yard on June 4, 1923, with Peirce Island across the Piscataqua. KHNM.*

The Rescue of the S-5

The *S-5*, a Portsmouth boat commissioned in March 1920, was engaged in test dives fifty-five miles off the Delaware Capes. She carried a crew of thirty-eight men. On September 2, 1920, at 1:00 P.M. she submerged on a crash dive and sank in 194 feet of water. Water flooded through the main induction valve and poured through four compartments.

Her commanding officer ordered the aft ballast and fuel tanks blown dry and the stern shot to the surface. With the stern sticking seventeen feet out of water, the crew managed to cut a three-inch hole through the hull, using the tools at hand. This took thirty-six hours. Through the hole, the crew saw ships pass without stopping. Finally the *Alanthus*, a wooden liberty ship, passed nearby. A sailor on watch spotted what he thought was a buoy through his binoculars, but the captain of the *Alanthus* knew that a buoy should not be that far out to sea and turned his vessel around to investigate. Approaching in a lifeboat, the Captain asked:

"What ship?"
"S-5."
"What nationality?"
"American."
"Where bound?"
"Hell by compass."[5]

The *Alanthus* sent out SOS signals and tried without success to enlarge the hole in the hull for an escape passage. Responding to the SOS signals, the steamship *General Goethals* arrived at sundown and pried a huge steel plate from the *S-5* hull. Within an hour all the submariners were out of their boat, some fifty-one hours after the ill-fated dive. The next morning dozens of navy ships came to the scene. The battleship *Ohio* secured lines to the *S-5* and pulled her free. After she had been under tow for about a mile, the *S-5* slipped her lines, capsized and sank in deep water. She was never raised.

Early in the 1920s the Yard shifted to construction of the new V-class subs (the Yard never built any T-class subs, which were plagued with engine problems, and the initial "U," too closely associated with the German U-boats, was never used to designate American submarines). On March 15, 1920, the Yard received authorization to build the *V-1*, *V-2*, and *V-3*. Construction began that fall. In the meantime, the last of the S-boats, still on the building ways, were being launched and commissioned.

On Monday, February 7, 1921, one launching brought an old friend back to the Yard. Franklin D. Roosevelt, formerly assistant secretary of the navy and now a private citizen, appeared with his family. His daughter, Anna E. Roosevelt, was the sponsor of the *S-11*. At noon she christened the boat with a bottle of sparkling cider, and the *S-11* slid into the Piscataqua without a hitch. Six months after the launching, Franklin Roosevelt was stricken with polio at his Campobello Island summer home.

A popular but probably apocryphal story about the launching contends that Anna Roosevelt missed the actual event because of illness, and that later she posed for a "launching" photograph so that she could dress in all the finery bought for the ceremony.[6]

Railroad Locomotives Pull the S-48

Bad weather frequently plagued the ill-starred S-boats. On the night of January 29, 1925, coming up from New London, the *S-48* and the *S-51*, two Lake Torpedo Company submarines, and their tender, the *Chewink*, approached Portsmouth Harbor in a blinding northeaster. The *S-51* and the *Chewink* rode out the storm at sea. The *S-48*, however, hit a ledge off Fort Stark, Jeffreys Point in New Castle. Drifting helplessly, the sub finally grounded on the mudflats at Frost Point, Little Harbor, Rye. Lieutenant Commander Stuart E. Bray, her skipper, sounded SOS calls with sirens and a whistle. Her distress signal was heard at the Yard, but tugs sent out to assist could not locate the crippled sub. Rescue crews battling snowdrifts and winds did not reach the *S-48* until the next morning.

Help arrived at the critical moment. The forward torpedo room and crew quarters were punctured and flooded, as the sub listed at a forty-five-degree angle to starboard. With the boat on the verge of breaking up, chlorine gas from the storage battery would have soon escaped and gassed the men. A Coast Guard dory made five trips and managed to bring ashore the forty-six men aboard the *S-48*. One sailor fell and was slightly injured. The rescued men were taken to Fort Stark, where they had a hot meal and wrapped themselves in blankets.[7] The only other casualty was the skipper's Airedale dog, "Sec," who sniffed chlorine gas, trembled, and made it ashore, but was never seen again.

After the blizzard abated, the *S-48* was floated on February 7 and tugs towed the battered sub to the Yard. There it lay idle for almost two years as naval officers wondered what to do with it. Many wanted to scrap her.

Lieutenant Junior Grade Carleton Shugg, a twenty-seven-year-

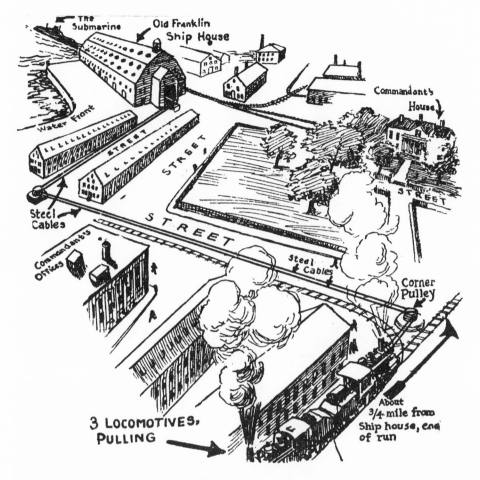

Map sketch depicting engineering strategy to haul S-48 into Franklin Shiphouse in 1927. PA.

old engineering officer at the Yard and a recent graduate of the Naval Academy, resolved to save the *S-48*. Many shipbuilding experts came to the Yard on February 3, 1927, to observe Shugg's rescue operation. The plan was to employ three Boston & Maine steam locomotives to pull the sub out of the water and into the Franklin Shiphouse. The three locomotives hitched in tandem, with an elaborate system of steel cables and pulley blocks which multiplied their hauling power several times, would pull the sub, which was housed in a wooden cradle.

At 12:10 P.M. Shugg ordered the first of three pulls. The first two were simply to pull up slack, while the last would haul the 700-ton submarine on heavily greased runners into the shiphouse. The locomotives moved ahead 2500 feet from their starting point and provided

*Preparations underway to haul S-48 into Franklin Shiphouse for repairs
in February 1927. Tug M. Mitchell Davis alongside sub as workmen
adjust pulling cables on right. Town of Kittery in background. PA.*

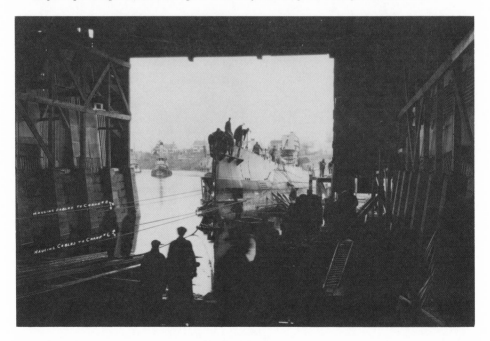

*S-48 approaching 30-foot incline to Shiphouse as three locomotives and
two cranes pull steel cables taut. Entire hauling operation required twenty
minutes. PA.*

power estimated at 85,700 pounds. Two cranes lent assistance. On the last pull the sub moved up a thirty-foot incline and into the Franklin shipways without a hitch. The entire operation took twenty minutes.[8]

Shugg began reconditioning the *S-48*. Workmen cut the boat in half and added thirty feet to her hull. On September 4, 1928, the *S-48* was launched from the shiphouse, and recommissioned on December 28 to rejoin the fleet.

The S-4 Initiates Reform

The *S-4*, so gloriously launched in 1919, was the last Portsmouth-built S-boat involved in a major accident. After her annual overhaul at the Yard, the *S-4* sailed from Portsmouth to Provincetown, Massachusetts, on December 15, 1927, to conduct trials and tests. On Saturday, December 17, the *S-4* left Provincetown and began making submerged runs over a measured mile. She carried a crew of forty. At 3:37 P.M. the U.S. Coast Guard destroyer *Paulding*, used to prevent rumrunning during Prohibition, rammed the submerged submarine. The *S-4* dropped, coming to rest at 102 feet on the mud bottom. The *Paulding* lowered a lifeboat, and waited for survivors, but none appeared.[9]

Notified of the sinking late that afternoon, the Portsmouth Yard recalled civilian and naval personnel to ready the tender *USS Bushnell* for sea. Despite the weekend liberties, a crew had the *Bushnell* under way at full steam by 7:00 P.M., carrying three deep-sea divers and a mass of equipment. The *Bushnell* arrived at the site of the sinking the next morning to join other ships for the salvage operations.

Captain Ernest J. King, later fleet admiral, took command. Heavy seas, gale winds and freezing temperatures prevented rescue operations for ten days. By then it was too late to save any of the crew. The *S-4* was finally raised in March and towed to Boston Navy Yard for dry docking.[10]

In June, the *S-4* arrived in tow at the Portsmouth Yard to be rebuilt with the latest experimental safety features. Notwithstanding her sinking and the loss of her crew, the legacy of the *S-4* is measured in the reforms she prompted which ultimately saved many lives. A presidential board investigated the accident and urged the adoption of safety equipment and procedures. Also by congressional enactment in 1928, submariners were granted a twenty-five-percent pay increase for hazardous duty, exactly what aviators received. Lieutenant Charles B. Momsen led a project which invented the Submarine Escape Appliance, better known as the "Momsen Lung." After testing, this device became standard equipment for all submarines. Momsen, Lieutenant Com-

Salvage operations underway for raising S-4 *off Provincetown, Massachusetts during March 1928. PM.*

mander Andrew I. McKee and Lieutenant Commander Allan R. McCann, collaborated in the design of the McCann Submarine Rescue Chamber, a decided improvement over the old diving bell.[11]

At the Yard, Lieutenant Shugg was in charge of refitting the *S-4* for its special mission. Under Shugg's direction, Yard employees removed the sub's entire power plant and outfitted the boat with the latest escape, rescue, and salvage devices. This equipment included improved quick-operating water-tight doors, telephone buoys and heavy compartment bulkheads. Since Shugg was eminently qualified to handle the *S-4*'s many new features, he was assigned second in command.

The *S-4* performed many tests and trials with the new equipment. In January 1932 Momsen became the skipper and took the refitted *S-4* on a training cruise. Submarine personnel received instruction in escape and rescue at naval bases at Panama, San Diego and Pearl Harbor. The use of chains and pontoons on the *S-4*'s hull in these demonstrations prevented damage to active submarines. The tour was successful. When the cruise was completed in September 1932, the *S-4* had performed well. "The *S-4* was decommissioned, towed out to sea," Momsen wrote, " and given a decent burial in 2000 fathoms of water."[12]

The V-Boats, the First Modern Submarines

The development of the V-boat, successor to the S-class sub, helped pull the Yard out of the doldrums of the early 1920s. The Yard built the first four V-boats and seven of the nine that were launched and commissioned. Profiting from the lessons learned from the S-boats, the V-boats mark the beginning of the modern submarine. Designed and fitted to accompany an American fleet under all conditions, these early "fleet" submarines employed the same basic architectural plan used in the later subs built by the navy to fight in the Pacific during World War II.[13].

In 1922 Congress ratified the Washington Naval Treaty between the United States, Great Britain, France, Italy, and Japan. The treaty addressed issues of limited tonnage and numbers of capital ships (battleships and carriers) but said nothing about the role or number of submarines, and therefore did not affect the Yard.[14]

In 1924 the Lake Torpedo Company went out of business. In the same year Electric Boat was preoccupied with shifting its operations from Massachusetts to Groton, Connecticut, across the Thames River from New London. The Electric Boat Company did not lay another submarine keel until 1931. The Portsmouth Yard continued its work without disruption.

While the V-boats were under construction during 1924, Andrew I. McKee and Charles A. Lockwood, two brilliant young submariners, were stationed at Portsmouth. McKee worked as a ship superintendent on submarines and eventually became the navy's foremost designer. In addition to studying all existing American designs, McKee examined many German U-boats brought to this country after World War I in order to incorporate their best features in his work. Lockwood served as a repair superintendent and was impressed by the Yard's booming appearance. These men eventually became the navy's leading submarine experts.[15]

The first three V-boats, better known as the *Barracuda*, *Bass* and *Bonita*, were launched during 1924 and 1925. Each cost about $7 million. These V-boats were 341 feet long with an operating depth of 200 feet. From the 1920s onward, workmen installed into most submarines a refrigerating plant, cold storage space and an air-conditioning plant which condensed as much as 100 gallons of water a day for washing.[16]

In the fall of 1924 the *V-1* embarked on a shakedown cruise to the Caribbean. The next year she traveled 17,000 miles on a five-month cruise for extended trials. The profile of her bow suggested "a shark with an anchor gripped in its jaws." The boat's power plant was a combination of

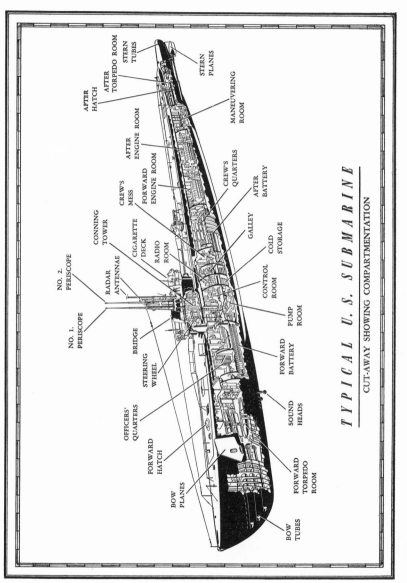

TYPICAL U.S. SUBMARINE
CUT-AWAY SHOWING COMPARTMENTATION

Diagram of typical U.S. Fleet Submarine, Navy's mainstay boat during World War II, showing equipment and compartments. USNI.

Inside building ways, Bonita (SS165) *awaits installation of decking. Note V-3 already painted on either side of conning tower. JPCC.*

Bow view of V-1 (Barracuda) *on launching ways on July 16, 1924. PA.*

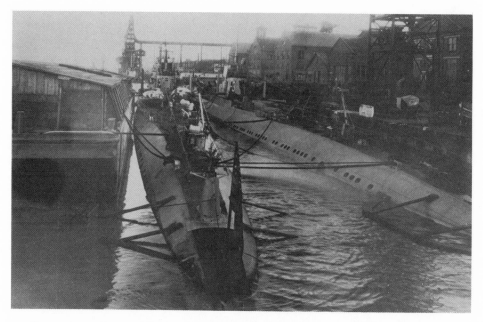

Stern views of V-2 (Bass) *and* V-3 (Bonita). *Note vents on side of Bonita for induction or expulsion of water. KHNM*

Bow view of V-2 and V-3. Note in center foreground V-2's bulbous bow with stem anchor giving V-boats an almost shark-like appearance. KHNM.

Two deck views of V-3, (top) looking aft from bow and (bottom) forward from amid-ships. KHNM.

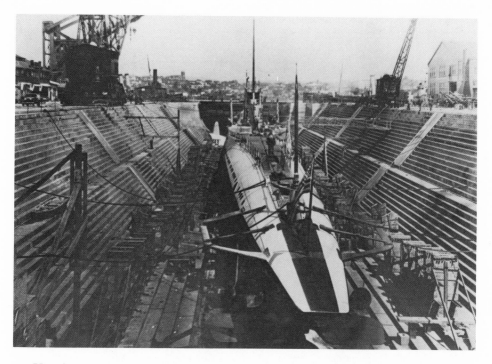

V-3 in dry dock with view of whole boat stern to forward, with close-ups of (left) bow with stem anchor and (right) stern with rudder. KHNM.

two diesels in the main engine room and two New York Navy Yard-built German-designed engines in the forward engine room. This arrangement was the initial step toward what later became standard design—diesel-electric drive which eliminated the previously troublesome main engine clutches.[17]

Despite such improvements, the early V-boats had many short-comings. Their fuel tanks leaked oil, leaving a telltale slick on the surface of the water. The V-boats never reached their design speed of twenty-one knots surfaced and eight knots submerged. Slow in diving, they maneu-vered poorly when submerged.

Designers believed a larger or more powerful diesel plant would eliminate these problems. This required a much larger hull. The Ports-mouth-built *V-4* and *V-5*, the second generation of V-boats, were enormous. The *V-4*, redesignated as the *Argonaut*, measured 381 feet long and weighed 2710 tons on the surface. She was the largest submarine built by the United States until after World War II. Launched in 1927 after two years of work, she was commissioned in April 1928. The *Argonaut* was unique among American submarines. Specifically designed as a minelaying submarine, she carried sixty mines in addition to her torpedoes.

The *V-5*, or *Narwhal*, was like the *Argonaut* in most respects, except that a heavier torpedo armament was substituted for the *Argo-naut*'s minelaying feature. Both subs were slow in speed and diving, and they were awkward when submerged. They could not maintain seventeen knots on the surface to accompany the fleet. Despite these shortcomings, the V-boats were safe compared with the S-class and went to sea during World War II.[18]

The development of the early V-boats suggested a new concept to submariners, who proposed a new mission for their boats. Their subs could act independently of the fleet and operate alone in gathering information on long-range scouting cruises. The navy called on Andrew McKee. Drawing from knowledge gained at the Yard and at the Bureau of Construction and Design in Washington, McKee assumed responsi-bility for the *V-7*, later called the *Dolphin*. McKee had no precedent for designing a sub specifically for long patrol operations in the Pacific. His design had to be original. One of his basic tenets was to keep superfluous equipment and material out of a submarine. McKee rearranged fuel tanks and trimmed existing features to save weight. The result was a smaller and lighter submarine than her predecessors, capable of remaining at sea for seventy-five days and of traveling up to 12,000 miles. The Portsmouth Yard was the logical place for McKee to build the *V-7*. After almost two years of construction, the experimental boat was

Against lower Manhatten skyline USS Argonaut *(SS166) passes
under Brooklyn Bridge on November 2, 1932. SB.*

commissioned in 1932. The *Dolphin*'s clean lines formed the prototype for
the standard fleet boats of World War II.[19]

A New Deal for the Yard and Her Submarines

On November 8, 1932, Yard employees were given time off in order to
vote in the national elections. Franklin D. Roosevelt, the Democratic
candidate, was elected president and assumed his duties the following
March. Throughout Roosevelt's New Deal administration, the fortunes of
the American Navy improved dramatically. International tensions in
Europe and in Asia alarmed President Roosevelt. The experience and
knowledge gained during his years as assistant secretary of the navy
convinced him of the need to expand the navy. In 1933 Congress
appropriated $238 million for new naval vessels, including the con-
struction of twenty-six submarines. During the next few years, the

Rolling plates for pressure hull of Cachalot *in 1932. Launched and commissioned a year later,* Cachalot *was one of the last of riveted hull subs. PA.*

Yard added employees and worked on the P-class and the *Salmon*-class submarines.[20]

During the early 1930s two institutions at the Yard came to an end. Links to the past, both Old Tom, a marine corps horse, and the Franklin Shiphouse were far better known than most of the submarines and the skippers who commanded them. Old Tom was born in 1892 and entered the corps in 1894. During the Spanish-American War he was the personal mount of Colonel William H. Huntington. He was wounded in action in Cuba. After many years of active service at the Yard, Old Tom was placed on the retired list in 1928 and spent his remaining days pampered with apples and lumps of sugar, watching the daily guard mount of the marines. Following his death on April 23, 1933, Old Tom received a military funeral, including a volley and taps. A stone marks the final resting place of Old Tom at the rear of the Navy Exchange.[21]

On Tuesday, March 10, 1936, heavy fog lay over the Piscataqua in the early morning. A red glow suddenly appeared, illuminating the

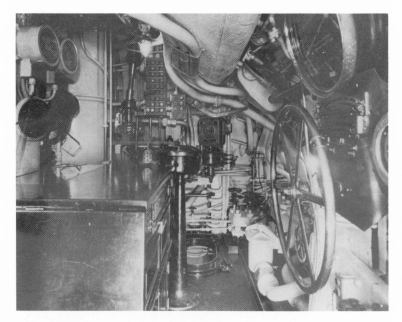

Interior of V-class subs was designed for the most efficient distribution of equipment and habitability for crew. Views illustrate tight quarters (above) in V-3's Control Room; (opposite top) Maneuvering Room; (opposite below) Forward Torpedo Room; and (below) Engine Room. KHNM.

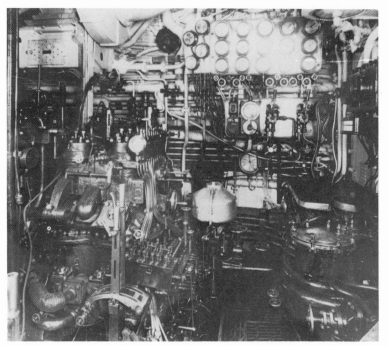

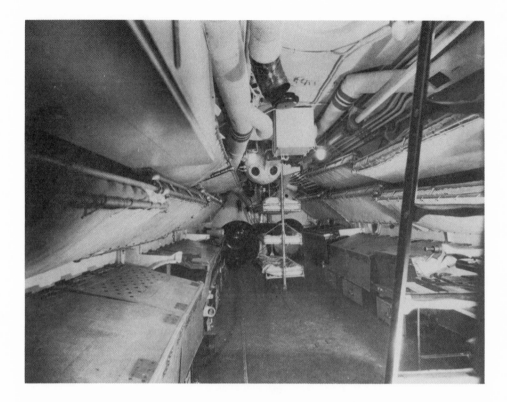

Compact sleeping quarters for crew in After Torpedo Room of V-3 *sub.*
KHNM.

countryside for miles. The blaze started at 5:00 A.M. and spread
throughout the Franklin Shiphouse. Despite the efforts of the Yard fire
department the building burned out of control, collapsed at 6:00 A.M.,
and smoldered for the rest of the day. The last of the original wooden
buildings of the Yard and the site of much of its history, the Franklin
Shiphouse was now ashes. To many visitors the building was a major
attraction. During its last years, the building was used for storage. The
cause of the the fire remains unknown. "Here the last of the old time wielders
of the sledge and adze labored," the *Portsmouth Herald* editorialized, "but
now its work is done and no more will shipwrights come to work or
'knock off' within its historic walls."[22]

The technology of the 1930s developed at the Yard left the old days
of horsepower and wooden ships far behind. Among new features were an
all-welded hull, bubble eliminator, and air conditioning in the sub's
original design.

Prompted by re-established rivalry with Electric Boat, the Yard
set aside initial skepticism to investigate the merits of producing an

Bow view of USS Snapper, *Navy's first all-welded submarine, undergoing overhaul in dry dock in 1939. PM.*

all-welded hull to replace riveting. In the early 1930s Yard employees practiced their welding skills and developed new welding procedures on garbage scows and derricks, where failures would not endanger the fleet. The Yard built a submarine hull section, half riveted and half welded, and conducted underwater explosion tests to compare the difference in fracture weaknesses. Such underwater tests were first developed at the Yard. "Every riveted joint popped," said one observer, "whereas the welded ones just bent like a tin can."[23]

On July 23, 1936, workmen laid the keel of the *USS Snapper* at the Yard, driving a rivet into the hull. But the original plan to make the *Snapper* a riveted-hull submarine was soon changed, for the ongoing underwater explosions demonstrated unquestionably that a welded hull was superior. Launched on August 24, 1937, the *Snapper*, the navy's first all-welded steel hull submarine, represented another Portsmouth-first milestone. This improvement enabled the sub to submerge to 300 feet operating depth and to withstand depth charge attacks much better. After the *Snapper*, the navy relied on welded construction for all their submarines.[24]

The Yard also introduced the invention of the bubble eliminator. Lieutenant Marshall M. "Heavy" Dana, an expert in diesel engineering, devised this improvement to prevent the escape of a bubble of air into the water when a torpedo was fired. Known later as the poppet valve, this device was installed on all American submarines to reduce the possibility of detection and counterattack during engagements with the enemy.[25]

Whether air conditioning would be part of an American submarine's standard equipment was settled in 1936 with the construction of the Portsmouth-built *Plunger*, the first American submarine with this feature provided in her original design. Air conditioning had drawbacks of additional weight and cost, but its good points outweighed these considerations. Without it, a submarine faced the possibility of both human and mechanical breakdown. In addition to the crew's exhaustion and heat rash in temperatures of 100 degrees F. or more, with almost 100 per cent humidity, "sweat" condensed on cold steel plates, which in turn corroded the metal and triggered short circuits in the electrical equipment.[26]

The torpedo data computer, a firepower control device, which automatically plotted the course of any enemy ship and set the proper angle in the torpedo to intercept it, was developed elsewhere. The TDC was quickly adopted for all submarines. Safety features, including a supply of Momsen Lungs and fittings on the escape hatches to lock on the McCann Rescue Chamber, also became standard equipment on all American subs.[27]

The Squalus *Becomes the* Sailfish

The keels of two "new S" class boats, the *USS Sculpin (SS 191)* and the *USS Squalus (SS 192)*, were laid during the fall of 1937. In that year Lieutenant Robert L. Evans reported to the Yard to serve as the ship superintendent for the keel laying, construction, launching and commissioning of both boats. Evans soon became acquainted with "Andy" McKee, who began another tour of duty at the Yard in 1938.

Evans made daily inspection rounds as construction on the two boats proceeded. One day he noticed a mistake. Misinterpreting the draftsman's plans of the *Sculpin*, a worker had drilled holes into the top of the hull to attach a sea chest for holding cooling waters. These holes were supposed to be drilled at the bottom of the hull. Evans ordered patches for the holes and steel back-up strips for a final sealing.

As the patching and welding neared completion, a particularly testy superior accompanied Evans on his inspection tour. The senior officer looked up and continued without stopping. "He didn't say anything," Evans said, "and I didn't say anything either." A sledge hammer tested the weld, following by air tests. The patches worked and never caused any problems.[28]

The *Sculpin* and the *Squalus* were both commissioned in early 1939. After completing her sea trials, the *Sculpin* was scheduled to leave the Yard for a shakedown cruise to South America on May 23. The *Squalus* had also performed well on her initial trials and was to complete several more tests on the same day. These included fast dives as submariners call them, or "crash" dives as they are known to civilians, although the *Squalus* had already successfully completed eighteen. Lieutenant Oliver Naquin, the skipper of the *Squalus*, saw Evans a day or so before sailing. "Come aboard, Bob," Naquin said. Evans declined, pressed with other responsibilities.

At 8:40 A.M. on Tuesday, May 23, the *Squalus* made her first fast dive of the day off the Isles of Shoals. She sank in 243 feet of water. Despite Naquin's order, "Blow main ballast," the *Squalus* failed to rise. The *Sculpin* departed the Yard at 11:30 A.M. and by a stroke of good fortune discovered the bobbing telephone buoy of her sister sub. The time was 12:41 P.M.[29]

Twenty-three men of the *Squalus* were trapped in the flooded compartments of the aft section, where they perished. Thirty-three others, including Naquin, crawled out of the forward battery compartment into the forward torpedo room. "We figured it [the battery compartment] would soon be filled with chlorine gas," said Electrician's Mate Second Class Gerald McLees. "It was cold there in the forward torpedo room. The sub was on emergency power. The crew was silent with no talking to conserve oxygen. There were no prayers. People were sick and throwing up."[30]

Charles B. Momsen arrived from Washington to lead the rescue attempt aboard the rescue ship *Falcon*, a converted World War I mine sweeper. A McCann Rescue Chamber made four trips down to the *Squalus* to bring the men in the forward compartment to the surface and safety. The fourth trip completed the rescue, perhaps the most remarkable in U.S. naval history, at 12:23 P.M. on May 25.

The survivors were taken to the Yard hospital. "I rested there for four or five days," McLees said. "They brought in a lot of food and candy from civilians. I was physically fit within a day or so." Restricted to the Portsmouth area, the survivors waited to testify before a board of inquiry.[31]

For days pieces of the cork insulation lining the interior of the sub's hull washed up on the coast of New Hampshire. The navy was determined to salvage the *Squalus*. McKee designed much of the special equipment for the salvage operation, including a cradle-like rig. After

Bow of USS Squalus *breaking water during abortive raising attempt to salvage boat, only to sink moments later. This famous photograph taken on July 13, 1939 by James A. Jones of the* Boston Post. *KHNM.*

many attempts, the *Squalus* was raised on September 13. The tug *Wandank* towed the sub to the Yard some 113 days after her fatal plunge. After workmen pumped the water out of the *Squalus*, a team of four navy doctors removed the bodies.

Employees floated the sub into dry dock. As the dock was pumped down, the *Squalus* settled on her wooden block cradle. The cause of the sinking appeared to be the failure of the lid or valve of the main induction — the air line which supplied air for the operation of the diesel engines while running on the surface — to shut during the dive.[32]

In a private letter, dated October 4, McKee asserted:

The thing that seems to be most inconsistent with any theory we may form is the fact that the valve operated satisfactorily when we tested it before it had been touched.

When we got the ship in dock we found the supply ventilation valve closed and the exhaust, which is also the engine induction valve, wide open. Just how this happened we do not know but there is no doubt but that the ship flooded through the open induction valve.

We have finally gotten rid of all Courts and Boards and the

After successful salvage operations off Isles of Shoals, disabled Squalus *in dry dock on September 15, 1939, awaiting repairs. KHNM.*

Yard is beginning to settle down to its normal pace. The week after the SQUALUS arrived in the Yard was by far the most hectic period of the whole salvage operation from the Yard's point of view. It took this long to get every working part out of the SQUALUS and slushed down to prevent further deterioration. We find, however, after this that the ship is in remarkably good condition and that very few things except electrical apparatus will have to be replaced. The bright steel working parts already had a small amount of soft rust on them but this cleaned off and in many cases hardly stained the piece...The hull itself had two small cracks...Neither hole was of any consequence...The propellers suffered only very slight nicks and bent edges and so far as we can now determine, the shafts were not injured at all. The rudder and diving planes also seem to be as good as new. Even delicate instruments like the gyro compass and data computer are in such condition that there is no doubt but that they can be salvaged at very reasonable cost. Our overall estimate for the reconditioning is $1,400,000, which includes a new battery.[33]

Commissioning on deck of USS Sailfish *(reconstructed* Squalus) *at the Navy Yard in May 1940, with skipper reading orders to officers and crew. Portsmouth skyline in background. KHNM.*

The navy officially decommissioned the *Squalus* on November 15, and a board of inquiry issued a report the following February concurring with McKee's opinion about a faulty induction valve. The board vindicated the officers and men of the *Squalus*.

New improved pressure valves, designed by Electric Boat, closed with sea pressure, not against it. From now on crew members in the control room at the indicator board, or "Christmas tree," with its panel of red and green lights, were assured that the valves were actually open or closed as the lights indicated.

At the dry dock the stripped parts of the submarine lay on the horseshoe stone rim. Trucks rolled into the Yard almost daily with replacement parts. "How can you ever get everything into the sub?" visitors asked Evans. "What a pile of material!" Since there was little structural damage, Evans and McKee directed their attention to the interior of the boat. Workmen were able to reinstall ninety percent of the original pipes in the refurbished submarine.[34]

On May 15, 1940, the completely reconditioned submarine was commissioned as the *Sailfish*. To the Navy the records of the *Squalus* were closed; a clean new log book of the *Sailfish* was ready for its first entry. Although virtually all the survivors volunteered to remain with the boat, only four received assignment to the *Sailfish*, among them Gerald McLees. He was a single man without responsibilities. "What the heck," McLees said, referring to his close call and decision to return. "I was too young to think about it."[35]

Others, however, did not share McLees's nonchalance. On August 20, 1940, the *Sailfish* left the Yard for her sea trials. The surface tests went without incident. The next phase would involve dives and sub-mergence tests. At this point several civilian experts and observers suddenly decided the surface trials were enough for the day, and, excusing themselves, boarded a tug to return to the Yard.

The *Sailfish* reached a position about ten miles southeast of Boon Island, Maine. McKee, Evans and the sub's crew conducted the *Sailfish*'s first dive. "Water gushed in and dripped down a fuel oil pipe," Evans said. "Otherwise the dive was mechanically sound." The *Sailfish* remained submerged for about an hour while the Navy tug *Wandank* stood by. Another version of the first dive declares the *Sailfish* hit bottom, some seven miles from the last dive of the *Squalus*, but was not damaged. Coming back into the caissons at the Yard, the *Sailfish* lurched heavily. Yard workers shook their heads and regarded her as jinxed.[36]

Transition to a Wartime Footing

The advent of World War II in 1939 accelerated the pace in the Yard. In June 1940 the American Congress authorized 21,000 additional tons of submarines. On July 19, after the fall of France, Congress passed the so-called "Two Navy Act," authorizing 70,000 more tons of submarines. Thanks to years of experimentation and planning, the navy was ready to implement mass production. At a cost of more than twenty-seven million dollars, more than 6000 employees were constructing submarines at the Yard in August 1940. Thirteen submarines were authorized, with three on the ways.[37]

President Roosevelt, underscoring the importance of this huge naval expansion, visited a number of vital national defense units in New England on a three-day tour. On August 10, 1940, at about 8:00 A.M., Roosevelt and his party arrived at the Portsmouth railroad station, and rode in an open car to the Yard, viewed by thousands of spectators along the way. A twenty-one gun salute boomed as he entered the Main Gate.

Five boats of Submarine Division One passing through Gatun Lock,
Panama Canal. PM.

During this first visit to the Yard since his daughter christened
the *S-11* almost twenty years earlier, Roosevelt took a keen interest in the
new construction. Stopping at the shipfitters building, he watched workmen welding the keel of a new submarine. Then the President viewed the
Sailfish at dock. Following a general tour of the bustling Yard, Roosevelt
arrived at the dock where the presidential yacht *Potomac* was moored.
His inspection required exactly thirty minutes. He boarded the *Potomac*
at 9:00 A.M., and began his cruise down the Piscataqua under the escort
of the naval tug *Penacook*. His destination was the Boston Navy Yard.[38]
Roosevelt had seen the most advanced American submarines up to
that time represented by the *Tambor* class, the last fleet boats built to
peacetime standards. A few days after the President's inspection, the
navy commissioned the *USS Triton* at the Yard. The *Triton* was one of
the twelve boats of her class which incorporated the best features of
earlier designs with many new improvements. Innovations included the

installation of six torpedo tubes forward, a larger conning tower, and the latest fire-control and sonar equipment. The *Triton* joined the fleet five and a half months ahead of her original schedule.

A year later the Yard marked another Portsmouth-first achievement. Electric Boat's *Tambor* and the Yard's *Trout* participated in the first live underwater explosion tests with the use of the two new operational submarines as targets.[39]

To ensure its investment in submarines from enemy attack, the Yard conducted its first blackout drill on September 8, 1940. At 8:00 P.M. every light in the Yard was out for a period of five minutes. The drill was a success. The *Portsmouth Herald* printed an exclusive photograph of the navy blackout, a solid black square mass. The *Herald* photographer reported he had hung by his heels from the War Memorial Bridge to get a detailed picture. As the moon refused to cooperate, he "blacked it out himself in the interests of good government."[40]

French and British Submarine Overhauls

Throughout 1941 the Yard continued to expand to meet an emergency building program. In that year the navy department placed contracts for seven new subs at Portsmouth. Workmen built new submarine barracks, an outside machine shop, piers and docks. The civilian force rose to 11,142 people. To relieve traffic congestion, the Yard built a second steel bridge, Gate #2, to Kittery, about a quarter mile east of the Main Gate.[41]

As well as building and overhauling its own subs, the Yard took on new responsibilities. The Lend-Lease Act of March 11, 1941 gave President Roosevelt broad powers to procure defense articles and "to sell, transfer title to, exchange, lease, lend, or otherwise dispose" of them to "the government of any country whose defense the President deems vital to the defense of the United States." A week later Secretary of the Navy Frank Knox, a former Manchester, New Hampshire, newspaper publisher, told reporters that the British had already requested use of American repair and overhaul facilities for war vessels. By June the first of three English subs arrived at the Yard; all had seen considerable action in the Mediterranean and required extensive refitting.[42]

The *Truant*, *Pandora* and *Parthian* were repaired at Portsmouth during the summer of 1941. One unusual feature of the British submarines was the appearance of a grill or oil-fired range under the aft of the boat's sail. The officers and crew could enjoy cookouts on deck as the cook worked at his grill. Around the Yard there was a story, undoubtedly apocryphal, that one of the British cooks had drowned during a fast dive.[43]

The Free French submarine *Surcouf* arrived at the Yard on July

Free French sub Surcouf *in Yard for overhaul and repairs in 1941. Note pair of eight-inch guns mounted in waterproof turret. UNH.*

27, 1941, for repair and overhaul. Launched at the Cherbourg Navy Yard in 1929, the *Surcouf* was the largest submarine of her time, 352 feet long with a surface displacement of 3304 tons. Designed to sail for as long as three months without refueling, the *Surcouf* was heavily armed and carried a scouting plane in a watertight hangar. After the fall of France, most of the French fleet remained in the hands of the Vichy government, controlled by Nazi Germany. The *Surcouf* escaped and symbolized the Free French naval forces. After docking at Plymouth, England, and Halifax, Canada, the *Surcouf* arrived at the Yard plagued with persistent engine trouble. Since the United States still maintained diplomatic relations with occupied France, the *Surcouf*'s presence at the Yard posed potential embarrassment for Washington. The sub was not officially received.[44]

While in Portsmouth, the officers and men of the *Surcouf* made many friends and became popular in town. Their jaunty red pompomed uniforms added an exotic flair to Portsmouth life. The employees at the Yard spoke highly of the sub. "She was a beautiful boat with beautiful workmanship," said Wilma "Bill" Letch, a mechanic who worked on her. Others admired her straight sides, the two eight-inch guns in her turret and her three decks. "The *Surcouf* had hammocks when she came in," said one worker, "and bunks when she left. A lot of money was spent on that boat." The sub carried live chickens and goats in her hull to provide fresh eggs, milk and meat for the ship's mess. Housed in crates or tied up, these animals—or their replacements—remained aboard for the *Sur-couf's* next voyage.

The officers' wardroom, made of mahogany and rosewood, became a popular meeting place (the United States avoided installing wood in submarines to reduce the chance of fire). When the *Surcouf* docked, American officials collected the French wine and liquor and locked up the bottles for safekeeping in the Yard's Officers' Club.[45]

Local reporters met the *Surcouf's* skipper, Lieutenant Commander Louis G. Blaison, in the sub's wardroom in early October. "We've been unlucky," Blaison said, "but we are hoping to make up for it," referring to the *Surcouf's* undistinguished war record. She had not sunk a single enemy target. At the end of the interview the reporters toured the boat. Due to the electric cables and debris on the deck while workmen swarmed around, one newsman could not tell when the boat would be ready for service again. "Even a finished submarine," he wrote, "looks unfinished to a layman." The Free French found it hard to believe that nearly every Yard worker had a car. Upon their arrival in port, they wanted to know if a conference was in progress.

Despite the hospitality they found in Portsmouth, an undercurrent of uneasiness stirred among the *Surcouf's* crew. The general feeling persisted among the sub's enlisted men that they would never see France again because a portion of her officers were pro-Nazi and intent on going over to the other side. Some men of the *Surcouf*, moreover, did not wish to return to sea. To delay their departure, these sailors stripped vital parts from the ship's machinery and threw them overboard. As soon as the Yard workers repaired the damage, sabotage occurred again. Divers sent down alongside the sub discovered missing parts. Shortly before sailing the French requested the return of their wine, only to learn that it was gone, confiscated by some unknown party. On October 29, 1941, with rumors still circulating that the boat was secretly in the service of Germany, the *Surcouf* sailed from Portsmouth.[46]

The Beginning of War

In addition to international concerns, the Yard had its own problems during 1941. In June the *O-6, O-9,* and *O-10* arrived at Portsmouth to drill on the regular testing area off the Isles of Shoals. All were World War I vintage boats, built in 1918 by the Fore River Ship Building Company for Electric Boat. As part of the program to increase the strength of the fleet, these old-timers were reactivated. The *O-9* had been used as a school training boat at New London and had been recommissioned a short time earlier.

The *O-9* submerged at 10:36 A.M. on June 20, diving in a "swept" area in 370 feet of water. She failed to surface. A massive search began for the sub and her crew of thirty-three men. A diver descended and located her crushed hull. The boat was never raised. On June 24, the *USS Grayling* dropped a floral wreath at the site of the tragedy with proper ceremony. A court of inquiry met and secretary Knox disclosed its findings on September 17. The court held that the *O-9* "was in satisfactory condition for the deep sea submergence test and that its crew was sufficiently trained for deep water operations." Found in 438 feet of water, the *O-9* evidently dove too deeply, collapsing her hull.[47]

On December 3, the Yard launched the *USS Halibut*, its fifth submarine of the year, in the fog with thirty-one-degree temperature. On December 7, news of the Japanese attack on Pearl Harbor arrived and the Yard immediately tightened its guard to secure the base.

On that Sunday afternoon Lieutenant Robert Evans, re-assigned to the Navy Department in Washington, was returning with his wife to their Virginia home after visiting friends. As they drove by Embassy Row on Massachusetts Avenue, they noticed bonfires burning in the backyard of the Japanese Embassy.[48]

The next morning, Monday, December 8, and for the next few days as he reported to his desk in Navy Department headquarters, Evans sensed gloom and dejection as he passed fellow officers on the stairwells and in the corridors. Only Admiral Ernest J. King, long experienced in submarines and recently appointed as Commander in Chief, United States Fleet, walked jauntily and wore an upbeat, determined look. It was widely reported that upon his appointment King remarked, "Yes, damn it, when they get in trouble they always send for the sons of bitches." To another officer King later admitted, "No, John, I didn't say it, but I wish I had." King must have known that it was going to take guts to win this war, and that the Portsmouth-built submarines would face their toughest test.[49]

III *Winning the War, 1941-1945*

The Dolphin *Fights Back at Pearl Harbor*

THE MORNING OF SUNDAY, December 7, 1941, began routinely at the submarine base at Pearl Harbor, Hawaii. Four subs, among them the Portsmouth-built *Dolphin* and *Narwhal*, were tied up at finger piers extending into the Southeast Loch of the harbor. A fifth sub, the Portsmouth boat *Cachalot*, was in the nearby navy yard undergoing overhaul.

The *Dolphin* and *Narwhal* recently returned from a forty-five day patrol to Wake Island, and were in for repair. It had been a grueling voyage and the twenty sailors unlucky enough to have weekend duty aboard the *Dolphin* were busy.[1]

Waldemar "Chuck" Hermenau, a sailor aboard the *Dolphin*, said:

> We left for a patrol in October, topped off with diesel oil, water, compressed air, so we knew that it wasn't an ordinary situation. The warheads and torpedoes arrived in two pieces and were loaded aboard the sub. Not the dummy torpedoes they used on previous missions. Two days out the air conditioning failed, a day later the refrigeration, and then finally the evaporator to make fresh water. If the air conditioning had failed at a critical depth, the sub would have blown up. All the fresh food began to spoil, the turkeys, the hams, chickens and beef. It began to be covered with a slime and stank so we jettisoned it. We began eating all canned foods, canned ham and Spam, called in the Navy 'horse-cock.' We were all sweaty and the bunk mattresses were all slime, dirt and oil. When we got to Pearl, all the mattresses were taken off.
>
> On Thanksgiving Day the ship's cook served us fried Spam. We crossed the International Date Line. The next day being the same date, he served us the exact same meal again. When I

Secured to finger pier at Pearl Harbor's South East Loch, Narwhal *gunners fire back during 1941 Japanese attack. USNI.*

returned to Pearl, my wife greeted me and served me fried Spam that evening. I was off a few days and had duty over the weekend.[2]

As the *Narwhal* leaked some 20,000 gallons of diesel oil during her voyage, leaving a telltale slick, she also needed repairs.

Rear Admiral Thomas "Tommy" Withers, Jr. was nominally in command of twenty-two submarines stationed at Pearl Harbor. But this number represented a paper figure; in November 1941 Withers actually had ten subs there. Five were on patrol duty, so Withers adhered to a weekend work schedule to ready the five subs in port for future assignments.

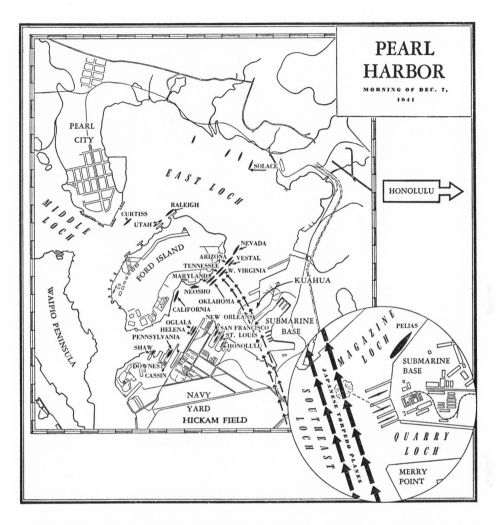

Map of Pearl Harbor showing location of American ships on morning of December 7, 1941. Note that American submarines lay directly in flight pattern of Japanese torpedo planes heading for Battleship Row off Ford Island. USNI.

On the deck of the *Dolphin* at 7:55 A.M. on Sunday, December 7, Hermenau was attaching a hose carrying distilled water to the sub's water tank as his crewmate handled the other end on the dock. Distilled water (compared with regular water which contains many impurities) prolonged the life of the battery by about three times.

"My buddy hated the navy," Hermenau said. "He always wanted to be in planes. Any time a plane flew overhead, he would automatically look up to observe it.'"

"'Look,' the buddy said, 'that plane dropped something.'"

Three planes were flying in formation. "Look," he said a second time and then a third. These were the first bombs dropped in the Pearl Harbor attack (bombs dropped earlier hit American airfields in northern Oahu). The two sailors watched the bombs land about half a mile away. The first dropped into the water, the second hit in the vicinity of a dry dock under construction, and the third exploded on a seaplane hangar. Smoke and flames erupted immediately out of every window in the building.[3]

"We saw a big tomato on the wings," Hermenau said, "and knew it was the Japanese. I went below and reported it to the officer of the deck. He couldn't believe it. We had no keys and had to break the lock on the powder magazine to get to the bands and clips of bullets."

The men rushed to the deck with their machine guns. The Japanese flight pattern took the planes over the Southeast Loch toward the east side of Ford Island and their targets on Battleship Row. One *Dolphin* gunner, an experienced hunter, fired at a Japanese plane with tracers. "The plane seemed to swallow the bullets," Hermenau said, "and wriggled and dipped as it went through the billowing smoke from our burning ships. He must have nabbed it. None of us were scared or frightened. We were mad, angry and wanted to get back at that guy. We were determined to make him pay in return."

From their homes in Honolulu and naval housing at the base, other officers and crew members of the *Dolphin* began arriving to join their shipmates. The executive officer arrived to oversee the operation. Crew members fired as others prepared clips of ammunition on the table in the crew's mess. The *Dolphin* remained at her pier throughout the attack. Because her hull was open for repairs to the evaporator, the boat could not dive. It was fruitless to consider getting under way.

Patrol boats picked up wounded from the water. They docked at a pier a short distance from the *Dolphin*. "Many men were covered with oil," Hermenau said. "Many were burned, many with limbs missing, some pulled out with just their skivvies on, their uniforms and clothes blown off in the explosions. There was rivalry and competition among the various boats and branches of the service, but this disappeared in an instant. Never have I seen people treated with such kindness and tenderness, as ambulances, trucks and private cars arrived at the pier, and loaded the wounded to be driven to the base hospital."[4]

During the attack the *Dolphin's* crew had no knowledge about damage or casualties to the American side. Each man, sub, ship and plane fought an individual battle.

That morning the cruiser *Minneapolis* lay off Barbers Point, the southwestern tip of Oahu. She was scheduled to dock at Pearl Harbor between 9:00 and 10:00 A.M. Seventeen year old Armand "Legs" Legare, a radioman third class, ate a quick breakfast at 5:00 A.M. His ambition was to be a code man and he studied in his spare time to win his commission. The night before he had run off the daily news on the ship's press. Instead of printing on both sides of one sheet, Legare used two separate sheets. He then realized his mistake. "I decided to make myself scarce below deck away from my boss officer," Legare said, "Then I heard a klaxon and orders for all hands to man their battle stations. I thought it was a dirty trick for my boss to pull in order to find me."[5]

But the alarm was no trick; an attack was on. The *Minneapolis* sent her two observation planes to investigate. For the next three days the cruiser searched for a non-existent Japanese ghost fleet in the seas surrounding the Hawaiian islands. On December 10, the *Minneapolis* returned. "Pearl Harbor was a mess, unbelievable," Legare said. "The *California* was upright; she beached herself rather than block the channel. The *Oklahoma* was turned over, with divers working frantically. The *Utah* and the *Arizona* were wrecked. The planes and the hangars [at Hickam Field] were still burning. No one told us anything. No informant came out. No one knew what was going on."[6]

The confusion, along with the smoke and dust, finally cleared. In addition to the loss of many ships, over 3000 navy and marine officers and men had been killed. The submarine force, on the other hand, escaped without damage. The sub base did not suffer a single hit. The Japanese pilots had overlooked the Pearl Harbor tank farms containing 140 million gallons of diesel oil. The torpedoes and magnetic exploders in storage were also left intact.

Sub crews worked at top speed day and night to ready the boats for departure. By December 11, Admiral Withers ordered EB's *Gudgeon* underway to carry the war to the enemy.[7]

The Yard Mobilizes

Reverberations from the exploding bombs dropped on Pearl Harbor reached halfway around the world to trigger an unprecedented building boom at the Portsmouth Navy Yard. The production of submarines, the number of employees, and the hectic pace of activity reached record peaks at the Yard from 1941 to the war's end in 1945. Establishing itself as the leading submarine builder in the country, the Yard delivered seventy-nine submarines during this period, one more than Electric Boat.

PORTSMOUTH'S WAR RECORD
Let Us Make It Better & Better
BUILDING TIME
ON WAYS   OVERBOARD

	KEEL LAID	LAUNCH	COMPLETE	
SS. 228 DRUM	243 days	226 days	469 days	
SS. 229 FLYFISH	215 days	213 days	428 days	*A*
SS. 230 FINBACK	201 days	206 days	407 days	RECORD
SS. 231 HADDOCK	203 days	179 days	382 days	*Another* RECORD
SS. 232 HALIBUT	201 days	161 days	362 days	DITTO
SS. 233 HERRING	184 days	146 days	330 days	DITTO
SS. 234 KINGFISH	185 days	106 days	291 days	DITTO
SS. 235 SHAD	173 days	91 days	264 days	DITTO
SS. 275 RUNNER	173 days	125 days	298 days	
SS. 276 SAWFISH	154 days	123 days	277 days	
SS. 277 SCAMP	136 days	123 days	259 days	
SS. 278 SCORPION	122 days	140 days	262 days	
SS. 279 SNOOK	120 days	133 days	253 days	
SS. 280 STEELH'D	102 days	120 days	222 days	

PORTSMOUTH'S WAR RECORD
Let Us Make It Better & Better!
BUILDING TIME
ON WAYS   OVERBOARD

	KEEL LAID	LAUNCH	COMPLETE
SS 285 BALAO	123 days	159 days	282 days
SS 286 BILLFISH	112 days	174 days	286 days
SS 287 BOWFIN	137 days	159 days	296 days
SS 288 CABRILLA	128 days	169 days	297 days
SS 289 CAPELIN	128 days	156 days	284 days
SS 290 CISCO	56 days	165 days	221 days
SS 291 CREVALLE	100 days	136 days	236 days
SS 308 APOGON	91 days	149 days	240 days
SS 309 ASPRO	101 days	134 days	235 days
SS 310 BATFISH	129 days	124 days	253 days
SS 311 ARCHER-FISH	126 days	116 days	242 days
SS 312 BURRFISH	114 days	115 days	229 days

Wartime billboards at the Yard display pride in reducing building time in half as submarine production became more streamlined and efficient. Note completion times of Crevalle, Batfish, Archerfish *and other famous boats. UNH.*

From a work force of slightly more than 11,000 in 1941, Yard employment almost doubled to more than 20,000 in 1943. Work went on three shifts a day, seven days a week. Referring to the time before the war, Kennard Palfrey, a pattern maker, said, "you knew everybody you met in the Yard then." Those days were over. War workers swarmed into the Portsmouth area and rented rooms, attics, and even cellars. "Quiet, Please, War Worker Sleeping" was a familiar sign in house windows. Despite blackout regulations, lights burned nightly at the Yard. This around-the-clock pace reduced the building time per submarine from 469 calendar days in 1941 to 173 calendar days in 1944.[8]

The mobilization of the Yard occurred literally before the sun set on December 7. The Yard doubled its guards and established a rigid censorship of all mail and communications. Naval officers halted all harbor shipping for examination. Marines at the Main Gate stopped cars even before they crossed the bridge to the guard house and conducted a complete search of every vehicle. The navy and other military branches cancelled all leaves and manned the Yard's and harbor defenses.

On December 15, Rear Admiral John D. Wainwright, Commandant of the Yard, addressed 8000 workers at a war rally. "We can replace the ships we lost at Pearl Harbor," Wainwright said, "but we cannot replace the lives that were lost. . . We must wipe the Japanese Navy from the face of the world. . . When you men go back to your machines today make them do double work. We need it. You need it."[9]

Within weeks the Yard was transformed for war. In December the navy mined the approaches to Portsmouth harbor and later installed a submarine net to prevent U-boats from coming up the Piscataqua. New Year's Day 1942 was merely another work day. In January the Yard tested its air raid apparatus in the open at full volume. The alarm was heard nearly eight miles away.[10]

The launching of the *USS Herring* on January 15, 1942, the first Portsmouth sub off the ways since the declaration of war against the Axis powers, reflected this grim mood. According to custom since World War I, the entire work force and Yard personnel always attended every launch on recess amidst a festive mood. As the *Herring* slid into the Piscataqua, however, only a small group of officers and those men actually engaged in her construction observed the brief ceremonies. Everyone else remained on the job at his machine, bench, or post. Such austere and lightly attended launchings, closed to the public, were standard for the rest of the war.[11]

The Mysterious Disappearance of the Surcouf

As the Yard strove to expand its production during the spring of 1942, military and civilian personnel received news of the sinking of the Free French sub *Surcouf,* to which they had devoted nearly five months of repair and overhaul the year before. Controversy continues to this day about the circumstances surrounding the *Surcouf*'s fate.

After leaving the Yard, the *Surcouf* participated during late December 1941 in the bloodless Free French seizure of the Vichy-ruled islands of St. Pierre and Miquelon, off the coast of Newfoundland. The *Surcouf* was then ordered to proceed to Tahiti via the Panama Canal. Leaving Bermuda on February 12, 1942, the sub was due at Colon, Panama, a week later. She never arrived. In April the Free French headquarters in London announced that "the submarine *Surcouf* is considerably overdue and must be considered lost." On April 18 the American press carried the story of the sub's disappearance. According to a subsequent U. S. Navy report, the *SS Thompson Lykes,* an American merchant ship "accidentally hit and sank a ship that it believes to be a submarine ... about 75 miles northeast of Colon at 0330 Feb. 19."[12]

Portsmouth felt the loss of the sub and all hands. On the Sunday following the announcement of the sub's demise, mourners placed flowers on the altar of St. John's Church in memory of their many acquaintances among the *Surcouf*'s officers and crew.

Rumors and whispers around the Yard, however, expressed skepticism about the official versions of the sub's sinking. One story current at the time asserted that a Coast Guard blimp spotted the *Surcouf* refueling a U-boat off Georges Bank, south of Cape Cod, Massachusetts, and that the blimp dropped bombs to sink them both. Another unofficial but persistent version of the sub's sinking circulated. When the *Surcouf* put out to sea with a full load of fuel, she returned shortly thereafter almost empty with the story that she had accidentally lost most of it. This pattern repeated itself several times. American naval officials became suspicious and sent two experimental subs, Portsmouth's *Marlin* and EB's *Mackerel,* to investigate. The American boats were said to discover that the *Surcouf* was refueling a U-boat and accordingly administered the "coup de grâce" to both. One rumor even claims that the *Surcouf* was carrying gold on her last voyage.

In 1967 diver Lee Prettyman, Jr. announced that he had located the sunken hull of the *Surcouf* in Long Island Sound but refused to elaborate or disclose the exact site. The French consul in Washington was offended. "I find it more than regrettable that 'legends' should be revived anew," he said. "They constitute an insult to the memory of the men aboard the *Surcouf*, all of whom gave their lives not only for France, but for the Allies."[13]

The English sub *Pandora*, another visitor to the Yard for an overhaul and refit, met a similar but less tragic end. She hit a mine off the island of Malta in the Mediterranean, and German ships fired on the disabled target. Blasts killed several English sailors in the engine room. The *Pandora* sank in about twenty feet of water. The rest of the crew, however, equipped with Momsen Lungs provided by the American Navy, escaped and survived.[14]

The Yard's Accelerated Building Program

The major objective of the Yard during the war was to construct submarines. It was difficult to make changes on the submarine's basic design while simultaneously attempting to turn out as many subs as possible. "Sub design didn't change much during the war," said Robert Evans, who served at the ship design section, Bureau of Ships, from 1940 to 1946. But Andy McKee, continuing as planning officer at the Yard until 1944, came up with some new ideas and refinements which saved many submarines and lives during their patrols.[15]

McKee proposed changes to the *Gato* class, developed and produced from 1941 to 1943. The new *Gato* class was virtually the same as the older *Tambor* class except for the addition of a watertight bulkhead to divide the engine compartment into two smaller and less vulnerable sections. To accommodate this change, the hull was lengthened by five feet. McKee was still not satisfied. Improving the *Gato* class, McKee made the most significant advance of submarine design developed during the war. His innovation was incorporated in the new *Balao* class.

In late 1941 McKee and another naval officer calculated they could increase the thickness of submarine hull plating and framing to practically double the sub's operating depth. By switching from mild steel to high-tensile steel, McKee increased the sub's operating depth from 300 to 400 feet. McKee was confident, moreover, that the new *Balao* class could dive to 600 feet, but did not recommend it unless skippers found themselves in dire emergency. These new boats, dubbed "thick skins," were one of the best-kept secrets of the war. Practically identical in outward appearance and in internal layout to the older type, these subs fooled Japanese naval experts. Unaware that there had been any change made in American subs, the Japanese set their depth charges to explode at the shallower depth capacity of the older boats. Since the new *Balao* class subs could dive much deeper, enemy depth charges exploded well above their targets.[16]

The decision to shift to a "thick skin" boat was made just after Pearl Harbor. The Yard achieved another "Portsmouth-first" in building the prototype of this new class. On October 27, 1942, the *USS Balao*, constructed in record time, slid down the ways exactly four months after her keel laying. The tenth submarine launched at the Yard in 1942, the *Balao* was a fit offering as a Navy Day present. Some 119 *Balao*-class subs were built during 1942-1945, forty-four of them Portsmouth boats.[17]

The commandant of the Yard during most of the war was Rear Admiral Withers. A 1906 graduate of the Naval Academy, Withers had served previously as the commanding officer of the Pacific Submarine Fleet during the Pearl Harbor attack. Transferred to the Yard in June 1942, the kindly, soft-spoken Withers served as commandant until his retirement from active duty in November 1945.[18]

The wartime emergency brought to the Yard new categories of employees never before hired in force. Men hired through the Civil Service Commission still constituted the vast majority of workers. But with so many men entering the armed forces the Yard sought other sources of labor. Women worked as welders, machinists and crane operators. Four "welderettes" in slacks and lumberjack clothes began work in early 1943. Mary E. "Mae" Adams, a twenty-seven year old, operated a three-ton wall crane. "Not many girls can stand climbing up fifty feet to the crane seat," she said, "but there are ten of us over here now. The height doesn't bother me at all."

Helen Lawrence was an electrician's helper. "Safety was lax during the war," she said. "No hard hats, safety shoes or ear plugs." Going down a submarine hatch for the first time, she gripped the rungs of the ladder. "Once I reached the bottom," she said, "my co-workers painted the heels of my boots yellow. It was a sign that I was initiated into their group."

Other women worked as pipefitters and clearers in the shops. During the mid-morning lunch periods volunteer shop bands entertained. "Rosie the Riveter and her boyfriend," the *Portsmouth Herald* reported, "are dancing in dungarees ... munching and lunching in time to swing music that echoes through the cavernous expanse of the yard's inside machine shop." On the wall a huge banner proclaimed, "Remember Pearl Harbor." Yard officials encouraged the melodic interlude during the lunch period to boost morale and encourage relaxation. Couples danced between the turret lathes and around pipes, axles and propeller screws. "Morale was good," Helen Lawrence said.[19]

During summer vacations high school students also found ready employment at the Yard. The minimum age was sixteen. "Some worked at fifteen, even fourteen years old, after changing their birth certificates," said Robert Harford, a worker in this special program. "The kids were assigned to older and more mature men, ran errands, picked up tools and took them to job sites. They crawled under work projects where a larger man would find difficulty." The students were assigned at random to any shop, earned $5.92 a day, and were promoted every month. After three months they earned $6.16 a day for top pay. "Some didn't want to go back to school," Harford said. "They preferred to work and earn good money."[20]

The inmates of the naval prison also performed useful work during the war. Under the supervision of an armed marine guard, these prisoners left the confines of the Castle to shovel snow, sweep floors, cut ice from South Pond, and work at special details around the Yard. One security rule was not to walk between the guard and his prisoners. After completing their work detail, the prisoners would often drag their shovels on the pavement to make a racket, thus irritating the guard as they walked back to the Castle.[21]

There was simply not enough room in the Yard to carry out all its assigned duties. Before the war, Shop 37 made 90 percent of the electrical boxes and switches of the U. S. Navy. The Bureau of Ships in Washington directed the Yard to double its production of these vital parts. To handle this increased load, the Yard purchased in early 1942 a vacant plant with 345,000 square feet of floor space at Somersworth, New Hampshire, eighteen miles to the northwest. The Electrical Manufacturing Shop (Shop 37) moved there in June with a minimum of lost time in production. From fifty-three men in the pre-war days, the shop swelled to more than 3750 men and women. At a formal dedication attended by 2500 people on August 15, 1942, Admiral Withers said:

> The submarine is the most valuable weapon we have at our command today. It can move into enemy territory and it is the only craft in the world that rides on its own all the time. Friend and enemy alike are trying to eliminate a submarine. When she leaves her home port she goes for two and three months. Everyone is after her. But I love the darned things.[22]

Withers's comments about the national importance of the Yard's submarines elicited strong support from the local community. Businesses with wartime contracts contributed their specialized goods. Kidder Press in Dover made valves, control parts and firing pins for torpedoes. One aspect of this arrangement was ironical. "A pacifist upstate built valves and pins," pattern maker Ken Palfrey said, "and sold them to Kidder Press, little realizing that his parts were eventually used in torpedoes." A steel foundry in Revere, Massachusetts, and a welding shop in South Berwick, Maine, also delivered parts to the Yard. The University of New Hampshire at nearby Durham sent professors to teach courses in mechanics and technology for Yard workmen. Often at the end of a class the mechanics would say, "That fellow [the U.N.H. professor] learned more than we did today."[23]

As commandant, Withers could fire people and possessed wartime emergency powers. Workers were civil service employees and were not allowed to strike. There was no union at the Yard then. "There was a sense of challenge during World War II," rigger Fred White said. "There were some deadheads and rummies around, but very few."[24]

Multiple Launchings

Patriotic spirit and hard work accelerated the delivery of the submarines to the fleet. From four subs in 1941, the Yard produced twelve in 1942, nineteen in 1943, thirty-two in 1944, and twelve through August 1945. To accomplish this task, the Yard expanded its industrial facilities. Workers built an emergency building basin (now Dry Dock #3) located on the back channel. A new dry dock (now Dry Dock #1) was constructed on the site of the old floating dock basin bordering the Piscataqua. Dry Dock #2, located on the site of the Jenkin's Gut channel, could accommodate six fleet boats. The old wooden shiphouse with two ways proved inadequate and in 1939 was removed. The steel shiphouse replacing it contained five ways and in 1942 was further expanded.[25]

The time required to deliver the boats to the fleet was also stream-lined. In the pre-war days this process took months: a week of builder's trials, preliminary trials at Provincetown, a shakedown cruise (usually to South America), and final trials at Provincetown, with each phase followed by periods of minor repairs and alterations at the Yard. The fleet's urgent need for subs resulted in a much faster procedure. After a one-day inspection alongside the docks, the newly completed boats spent sixteen days in the Portsmouth area in training and for minor adjustments. The subs then proceeded to Newport and New London for another sixteen days of advanced training, after which they departed for the fleet.[26]

This quickened pace resulted in many unprecedented events at the Yard. On June 23, 1942, for example, the *Sawfish* slid down the ways in darkness at 8:40 P.M., the first night launching of an undersea craft in history. A month later, on July 20, 1942, the first double launching of American subs occurred when the *Scamp* followed by the *Scorpion* splashed into the Piscataqua. The Yard's sixth and seventh subs for 1942 were constructed on parallel ways. Planning officer Andy McKee watched proudly for a special reason—his daughter was the sponsor of the *Scamp*.[27]

Bow view of Scorpion (SS278) *underway on Piscataqua in 1942. Note U.S. Naval Prison ("the Castle") in background. PA.*

On October 27, 1943, the Yard joined the nation in saluting Navy Day with the first triple launching of submarines in history. From the new building basin at 10:30 A.M., the *Sterlet* and the *Pomfret* were floated into the Piscataqua. From the nearby huge construction shed the *Piranha* slid down the ways at 11:15 A.M. After their christening with champagne as well as with plain rain water, the three boats were then tied up at fitting-out piers. The building of *Sterlet* and *Pomfret* also represented a new development. Unlike earlier boats built under protective sheds, they were constructed entirely within the open building basin, exposed to the elements. Once the hull was welded together, the crews could work under cover in relative comfort.[28]

The biggest launch day ever was approaching in early 1944. Three boats, the *Razorback*, *Redfish* and *Ronquil*, were nearing completion in the building basin, while the *Scabbardfish* lay on the ways "on the hill" in the steel shiphouse. Job specialists worked on one sub for a few days and then moved to another. The prospective commanding officer (PCO), Louis D. "Sandy" McGregor, Jr. of the *Redfish*, arrived months in advance at the Yard. Going through the shops and talking to the workers, McGregor wanted to learn from personal observation the capabilities of his assigned sub. "Let's look at the boat," he said to his crew. McGregor arranged for the workers to install sixteen vent flood holes (eight on each side of the hull, twice the usual amount) so that she could dive faster. Daniel MacIsaac, a torpedoman, was the seventh man assigned to the *Redfish*. Calling the *Redfish* "the Queen of the fleet," MacIsaac was happy as he anticipated serving on this new boat. His previous duty had been aboard two older subs, the *R-2* and the *Bonita*. "I felt confident about serving on the *Redfish*, a thickskin," MacIsaac said. "I felt nothing could happen to me."[29]

On January 27, 1944, Admiral Withers spoke to the group in the launching stand. "In the launching of four submarines in a single day," Withers said, "the Portsmouth Navy Yard sets another record in the submarine program." The *Redfish*, *Ronquil* and *Razorback* floated out of their basin at 1:00 P.M.; the *Scabbardfish* hit the water an hour later. After tying the boats at their piers, workmen prepared to move the stacked sections of steel for the next pair of subs down into the building basin.[30]

On April 1, 1944, the Yard laid the keel of the *USS Tench*, the prototype for the new *Tench* class and the last type of fleet submarine built before the end of the war. This class represented a refinement of the *Balao*-type hull with a more efficient arrangement of various fuel and water tanks as well as newer engines and equipment.

Yard workers displayed their flexibility during 1944 by completing the *Lionfish* and the *Manta*, two unfinished boats brought up from the faltering Cramp Shipbuilding Company in Philadelphia. In addition, other boats arrived. The Italian submarines *Speri*, *Mameli*, *Dandola*, *Marea* and *Ornice*, "repatriated" after the fall of the regime of Benito Mussolini, arrived at the Yard during 1944-1945 for successful overhauls and refits.[31]

The legacy of hard work and building experience did not end at the Yard's boundaries. During the war Captain Edgar Ladd, a former Yard master electrician, served in his activated National Guard unit on a remote Pacific island. An American sub limped into the island's port

Razorback, Redfish, *and* Ronquil *(left to right) awaiting triple launching from Yard's Dry Dock #1 on January 27, 1944.* Scabbardfish, *launched an hour later from Building Ways, completed record four launches in one day.* UNH.

Christening of Redfish *on January 27, 1944, during record launching of four boats in one day. Note dry dock has been filled with water preparatory to floating subs into Piscataqua. PA.*

Trout docked at base prior to World War II. All numerals on Navy ships, such as "202" illustrated here, were removed for wartime service to avoid ship's identification by the enemy. PA.

with her wiring burned out. The Portsmouth-built sub was virtually paralyzed since the sub's crew and the workmen on the island were unable to make repairs. There were no naval electricians within several thousand miles who were familiar with the sub's equipment. Naval officials contacted the New Hampshire National Guard unit in hopes that among this contingent someone might have worked at the Yard. Ladd responded. When he started to work on the burned-out equipment, he found it was the same apparatus he had installed earlier, 15,000 miles away.

"It was just like old times," Ladd wrote to Withers. "In a few short hours I managed to rig something from the boat's emergency equipment and everything was soon shipshape." After Ladd's repairs the sub refueled and went back on patrol to hunt for Japanese targets.[32]

President Franklin D. Roosevelt did not live to see final victory. The nation's commander-in-chief and the Yard's friend through the years died on April 12, 1945. In tribute, Admiral Withers spoke for the Yard:

> The sudden and untimely death of Franklin Delano Roosevelt is a great loss to the navy. His understanding and interest in naval matters has contributed more than anything else to the great expansion which has been accomplished during the present conflict. That he will not see the vast fleets that he helped so materially to create conclude the task for which they were constructed is indeed unfortunate. He would wish no greater tribute than the final victory for which he has built. The navy will continue to move toward that goal.[33]

With the flag at half-mast, the Yard conducted memorial services for the late president on April 15 on the parade grounds in front of the marine barracks.

The Surrender of the U-Boats

The next month brought half of the final victory pledged by Admiral Withers. When Nazi Germany capitulated on May 7, 1945, her submarines on the high seas surrendered. As the largest American submarine base on the Atlantic coast, the Yard was ideally suited to receive these captured boats. At least seven U-boats were towed or escorted to Portsmouth during 1945. The German submarine design, the most advanced in the world, elicited paramount attention. The German U-boat prisoners, housed at the Castle, were required to work on their boats and to explain their systems to American authorities.[34]

The excitement surrounding the arrival of the U-boats generated the greatest press coverage in the Portsmouth area since the sinking of the *O-9* in 1941. The story was national news. The *USS Dekanisora*, a navy tug, served as a press boat to convey the many reporters and photographers out to X-ray Buoy, eighteen miles off the coast. During five days in mid-May, four captured U-boats, the *U-805*, *U-873*, *U-1228* and *U-234*, arrived under escort at the Yard, and their crews were removed to the naval prison. Prior to their surrender, German skippers threw log books and documents overboard. The boats showed the wear of their last voyages. Most were dirty inside. Their hulls were rusted, with huge strips of paint peeling off the conning towers. The scarred condition of the boats' paint indicated they had been submerged for most of the time during their final cruises.

The German submariners were young men in fine physical condition. Their faces had a yellowish-white tinge, produced during many days of submergence without sunlight. They wore rubber suits. Their submarine service reaped the benefits of the best provisions their country could offer; there was plenty of excellent food aboard as well as cognac, brandy, and other alcoholic beverages. Prison officials searched the men and found among their personal belongings eleven cents in American coins, German and Dutch paper money, family photographs, and pictures of girl friends and pin-up girls. One prisoner, stricken with appendicitis, was taken immediately to the base hospital, where doctors performed a successful operation.[35]

At the prison the Germans took showers, recieved clean POW outfits and appeared at the mess hall for their meals. The marine guards, many of them Pacific combat veterans, handled the prisoners in a fair but stern manner. The skipper of the *U-805* protested about the food and argued that he should not be made to eat with his men. He demanded service while his crew was eating cafeteria style. After the skipper waited in vain, he finally walked up and served himself at the cafeteria line. An unconcerned guard looked on and explained such officers would eat their food when they were ready. "They always do," he said.

With the other German officers, *U-873* skipper Fritz Steinhoff was taken to the Charles Street jail in Boston, pending his transfer to the Fort Devens prisoner-of-war camp. On May 19 in his cell Steinhoff broke his spectacles and with a jagged piece of the lens slashed one of his wrists. Taken to a hospital, he died shortly after his arrival. Army officials at the jail took precautions to prevent similar suicide attempts.[36]

The huge 1600-ton *U-234* was the chief prize. Surrendering to two American destroyer escorts 500 miles off the coast of Newfoundland, the German sub arrived at the Yard on May 19. En route to Japan, the *U-234* contained uranium oxide and blueprints for jet planes. Two Japanese aviation experts aboard committed suicide by drinking Luminal. Other important passengers aboard the sub included a German civilian V-2 rocket technician and three Luftwaffe generals. One was General Ulrich Kessler, the English-speaking commander of the German Air Force who had directed the 1939 Poland blitz.

Hoping to discover German secrets which might be of value to the American sub fleet still fighting in the Pacific, American naval officials and technicians examined the special equipment on the *U-234*. The sub possessed a snorkel which enabled the boat to charge its batteries for its diesel engines without surfacing. The snorkel supplied oxygen for the engines, but had nothing to do with the air the men breathed inside the hull. In late June the Yard inspectors discovered an unusual cargo aboard the *U-234* which had completely escaped their attention. Stripping the

American sailor checks through interior of captured German U-boat under study at the Yard. UNH.

boat, the Yard crews found $5 million worth of mercury in flasks hidden between the inner and outer hulls on either side of the keel. This cargo served as a ballast, and if the sub had reached Japan, the mercury would have been used in making alloys.[37]

In September 1945, the *U-3008* and *U-2513*, two sister boats, arrived at the Yard, minus their German crews, for detailed study of their advanced technical features. The "Thirty-Oh-Eight," as she was known, remained at the Yard a long time. The world's most advanced sub was put on blocks and given a minute examination. "The navy studied every inch of her," wrote one Yard worker. "It lifted her lines and studied her ballasting, torpedo handling, optical and structural systems." The Americans studied the sub's increased battery power, streamlined hull, snorkel, and super-silent "creeping motor." The last feature enabled her to slip away, unheard, from a depth-charge attack. On July 24, 1946, the American Navy commissioned the boat at the Yard as the *3008*. After

German submarines, U-2513, U-3008 *and* U-505 *(left to right) at berths in Yard following surrender after World War II. Note Memorial Bridge and old Portsmouth waterfront in background. UNH.*

two years of service, she was decommissioned. She was not towed from Portsmouth for "final disposition" until 1951.[38]

The *U-505* was perhaps the best known German U-boat associated with the Yard. Seized by the American Navy in June 1944 off the coast of French West Africa, the German sub made naval history. Her capture marked the first time since 1812 that the U. S. Navy had taken an enemy man-of-war on the high seas. Its capture was kept secret until after the war because the Americans had found a German naval code book which enabled the Allied intelligence to follow Nazi war moves.

Brought to Portsmouth in September 1945 and docked at the foot of Daniel Street near the Memorial Bridge, the U-boat was open to the public to promote a Victory Bond drive. The American crew bringing the *U-505* to the United States had already stripped the boat for souvenirs — name plates, gauges, and small pieces of equipment which were not double riveted to the hull. After a week at Portsmouth, the boat toured other Atlantic and Gulf ports and eventually returned the same year. Remaining at the Yard at her Back Channel mooring until 1954, the *U-505* rusted in neglect. The city of Chicago finally decided to acquire the sub as a war memorial for the Museum of Science and Industry located five hundred feet from Lake Michigan. On May 14, 1954, the *U-505* began her journey to Chicago via the St. Lawrence River, Welland Canal, and the Great Lakes, a distance of 2500 miles. A Portsmouth tug, *Pauline L. Moran*, towed the sub to Lake Erie for the first leg of her journey, where a Coast Guard cutter took over. In late June the U-boat arrived at Chicago, becoming the first sub to cross the Great Lakes. There the *U-505* remains to this day as one of the prime attractions of the museum.[39]

Fighting Submariners

When Pearl Harbor was bombed, the United States had 111 operational submarines in commission and another seventy-three under construction. At war's end in mid-August 1945, the navy had a force of 260 commissioned subs, 202 of them delivered during the war.

Portsmouth-built *USS Grayling (SS-209)* participated in a symbolic first step on the long road to victory. Leaving San Diego on December 17, 1941, the sub arrived at Pearl Harbor a week later. Her deck was soon chosen as the site of an historic change of command ceremony. A signed photograph of the *Grayling* bears the following inscription:

> At Pearl Harbor on 31 December 1941 [I] hoisted 4-star Admiral's flag on *U.S.S. Grayling* and took command of the U. S. Pacific Fleet.
> [signed]   C.W. Nimitz, Fleet Admiral, U.S.N.

After this honor by the Navy and Admiral Chester W. Nimitz, the *Grayling* left on her first war patrol a few days later.[40]

The Portsmouth-built *Pollack* soon achieved another historic distinction. On January 7, 1942, off the coast of Honshu, the *Pollack* sank the Japanese cargo ship *Unkai Maru No. 1*, the first officially confirmed victim of the Pacific Fleet Submarine Force.

In 1942 Rear Admiral Charles A. Lockwood, Jr., assumed command of the submarines of the Asiatic Force. The next year he was promoted to vice admiral with an even greater assignment—Commander, Submarine Force, U.S. Pacific Fleet. Once stationed at the Yard in the 1920s and a well known submariner, Lockwood was popular among his

Admiral Chester W. Nimitz (center with "scrambled eggs" on cap) taking
command of U.S. Pacific Fleet aboard Grayling *at Pearl Harbor in*
December 1941. PA.

men. "He was a legend," Daniel MacIsaac of the *Redfish* said. "We knew
him as 'Uncle Charlie.'" Lockwood helped to secure the leasing of the
Royal Hawaiian Hotel at Waikiki Beach, Honolulu, as a rest camp for
submariners and aviators back from war operations. "Nothing was too
good for his boys," MacIsaac said.[41]

For Lockwood and his men, the mission was simple and direct:
destroy the Japanese fleet and end the war in the Pacific. As Lockwood
entered the lobby of an Albany, Western Australia, hotel in 1942, he
heard a dozen American submarine officers and their girls singing at the
top of their lungs:

> Sink 'em all, sink 'em all
> Tojo and Hitler and all:
> Sink all their cruisers and carriers too,
> Sink all their tin cans and their stinking crews.

Sung to the tune of an Australian song, "Bless 'Em All," these verses set the mood and tone for the American submariners in their fight against the Japanese empire. "Good luck and good hunting" was the popular saying in the submarine service. The sneak attack against Pearl Harbor, the Bataan death march, and rumors about conditions in Japanese prisoner-of-war camps incensed the sub skippers. "Any man who does not hate the Japanese," said skipper Sandy McGregor of the *Redfish* upon meeting his crew for the first time in 1944, "need not serve on this vessel." As submariners have always asserted, "There are two kinds of ships in the navy. Submarines and targets."[42]

The Routine of War Patrols in the Pacific

Virtually all the targets were, in fact, Japanese ships in the Pacific. American submarines enjoyed relatively few opportunities to destroy the capital ships of Germany and Italy. The warships of these other Axis powers were usually bottled up at North, Baltic and Mediterranean Sea ports and Norwegian fjords.

The patrols of Submarine Squadron Fifty, formed at New London in September 1942, represent the limited activities of American fleet boats in the Atlantic theatre of war. In late October the six new submarines of the squadron, among them Portsmouth-built *Herring* and *Shad*, sailed for a base in Scotland. The boats were then deployed to the coast of northern Africa to provide reconnaissance for "Operation Torch," the Anglo-American invasion of that area. During November as the two Portsmouth boats patrolled off the Moroccan coast, the *Herring* sank a Vichy French merchantman off Casablanca.

In operations during the winter of 1942-1943, the squadron submarines concentrated on the Bay of Biscay off the Spanish Atlantic coast. The *Shad* sunk a barge. In the same area the *Herring* attacked and sent the Nazi submarine *U-163* to the bottom.

In mid-1943 the United States decided to withdraw her fleet boats from the European war zone for use in the Pacific. En route back to New London the six submarines conducted a sweep through Norwegian and Icelandic waters but encountered no targets. During their twenty-seven war patrols, including the "Operation Torch" operation, American submarines tangled with U-boats and fired torpedoes and shots at Axis merchant ships. Postwar records credit few positive sinkings, with several in dispute. Thereafter American fleet boats did not operate off the coasts of Europe and Africa. The U.S. Navy concentrated solely on the many Japanese targets in the rich hunting grounds of the Pacific.

To conduct these Pacific patrols, Admirals Nimitz and Lockwood relied upon an outstanding group of submarine officers. A typical skipper

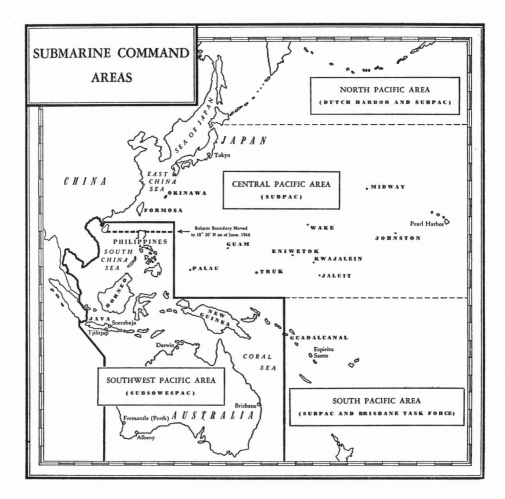

Pacific War Zones assigned to skippers of American subs who located the majority of their targets at straits, shipping lanes, Japanese homeports and island bases. USNI.

was a graduate of the Academy and held the rank of lieutenant commander. Known as "captain" to his officers and the "old man" to his crew, he was usually a man in his early thirties. Submarining with its many pressures was a young man's profession. Second in command, the executive officer or "exec" also served as the navigator. In case something happened to the skipper, the "exec" would assume command. Others served in specialized capacities as the torpedo, gunnery, communications or engineering officers.

"One is well prepared to be a skipper and knows all the jobs," said submarine commanding officer Sam Francis. "The skipper provides the

Two Pampanito *shipmates relax beside deck gun during World War II. PA.*

leadership and the incentive and makes it the best sub. He supplies the morale and leadership that meld it together." Such an example brought respect. "The officers were down to earth," electrician Gerald McLees said. "You could talk to them."[43]

In addition to the officers, about seventy-five enlisted men made up the sub's complement. The chief of the boat, the sub's equivalent to the army's first sergeant, led the crew, assisted by a half dozen petty officers long experienced in submarines. But those on a war patrol worked as a team without recourse to the protocol of rank. All submariners were volunteers, highly intelligent, socially compatible and trained in dual or triple capacities. "Do what you were told and get along with your shipmates," was the advice of *Grenadier* radioman Edgar Poss. "Otherwise those who didn't get along would get off the boat."[44]

Submariners developed their own special language, calling torpedoes "fish," and referring to enemy ships in the masculine as "he." "Tin cans" were destroyers which dropped "ash cans" or depth charges. As the Japanese used the suffix, "maru," as part of the name for their merchant vessels, American submariners used the same term to refer to any Japanese ship except a warship.

Morale among submariners was high, perhaps in part because they received 50 percent extra pay for their service. "Submariners stick together," said Joseph Enright, skipper of the *Archerfish*. Gerald McLees served briefly aboard surface ships but found them too impersonal. "It was like living in a big city," he said. "On a submarine you know everybody, what their girl friend's name is, how their parents are."[45]

The submariners' pride in their boat was reflected in the fanciful emblem, usually a caricature of the fish or sea creature after which the boat was named. The crewmen put the emblem on stationery, patches adorning their foul-weather jackets, and battle flags. Walt Disney Studios and artist Ray Young of Wisconsin created many emblems. The crews delighted in the pugnacious look of the fish. "The more vicious you could make them," Young said, "the better they liked them."[46]

Assigning names to the boats themselves was the responsibility of William F. Calkins, an officer in Washington during the war. Submarines were named for fish, and during the height of its shipbuilding program the Navy had about 500 in action, under construction, or on the planning boards. "There are not as many fish as you think," Calkins wrote. Before he took over the job, such obvious names as *Trout, Bass, Salmon*, and *Shark* had been used. "I was reduced," he continued, "to scrambling around for names like *Spinax, Irex, Mero*, and *Sirago*. You wouldn't want to call a naval vessel the *USS Big-Eyed Scad*."

There were several ways around this dilemma. If the sub was named *Shark*, there could be another named *Tiburon*, which is Spanish for shark. Others were the *Jack*, the *Amberjack* and the *Ulua*, three names for the identical fish. "There were the *Chub* and the *Hardhead*," Calkins wrote, "both minnows, but we couldn't name a fighting ship the *USS Minnow*. We decided we could not put the *Sardine* on the navy list, but we named the *USS Sarda*—same fish."[47]

Once underway on their patrols, the officers and crew operated as a professional team. Submarine duty demanded by far the most technical skills of any branch of the U.S. Navy. "There is room aboard a submarine for everything but a mistake," one saying went. The dive represented the most critical test for a crew, since most accidents occurred then. Diving included both to "periscope depth," with the eye a foot or two above water and the keel thirty feet down, and to "pressure depth" which was about 300 feet down. Upon the skipper's orders, passed through the sub by voice and telephone, all hands sprang immediately to their diving stations. Talk ceased entirely; smoking stopped. Everyone had a definite sequence of duties down to the cook who had to secure the kitchen sink.

"We practiced these maneuvers time and again," said Jack Sousae, a veteran submariner. "With the diving alarm, those on deck must be off in thirty seconds and in one minute the boat went to periscope depth. Seven people had to jump through the hatch. There were many bloody noses as men squeezed through with a nose between them and a pair of binoculars. Then the O.D. [officer of the deck] pulled the hatch." Once inside the men still counted on their agility. "No one put his hands on the rungs," MacIsaac said. "Otherwise your hands would be stepped on. Once on the bottom, one leaped out of the way."[48]

On the ninety-day wartime patrols, no one took a shower, just a rubdown with alcohol. Officers and crew alike walked around in boxer shorts and sneakers. Little of the routine aboard the boat was ever recorded. "Diaries were not permitted," said William Gray, Chief of the Boat on the *Sailfish*. "All your mail was censored. My wife complained, 'What's the matter? You never tell me anything.'" MacIsaac numbered each letter and wrote twenty-five letters on one patrol. Upon reaching port he received eighty-seven letters in one lump. "I sorted my girl friends out by the postmark." he said.[49]

For purposes of watch-standing, the officers and crew, except the skipper, stood watches eight hours on and four off. The captain remained constantly on call. For the enlisted men the cramped quarters in the sub did not permit the luxury of individual sleeping quarters. The crew used the "hot bunk" method in which the man going off watch would wake up his successor and then sleep in his buddy's rack.

The quartermaster on watch wrote the rough log, which was the responsibility of the duty officer. The captain then edited the log, possibly adding and deleting. Within twenty-four hours the duty officer finally finished the "smooth log," which was ultimately forwarded to the Navy Department in Washington. The first watch on New Year's Day, from midnight to 0400 (4:00 A.M.) was a special occasion. "It's a navy tradition," MacIsaac said, "to write a poem for that watch describing the boat's position and weather."[50]

The food served aboard the sub during the war patrols was the best. Before the boat left for sea, the men carried on fresh provisions, milk, bread, fruit, and cases of canned goods. They stashed the food everywhere, in the passageways and in the hatch in the mess hall. "One skipper I had insisted the torpedo tube be filled with potatoes," said Chuck Hermenau, "because he loved the spuds. He was a fat man like a smiling Buddha." By the end of the patrol, however, provisions were low and they would be eating powdered eggs. "A bad cook doesn't last long, MacIsaac said. "They would get rid of him. The cook is the morale builder of the boat." Gerald McLees took no chances. "We put the canned shrimp in the maneuvering room so that we electricians could snack on it." Since boats were often submerged during daylight, the main meal of the day occurred at midnight when the boat surfaced to recharge her batteries. At 4:00 A.M. the sub would submerge again.[51]

On patrol the men often endured weeks of boredom broken by periods of furious action. "We might have twelve to sixteen hours of battle station," McLees said, "and then pull guard watch for four hours." Recreation was limited, but the officers and men found ways to relax. They watched movies, read, wrote letters, and slept. After meals they played cards or acey-deucey, a version of backgammon. Poker games in the crew's mess hall went on continuously as the place served as a twenty-four-hour center for snacks and coffee. The "joe" pot, or coffee urn, was always being refilled. The officers' wardroom was also a busy place. Armand "Legs" Legare played many games of cribbage in the wardroom. For luck he always laid his string of rosary beads out on the table. His cribbage opponent would remark, "I've got to beat Him and you too!"[52]

If the patrol was successful, crew members hoisted battle flags as they approached home base. Preparation of the flag of the *Redfish* followed a standard procedure. "We used meatballs for tankers and freighters," MacIsaac said, "and a rising sun for a man-of-war." To dramatize their victories even more, American submariners revived an old naval custom. Skippers lashed brooms to their periscopes to signify a "sweep" of enemy shipping, a tradition dating from the seventeenth century when the Dutch Admiral Maarten Harpertszoon Tromp hoisted a broom to his masthead to symbolize his intent to sweep the English from the sea.[53]

As the subs approached their home ports in Australia, Midway or Pearl, liberty boats (used to take crews ashore for liberty or leave) came out in the harbor with fresh milk, orange juice, and ice cream. By naval tradition these boats supplied treats for the sub's crew even before the distribution of mail. In other ports bumboats run by native peddlers often appeared, offering provisions or trinkets for sale. Upon landing the officers and men had two weeks of leave to relax in the leading hotels in

Australia or Hawaii. "We had good times in port," McLees said. In Perth, Australia, the U.S. Navy leased four hotels for American sub crews, including the fashionable King Edward Hotel.

Admiral Lockwood ignored talk in some quarters of pampering as he felt "the rehabilitation of our crews throughout the war paid large dividends in the form of better performance on patrol, better physical and mental health," As a result of this policy, Lockwood was convinced that "we lost fewer submarines."[54]

The Lucky Sailfish Returns Home

Many Portsmouth boats achieved fame with their outstanding patrols and exploits during the war. Some are subjects of full-length books, among them the *Batfish*, *Bowfin*, and *Seawolf*. The *Batfish* sank three Japanese submarines within a four-day period. The heroic deeds of the *Parche* and the *Tirante* earned congressional medal of honor awards for their daring skippers. But for sheer drama coupled with a compelling identity with the Yard and the people of New Hampshire and Maine, the saga of the legendary *Squalus/Sailfish* still retains a unique place in the history of the submarine service. The *Sailfish* gradually overcame her *Squalus* jinx to compile a brilliant war record. Because the boat represented so much history, the superstructure of the *Sailfish* became after the war a permanent memorial at the Yard.

On the morning of December 8, 1941, Manila time, news of the Japanese attack on Pearl Harbor reached the American naval command in the Philippines. The *Sailfish* was then moored at Cavite in Manila Bay. Morton C. Mumma, Jr., the boat's skipper, awakened the crew at 4:00 A.M. and ordered every man to the deck. "Pearl Harbor has been bombed," Mumma said. Shortly thereafter the *Sailfish* left on patrol. A stern disciplinarian, Mumma would not tolerate nonsense. After one sailor had informally christened the rebuilt boat as "Squailfish," Mumma was firm. Anyone referring to his boat by that name would be court-martialed.[55]

Along the west coast of Luzon on December 13, Mumma sighted three Japanese destroyers. After diving and firing torpedoes, the *Sailfish* was subjected to a depth-charge attack. Although none were dropped close enough to cause damage, Mumma's nerves shattered under the stress. He ordered his "exec" to assume command of the boat. Retiring to his stateroom, Mumma stayed there for the duration of the patrol. "We didn't know about it," Gerald McLees, an electrician, said, "until we got back into port."

On December 17 the *Sailfish* returned to Manila Bay under cover of darkness. "There was a blackout coming back into the channel," McLees said. "The channel light buoys flashed, were on for a few seconds, and one would get his bearings to navigate the channel." Mumma was relieved of command of the *Sailfish* and spent the rest of the war on shore duty.[56]

Following other patrols conducted from Australian ports, the *Sailfish* was overhauled at Mare Island, California, and refitted at Pearl Harbor. She left on her eighth war patrol from Midway on May 21, 1943. Her last two patrols had been unproductive.

On June 15, the *Sailfish* sighted two cargo ships off northern Honshu, Japan. After sinking one, the sub had to clear the area when escort ships dropped thirty-six depth charges. Ten days later the *Sailfish* picked up another convoy and sent a maru to the bottom. This time the sub's escape was imperiled; three Japanese escort destroyers appeared out of nowhere and delivered a devastating attack. In ten hours the enemy dropped ninety-eight depth charges. "The *Sailfish* had been through a lot," said William Gray, chief of the boat, "and many feared this attack would finish her. It was hard to breathe. We thought this might be a permanent address. The men were trembling. One officer was pacing back and forth through the sub. 'Sit down,' I said, 'you're making the crew nervous.'"[57]

The hard luck often associated with the *Sailfish* reversed. A storm came up. "When it rained," Gray said, "the sound gear on the Japanese surface ships wasn't too good." It was the right time to exploit this weakness of the enemy. "We've got to go up," the *Sailfish* skipper said. The boat surfaced and made a run for it. Her luck held. After her escape the *Sailfish* headed for Midway. Although the sub had sighted thirty-one ships exclusive of escorts, she was able to fire torpedoes only at two targets. "If you had a lousy, non-productive patrol," Gray said, "you might as well have stayed out there. The word got along through the grapevine."

The rumors circulating around Midway in this particular case held that the *Sailfish* could not have survived the heavy attack and undoubtedly had sunk. On July 3, the *Sailfish* arrived at Midway. "What boat is it?" asked the American naval personnel on the island.

"*Sailfish!*"

"Horsefeathers!"[58]

Robert Ward, an aggressive skipper, led the *Sailfish* on her tenth patrol. Determined to restore morale, Ward called the crew together. "Our craft was lucky," Ward said to them, "for they'd tried to keep her down and couldn't."[59]

On December 3, 1943, Bob Ward approached the Japanese coast in a winter typhoon. The sea was high in a driving rain with fifty-knot winds. A Japanese convoy neared home but had abandoned the usual zigzagging; its commander believed his ships were safe in such foul weather. At midnight Ward fired his torpedoes at the largest target, hearing two distinct hits. With the coming morning light, Ward attacked again. Finally at 7:58 A.M., December 4, Ward glimpsed his target through the periscope. "The picture now indicates," he wrote in the log, "that we have a badly damaged carrier...I am convinced the carrier is a dead duck....He has many planes on deck forward and enough people on deck aft to populate a fair size village....The number of people on deck indicates they are prepared to abandon ship — a reassuring picture."[60]

Ward fired three more torpedoes to hasten the carrier's demise. Heavy seas prevented visual confirmation of the sinking. Ward's entry at midnight reads, "One full day's work completed." Upon returning to Pearl Harbor, Ward saw Admiral Lockwood standing on the pier with a smile to personally greet the boat. Ward received the Navy Cross for conducting the most outstanding war patrol to date—three ships totaling 29,571 tons.

Ward had sunk the 20,000-ton *Chuyo*, the first Japanese aircraft carrier sunk by an American submarine. Unknown at the time to Ward and his men, the *Chuyo* was carrying aboard twenty-one American prisoners of war, one of two groups of survivors of the *USS Sculpin*. After the *Sculpin* was scuttled and sunk in mid-November during a one-sided battle with a Japanese destroyer, these twenty-one American men were en route to prison camps in Japan. By an irony of fate the *Sailfish* had killed all but one of the survivors in the group of the *Sculpin*, her sister sub which had come to her aid off the Isles of Shoals in 1939. But none of the *Sculpin* victims were members of the crew who discovered the *Squalus* four and a half years earlier; the 1939 *Sculpin* crew had long before been rotated to other assignments.[61]

During his patrols on periodic lifeguard duty Ward rescued at least twelve American pilots who had been shot down. When hit, the pilots would radio to indicate their location. Once, on a dark night, *Sailfish* couldn't find the rubber raft and the pilot. The next morning she surfaced and found the rubber boat with the pilot fishing with a line extending from his toe. "Those rescued pilots," Gray said of his service aboard the *Sailfish* and *Batfish*, "stayed for the duration of the patrol. They wanted to do something, offered to and did stand watches and decode messages."[62]

Bob Ward also conducted two more successful war patrols with several confirmed sinkings. In her eleventh patrol in July 1944, the engineering officer of the *Sailfish* decided to conduct a routine trim dive. For some reason he neglected to compensate for the twelve torpedoes which had been taken aboard and loaded forward. The sub dove and went out of control. Everyone immediately recalled the *Squalus* incident.

The sub continued to dive at a dangerous angle until all hands moved aft. Then she leveled off slowly and then nosed down again. Finally someone recalled the engineering officer had apparently forgotten the location of the recently loaded torpedoes and passed the word on to him. Hurriedly making trim adjustments, the engineering officer brought the *Sailfish* back on an even keel. Everyone breathed more easily.[63]

After her twelfth patrol, the Navy decided to retire the *Sailfish* from combat and assigned her to New London as a training submarine. In mid-October, 1945, the famed sub was docked at the Philadelphia Navy Yard.[64]

A groundswell of Portsmouth-area citizens urged that the *Sailfish* return home for her decommissioning. The Portsmouth mayor, city council, chamber of commerce, military and civilian groups dispatched telegrams to the president of the United States, secretary of the navy, and senators and representatives. "She is one of our proudest subs," said one local leader in the "Save the *Sailfish*" campaign. "At least it is only fitting that she come home to die."

William Gray was aboard the boat in Philadelphia as her skeleton crew awaited authorization to put the boat out of commission. Washington officials finally relented and granted the *Sailfish*'s removal to the Portsmouth Navy Yard. "The boat was already rid of fuel oil and tools," Gray said. "We grabbed a couple of wrenches and hammers and headed for Portsmouth."[65]

On Saturday, October 27, 1945, nearly 15,000 persons visited the Yard to observe the decommissioning ceremonies for the *Sailfish*. At 11:00 A.M. the boat made her last dive as she blew her tanks. Harold Preble, a civilian survivor of the *Squalus* sinking, pulled the vents. The bow remained up as the stern pitched down awkwardly; the unruly *Sailfish* stayed in character to the very end. She was unable to submerge completely in twenty-five feet of water in the channel leading into the old dry dock.

At 2:00 P.M. the *Sailfish* was decommissioned. As the crew hauled down the colors and emblems from the old *SS 192*, many observers wept. An old chief petty officer raised his hand in salute to the *Sailfish* as her ensigns were taken down. "May God let her rest in peace," he said. "She sure paid for herself."[66]

But the battle to save the *Sailfish* still had not been won. Portsmouth-area organizations pressured Washington officials to introduce a bill for the memorialization of the sub. The original reaction of the navy was to use the boat in atomic bomb tests. "Extensive experiments must be made," wrote an admiral in Washington, "and these require every surplus ship which embodies certain characteristics of design, as

Triumphal return of Sailfish *to the Yard in fall of 1945, following her outstanding war record in the Pacific. Note painted emblems, representing sunken Japanese merchant and man-of-war ships, above "192" numerals.* Thornback (SS418) *docked in background. PA.*

the *Sailfish* does." He declared further that retaining the *Sailfish* as an historical memorial would be of "doubtful propriety."[67]

Portsmouth citizens opposed any policy of scrapping or use as a target. The final disposition was a compromise. In January 1946 the navy authorized the removal of the boat's superstructure, consisting of the bridge and conning tower, as a suitable memorial.[68]

In August 1946 work on the *Sailfish* war memorial started at the Yard at the cost of about $10,000, appropriated from congressional funds. Employees of the public works and production departments prepared a foundation in the Mall in front of the commandant's residence and opposite Building 86, housing administrative offices. The superstructure was then mounted on a base of concrete.

On Armistice Day, November 11, 1946, Secretary of the Navy John L. Sullivan spoke at the official dedication before 2000 people. Sullivan quoted the words of the late President Roosevelt, who had said in

April 1942, "It is heartening to known that the *Squalus*, once given up as lost, rose from the depths to fight for our country in time of peril." William Gray, representing his shipmates, uncovered the steel plaque mounted on the bridge, which reads in part:

THIS MEMORIAL IS DEDICATED TO ALL MEN OF THE U. S. SUBMARINE FORCE

On April 30, 1948, the *Sailfish* was struck from the navy list. She was sold as scrap at auction for $43,167 at the Brooklyn Navy Yard on May 3, 1948, to Luria Brothers & Company, a Philadelphia metal firm.[69]

The *Sailfish* memorial on the Mall remains as an impressive landmark in the Yard. Many official functions are held yearly on her bridge, marking change of command, retirement, or other naval ceremonies. Every May 23rd or thereabouts the surviving members of the *Squalus/Sailfish* and other submariners gather at the memorial to honor their old shipmates. Longtime workers, naval personnel and visitors to the Yard pay their respects at the gray superstructure with its conning tower adorned with red and white emblems representing sunken Japanese merchant and man-of-war ships. The spirit of the submarine service, both of the living and the dead, radiates out from the *Sailfish's* ghostly cold steel and paint.

Special Missions of the Trout, Grenadier and Crevalle

In addition to war patrols to sink shipping, the American submarines frequently undertook special missions. They conducted photographic and sounding reconaissances, landed marine commandos on islands, evacuated civilians and American military personnel, and delivered supplies and equipment. Other duties included laying mines, detecting minefields, searching for air force crews in "lifeguarding" missions, performing anti-picket boat sweeps, and reconnoitering coasts, shoals and bays. Portsmouth subs participated in many such missions, three of them especially noteworthy.[70]

Frank W. "Mike" Fenno, skipper of the *USS Trout*, headed for the Philippines on the boat's second war patrol. Arriving at Corregidor in February 1942, Fenno delivered 3500 rounds of antiaircraft shells for the hard-pressed defenders of the island. The *Trout's* log tersely states,

> On February 3 we effected a rendezvous with a motor torpedo boat off CORREGIDOR at 1830 [6:30 P.M.] and were escorted in around the north of the Island to South Dock where we unloaded the ammunition, fueled, obtained two torpedoes and 20 tons of gold and silver, mail, securities and State Department

mail. At 0400 [4:00 A.M.], cleared the dock and bottomed in Manila Bay until the next evening when more mail and securities were brought out to us and we were escorted clear of the mine field.[71]

The gold ballast of the *Trout* marked one of the most fascinating events of World War II. After the Japanese advance toward Manila, Philippine and American officials collected a vast amount of gold, silver and securities and sent this wealth for safekeeping to the "Rock," or Corregidor Island fortress. When Fenno arrived there, he unloaded the 3500 rounds of shells and all the food, cigarettes, and medical supplies he could spare. For the remainder of the patrol, the *Trout*'s cooks were compelled to serve spaghetti for almost every meal. To replace the weight lost by the removal of the heavy projectiles, Fenno asked for twenty-five tons of ballast in the form of sand bags or crushed rock. Such items, however, were needed for the defense of Corregidor. A practical bargain was struck. The *Trout* would receive her ballast in the form of gold bars and silver coins which the Philippine and American authorities wanted to send to the United States for the duration of the war.[72]

The gold and silver cargo amounted to about $10 million (by 1942 international monetary standards). During the night 583 gold bars, most of them weighing forty pounds and valued at $23,000 apiece, arrived on flatbed trucks. They were passed from hand to hand and taken aboard the sub and stacked in the bilges as officials kept inventory. The second load consisted of eighteen tons of silver coins in heavy sacks. Fenno signed a receipt, but added a note that he could not personally verify the exact amount of the treasure.

This expensive ballast did not alter the basic purpose of his patrol. En route back to Pearl Harbor, Fenno looked for targets. Patrolling northward through the Formosa Strait and the Bonin Islands, the *Trout* sank a maru and a small patrol vessel.

On March 3, 1942, the sub arrived at Pearl Harbor and transferred her cargo to treasury officials. The press lionized Mike Fenno as a hero in a time of generally dismal war news for the American forces. President Roosevelt directed that Fenno and his crew receive appropriate medals and citations. Every bar was accounted for except for a $14,500 ingot. An inch-by-inch search of the *Trout* finally located the missing bar. The gold ingot was in the galley; one of the cooks was using it as a paperweight.[73]

A year later the *USS Grenadier* undertook a special assignment. On his second patrol in the boat, skipper John Fitzgerald was exploring the Straits of Malacca, an area heretofore unknown to American subs during the war. This body of water lying between the Malay Peninsula and Sumatra was known to be shallow and confined. One American submariner, in fact, was opposed to conducting patrols there. However, since this

During March 1942 at Pearl Harbor, crew of Trout *form chain line to unload gold bricks of Philippine treasury. UNH.*

strait would be the logical place to intercept any Japanese shipping between Rangoon and Singapore, he was overruled. Normally the strait was under British control, but they did not have the seapower to maintain supremacy in this area and had requested American assistance.

On the morning of April 21, 1943, the *Grenadier*, with seventy six aboard, closed the port of Penang on the west coast of the Malay Peninsula. Fitzgerald's lookouts then sighted a two-ship convoy. Remaining on the surface, the *Grenadier* gave chase within sight of the coast. At 8:35 A.M. the lookouts spotted a plane. The officer of the deck gave the order, "Dive, dive, this is not a drill." At the depth of 120 feet the sub appeared to be out of danger. "We ought to be safe now," one officer said.

Then a violent explosion rocked the boat and sent her to the bottom. The hull was badly damaged by an exploding bomb. The flooding sub lay at 270 feet. Fires broke out as the result of electrical short circuits. Work parties, suffering heat prostration and exhaustion, made repairs.

Men passed out from fatigue, heat, and foul air. Finally at 9:30 P.M. the *Grenadier* surfaced. Despite every effort throughout the night, the boat could not regain propulsion. Fitzgerald decided to rig up mattress covers to the periscope as sails, hoping wind could blow the boat close to the Malayan shore, either to make her seaworthy or to allow the crew to escape into the jungle.

A dead calm reigned and the sub did not move. Shortly after 8:00 A.M. a Japanese dive plane approached and strafed the starboard side. The crew fought back with two 20mm guns, machine guns, a few rifles, pistols, and tommy guns. A commissary steward threw potatoes that he had brought topside in his effort to bring the plane down. The Japanese pilot released his bomb, which exploded harmlessly 200 yards off the starboard bow.

By this time Japanese ships approached the motionless sub. The *Grenadier*'s crew destroyed the codes, smashed radio gear and threw weighted bags containing documents over the side. The chief of the boat pulled the vents and scuttled the sub. The men jumped to swim for their lives. An armed Japanese merchant vessel picked them up and took them to Penang. There at a commandeered Catholic school the submariners were immediately and systematically beaten and tortured. Fitzgerald, in particular, suffered at the hands of his Japanese interrogators. But the skipper would not break.[74]

Taken to Japan, the officers and men were separated. About twenty-five sailors of the *Grenadier* found themselves at the Ashio copper mines, where they remained for the rest of the war.

Edgar Poss, a radioman, was one of the *Grenadier* prisoners at the 250-man camp. "It was hell," Poss said. "They starved, beat and worked you." The prisoners received 700 calories of food a day, a gruel of Korean maize, cane seed, barley and rice. There was a doctor on duty, but he had no medicine. Subjected to hard physical labor, the prisoners' job was to recover the copper from a mud-flat pond after the water had been pumped out, raking and shoveling the concentrate. During their twenty-seven months of internment, the prisoners heard vague rumors about the war but nothing definite.

"One day at noon time we knocked off for lunch," Poss said. "Fifteen or twenty minutes after lunch a guard came down, stopped the work, and marched us up to our quarters. This was a break from our usual routine. At the end of a work shift we always washed up the tools, shovels, and rakes."

As the prisoners stood around, they saw the guards listening to the radio in command headquarters. "Many came out crying," Poss said. "The prisoners waited to see if the night crew would go out. They would not work that night. We knew then that the war was over. It was August 15, 1945. It was the happiest day in my life."[75]

During the following days the Japanese increased the food rations and provided better treatment. On September 4, 1945, special Japanese military guards fluent in English escorted the American POW's on the railroad down to Yokohama. Poss boarded the LST *Ozark* and arrived at San Francisco, where he entered the naval hospital for a few days. In October he left for his home. At 3:30 A.M. he arrived at Dover, New Hampshire, for a reunion with his girl friend. During his years in the POW camp he had absolutely no communication with her. They were married shortly thereafter. Poss was awarded several long leaves and thereafter resumed active duty.

Of the seventy-six *Grenadier* prisoners, all but four survived their ordeal in the Japanese POW camps. Fitzgerald was awarded the Navy Cross. The *Grenadier* mission had been performed at a cost of great human suffering.[76]

The *USS Crevalle* was a luckier boat. Launched at the Yard in February 1943 and commissioned in June, the *Crevalle* operated out of Fremantle and Darwin, Australia. On her first war patrol in November the sub sank a Japanese freighter and shortly afterward surfaced to interrogate the crew of a Filipino fishing boat about the Japanese shipping traffic. Terrified by the incident, the fishermen insisted that the *Crevalle's* skipper accept a sickly chicken as a peace offering. The *Crevalle* crew adopted the bird as a mascot, feeding it the best bread crumbs and cornmeal in hopes of producing fresh eggs. "The quartermaster sewed up some clothes for the chicken," said Gerald McLees, serving aboard the *Crevalle*. "He made a dress for it. The bird lived in the forward torpedo room and went back to Australia with us." After one shell-less attempt, the chicken the next day laid a hard-shell egg, and more importantly, provided an omen of good luck for the *Crevalle's* special mission the following year.[77]

On the *Crevalle's* third patrol during April and May 1944, she cruised off the west coast of Borneo. On May 6 the *Crevalle* torpedoed and sank the *Nisshin Maru*, the largest Japanese tanker sunk during the war. The sub dove to the bottom in 174 feet of water to escape a violent counterattack of depth charges dropped by the tanker's escorts. The Japanese even used grappling hooks in an attempt to snare the *Crevalle*. The men aboard the sub could hear scraping sounds along the outer hull, but the *Crevalle's* luck held and she got away safely.

Then she received orders for her special mission: to proceed northward to Negros Island, Philippines, to evacuate refugees and pick up intelligence information. "There was a big sheet on the mountain top,"

McLees said, "a signal that the coast was clear. The evacuees came out in rowboats and bumboats. We were on the lookout for planes overhead; otherwise we would have had to submerge immediately."[78]

The evacuation was timed perfectly. On May 11 the *Crevalle* took aboard more than forty people, including about thirty women and children. Four of the men had escaped from the Bataan death march by fleeing into the jungles. "The refugees were overjoyed upon being picked up," McLees said. "The women and kids moved into the forward torpedo room and the chiefs moved out. One woman was pregnant."

The *Crevalle* headed south for Darwin. On the way home the sub picked up a Japanese convoy. Before the *Crevalle* could fire torpedoes, a destroyer dropped eight depth charges on top of the boat, the worst bombardment the *Crevalle* received during the war. The adult passengers were terrified.

"The kids heard it," McLees said, "and were excited. 'Did we hit something?' was their reaction. The youngsters thought it was part of a game and were more amused than scared." Damage to the boat was heavy. "Both the gyro compass and the glass in the periscope were smashed," McLees said. "We were 'flying blind' with no sight, only sounds. When we landed at Darwin, the forty refugees were the happiest people in the world."[79]

The Redfish *and the* Picuda *Go Wolf-Packing*

During the spring of 1944 the naval war in the Pacific had entered a new phase as the *Redfish* and the *Picuda*, two of the newer Yard boats, met at Pearl Harbor. American submariners adopted a new strategy. The individual "lone wolf" patrol was merging to become part of a "wolf pack" attack group. Wolf-packing quickly emerged as the most successful method against Japanese convoys. By 1944 the war's arena in the Pacific was rapidly shrinking, with the elimination of some Japanese sea lanes and the shortening of others. Forced to operate in contracted areas, Japanese convoys presented inviting targets, especially in the bottleneck of Luzon Strait, between Luzon and Formosa. The concept of wolf-packing brought together the firepower of several submarines and mutual defensive support. The new Mark XVIII electric torpedo proved to be a superior weapon.[80]

During June 1944 the *Redfish*, *Picuda*, and Mare Island's *Spadefish* participated in mock attacks on convoys near Pearl Harbor. "The exercises went on for more than a month," Daniel MacIsaac of the *Redfish* said. "Our coordinator was 'Wild Bill' Donaho. He was immaculate in appearance, a slim build, with a mustache and ramrod straight." In command of the *Picuda*, Glynn R. "Donc" Donaho was a veteran of six previous patrols. "Donc Donaho had a reputation," Charlie Barfield, a radioman on the *Picuda*, said, "of getting you out there and then getting you back. He appeared in clean khaki dress every day." On July 23 this pack, known as "Donc's Devils," left Pearl Harbor for its battle station in the vicinity of the Luzon Strait.[81]

During the first phase of their patrol, all three submarines sank Japanese destroyers, tankers, and cargo ships. The *Redfish*, skippered by Sandy McGregor, sank a maru on August 25. Surfacing after the battle the *Redfish* rescued a Japanese crew member from the water. The prisoner was afforded good treatment and was clad in a G-string to prevent concealment of weapons. His American guard taught him a few words of English, "To hell with the marines!" knowing that the prisoner would be turned over to them once the boat came into port. The *Picuda* also attempted to pick up prisoners. "The Japanese would swim away from a surfaced submarine," Barfield said. "They preferred death to boarding an American sub. Any Japanese survivor who attempted to swim toward an American sub would find his buddies pulling him back. One managed to evade his buddies and he was taken aboard the *Picuda*. The prisoner was kept under guard in the forward torpedo room and escorted to his meals in the mess room."[82]

The pack had expended all its torpedoes and left its battle station zone on August 27. "The *Picuda* headed for Saipan which the marines had just secured," Barfield said. "They turned the prisoner over to the marines. Then there was a big beer party on Saipan." Once the site of a major Japanese base, Saipan fell to American forces after a bitter struggle. On August 9 the marines had control of the island; less than three weeks later "Donc's Devils" came in for their reload. The sub tender *USS Holland* was there with torpedoes and fuel. Admiral Lockwood had wasted no time re-building the facilities on Saipan to establish a large submarine base for his boats.[83]

On September 5 the *Redfish*, *Picuda* and *Spadefish* resumed their patrol. A few days later the *Spadefish* fired twenty torpedoes to sink four Japanese cargo ships. Again emptied of torpedoes, she left, with Donaho's permission, for Pearl Harbor. On September 16 the *Picuda* and *Redfish* had an exceptionally busy day. Donaho found a convoy and sank a tanker. The convoy continued on, only to be picked up by McGregor. The *Redfish*, while it was surfaced, counted thirty-four Japanese airplane sightings on that day from two separate convoys, of which the first got away and "went over the hill" in McGregor's words. At 3:15 P.M. a Japanese plane dropped two bombs just as the *Redfish* was submerging to periscope depth. A tremendous explosion shook the boat "like you would crack a whip," as

MacIsaac said. McGregor saw two round circles of white water, but the *Redfish* was not damaged.

"Take me down, for that damn plane is coming back," McGregor said.

At that moment McGregor sighted a tanker through his periscope sight. The bridge of the tanker was crowded with white uniforms. "All the people in white uniforms are pointing," McGregor said, "and probably laughing for they could see something I couldn't." He made a quick final periscope observation. "They [the white uniforms] are still there. Fire one, fire two. Well, will you look at that. They see the torpedoes and look at them scatter. They are even climbing the masts."

The torpedoes crashed into the *Ogura Maru No. 2*, a 7311-ton tanker, sending her to the bottom.

On September 21, Donaho and McGregor attacked another convoy with two more kills. Then they headed to Midway for a refit. The two forays of this triple-barreled patrol marked the most successful wolf-pack record of the war. The *Spadefish*, *Redfish* and *Picuda* sank thirteen ships for almost 65,000 tons.[84]

A month later the *Redfish* left Midway on another patrol. McGregor commanded a pack called "Sandy's Sluggers," consisting of three Portsmouth boats, the *Redfish*, *Shad*, and *Bang*. After a successful foray off Formosa, the three subs returned to Saipan. With a reload of torpedoes and a few days' rest the *Redfish* left alone on December 1 for the East China Sea. There a total of five subs rendezvoused.[85]

On the night of December 8 McGregor located on radar an enemy force fifteen miles away. He reported this information to the other subs and began tracking. The *Sea Devil*, a Portsmouth sub, reached the convoy first and fired four torpedoes at the largest target, the light aircraft carrier *Junyo*. Two of the shots hit the boat, but the *Junyo* limped away. At 1:34 A.M. on December 9, McGregor's log reads: "Heard two separate explosions far enough apart to be torpedo hits. Aircraft carrier slows down .... He must be hurt!"

The *Redfish* stalked the stricken carrier. After 3:00 A.M. the sub caught up and headed in for attack. Two torpedoes found their marks. At 3:36 A.M. the log reads: "Explosion. We are retiring at flank speed; carrier appears to be maintaining his speed of 12 knots. Sound continues to report loud rumbling noises from direction of carrier....He was definitely lower in the water." The *Junyo* managed to get away. "Daylight was coming," MacIsaac said, "the water was shallow and we had to break off the attack. We had four torpedoes left."

McGregor viewed the carrier's escape as a personal loss, noting, "Feel bad about not sinking that carrier, but maybe he'll blow before he hits port." The *Junyo* limped into Nagasaki, but the ship was so badly damaged that she never returned to action for the duration of the war.[86]

McGregor's disappointment was shortlived. In mid-December General Douglas A. MacArthur's forces landed on the strategic island of Mindoro, south of Luzon. The Japanese reacted with alarm and dispatched the newly built 18,500-ton carrier *Unryu* to fend off the American invasion. On December 19 McGregor picked up the Unryu on her maiden voyage.[87]

Sighting the carrier with its three-destroyer escort at 4:27 P.M., the *Redfish* fired the first of her last four torpedoes just seven minutes later. The *Unryu* stopped in her tracks, listed twenty degrees to starboard, and began burning furiously. The last torpedo hit the carrier at 4:50 P.M. "The sharp crack of the torpedo explosion," McGregor wrote, "was followed instantly by thundering explosions apparently from magazine or gasoline stowage . . . . Huge clouds of smoke, flame and debris burst into the air completely enveloping the carrier." When McGregor raised his periscope at 4:59 P.M., he noted, "Took good sweep around, unable to see aircraft carrier. He has sunk!" Only thirty-two minutes had elapsed from the first sighting of the *Unryu* until the sinking.[88]

About ten minutes later the great career of the *Redfish* almost ended in the East China Sea. The *Unryu's* escort destroyers sought to avenge the loss. Seven depth charges exploded near the *Redfish* as she was running submerged at 150 feet. One charge exploded under the boat about seven feet from the hull. The *Redfish* evidently had ridden over the top of the charge. If the explosion had been to either side or above, the damage would have been much less.

MacIsaac said:

> We hit the bottom [242 feet] without control. No power. I was knocked out, up in the air horizontal with my feet straight out and with big bulging eyes. Bunks and mattresses were on top of me. Water was pouring in, screening in under pressure. There were leaking valves and the sanitary tanks ruptured. The shocks sprung out.
>
> I said to myself, 'What the heck. Fix the thing.'
>
> One guy was sitting with rags over his ears. One guy was praying, one guy crying on his hands and knees, exclaiming, 'They got us, Mac.' One guy was doing a correspondence course.
>
> I worked with a crescent wrench, with my hands covered with oil. Men spoke in whispers. Another man dropped his wrench with a big clang. He incurred the hostility of his shipmates.
>
> The sub lay there for four hours. They pounded us for those four hours with fifty depth charges dropped. The sub settled into fifteen to twenty feet of mud. We could hear the 'click, click' of the

detonator as the firing pin hits the detonator. If the charge exploded in water, there was a clear ringing sound. If in mud, it was a sickly noise.[89]

The men of the *Redfish* remained as silent as possible to avoid revealing the boat's position to the enemy. To escape such depth-charge attacks, American submariners liked to escape into a huge noisy school of shrimp or fish, but that option was impossible in this situation.

"With depth charges," one submariner explained, "there is a tremendous shock wave. Every joint in one's body aches. Everything moves, cork breaks and light bulbs shatter. The whole hull is compressed and creaks like creaking leather. The next one [depth charge] is always scary. The thought remains: 'If the last one is closer than before, the next one is going to get us.' There is anxiety in waiting to see if the next one will be closer or farther away."[90]

No more depth charges, however, hit the *Redfish*. Damage was extensive, including jammed steering gear, inoperative sound gear, and cracked pressure hull with water and oil leaks throughout the boat. Radio, electrical, and sonar equipment was broken.

Two men had fillings knocked out of their teeth by the impact of the explosion. "Two sailors were injured," MacIsaac said. "A 500-pound bulkhead door slammed shut. A sailor's ear was severed as he was walking through. The medic aboard stitched and sewed the ear back on and the Navy awarded a Purple Heart. The other injured sailor was carrying some dental bridge work in his hip pocket. With the tremendous jolt to the boat, the teeth bit into him and left their impression on his rump."[91]

After dark in the winter evening McGregor was able to surface. The closest Japanese destroyer was 9000 yards away. The *Redfish* opened the distance from the enemy. McGregor saw many searchlights from the destroyers playing on the water and soon realized the lights were not searching for the *Redfish* but were looking for Japanese survivors from the carrier. It required three days for the *Redfish* to leave the East China Sea. "We went through the Coinett Strait," MacIsaac said. "There were five American subs waiting to get out and seven to go through." He and the crew then sensed the strength and presence of the American navy in the Pacific. On December 25, "All hands enjoyed a delicious Christmas dinner," McGregor wrote, "and have begun to breathe easier." Four days later the *Redfish* arrived at Midway and was "met by a truck load of much appreciated mail and promises of beer for all hands."[92]

The *Redfish* remained at Midway only half a day to receive these morale builders and fuel. She was underway that afternoon for Pearl Harbor in company of another submarine. Upon her arrival in January

1945, Lockwood conducted a personal inspection. During his tour below, Lockwood met with the crew. "You are damaged bad enough to go back to the States," he said with a wink. The crew gave him a big grin.[93]

On February 17, 1945, the *Redfish* arrived back at the Portsmouth Navy Yard, which she had left as a new boat the previous May. As the first locally built sub to return during the war, the *Redfish* received a hero's welcome. "A band was out to greet us," MacIsaac said. "Workmen came down to see the boat and were proud of her." A large crowd of workmen at the dock boarded the *Redfish* and hurried immediately to the areas they had built to examine the section for themselves. "Yes, sir," one workman would remark to another, "my welds held together." It was an emotional moment for the officers and crew of the *Redfish* who observed these scenes, many of them survivors of the nearly fatal depth charge attack.[94]

Repairs on the *Redfish* began the same day she arrived. After extensive work, an overhaul and sea trials, the boat was underway once again on July 2 for her long voyage to the Pacific. Arriving at Pearl Harbor in late July, she was completing her training period to resume war patrols when the United States government announced the end of hostilities. The dramatic history of this boat was shared by Yard worker and navy man alike.[95]

The Archerfish *Sinks the Giant* Shinano

In another night launching, on May 28, 1943, the *USS Archer-fish* slid down the ways at 8:20 P.M. into the calm black waters of the Piscataqua. Later designated as the *Archerfish,* she conducted four moderately successful war patrols in the Pacific. In late September 1944 the boat docked at Pearl Harbor. There Joseph F. Enright, a thirty-four-year-old career officer, assumed command. Under his leadership, the *Archerfish* made naval history.[96]

Born and educated on the plains of North Dakota, Enright graduated from the Academy in 1933. After attending Submarine School at New London, he commanded the *O-10*, gaining the nickname "Hobo Joe of the O-One-O."

In 1943 Joe Enright became skipper of the new *USS Dace* and instituted a morale-booster reform. Obtaining a slot machine, Enright had the gambling device put on deck during the *Dace*'s stops in Panama, Pearl Harbor, and Midway for the amusement of local relief crews. It collected enormous illegal sums, often $150.00 a day, which went into a slush fund for such luxuries as expensive canned seafood, tobacco and beer and liquor that the crew could consume ashore.[97]

After one war patrol aboard the *Dace* and nearly a year of shore duty, mostly at Midway, Enright joined the *Archerfish* at Pearl Harbor where she was undergoing a refit. In late October 1944 the regular crew moved back aboard and conducted an eight-day training exercise. Leaving on her fifth war patrol, the *Archerfish* stopped at Saipan for a "topping off" of fuel and provisions. Enright flew to Guam to see Admiral Lockwood and received his assigned location and instructions in person. "We would act as lifeguard," Enright said, "listen to the radio and send in weather reports." The *Archerfish*'s primary mission was to rescue downed American pilots forced to ditch off the main Japanese home island of Honshu. With B-29 bombers attacking Japan from American fields in the Marianas, the placing of submarines along the route in a lifeguarding capacity saved the lives of many pilots.[98]

On November 11 the *Archerfish* left Saipan on her patrol. On that same day the Japanese aircraft carrier *Shinano*, under construction since 1940, was launched at the Yokosuka Navy Yard. The ship was built in a specially constructed dry dock concealed behind high sandstone cliffs and huge elaborate screen fences. Such security made the *Shinano* one of the best-kept Japanese secrets of the war. Named for one of the provinces of old Japan, the *Shinano* was built in its early stages as a super-battleship in the giant *Yamato* class.

The loss of four aircraft carriers at the Battle of Midway in 1942 demonstrated to the Japanese military command the need for more carriers. They decided to convert the *Shinano*, half completed at the time, to a super-carrier. Statistics concerning the *Shinano* were staggering. The ship displaced 71,000 tons and carried a complement of 1900 officers and crew.

After her launching on November 11, the huge ship left port for builder's trials without aircraft on board. She cruised at twenty-four knots. Captain Toshibo Abe, the *Shinano*'s commander, was a torpedo expert who was ambitious to make admiral. On November 16, Abe returned to Yokosuka, believing he had been sighted.

Two days later the *Shinano* was commissioned. Officials hung a large portrait of Emperor Hirohito on the flying bridge. But the ceremonial celebration was short-lived. The massive American bombing of the Tokyo area on November 24 convinced the Japanese Naval Ministry that the *Shinano* was in grave danger. Its officials ordered Abe to move his uncompleted warship to the Inland Sea, the relatively well-protected body of water between three large Japanese islands, for final fitting out and its air complement. The *Shinano* left on her maiden voyage under heavy escort at 6:00 P.M. on November 28 for a high-speed 300-mile night voyage.[99]

On that same evening the *Archerfish* was approaching Tokyo Bay. So far Enright and his men, preoccupied with their lifeguarding mission during their patrol, had not encountered any targets. With his executive officer, Enright decided to postpone Thanksgiving celebration until the end of the month in hopes of finding success in the meantime. On November 27 they learned that all planes had returned safely from a Tokyo raid. The scheduled American bombing attacks of November 28 and 29 were cancelled. "The weather was bad," Enright said. Another factor contributed to the lifting of his lifeguarding role. "[Admiral William F. "Bull"] Halsey had to cancel the raid as the result of the Battle of Leyte Gulf. As the raid was off, we could go and look. We decided to go to Tokyo Bay and look for targets."

Submerged during the day, the *Archerfish* surfaced in the late afternoon and at 8:34 P.M. spotted Inamba Shima, an island near the Bay's entrance. The radar officer picked up a contact at 030 degrees. Enright responded harshly that the island was at 060 degrees and that the radar was working improperly. A few minutes later the radar officer reported back. "Your island is at 028 degrees and moving at 20 knots."[100]

"We thought it was a tanker," Enright said. "It had a long profile. One escort came out, then another and then a third. The ship was going about twenty knots. Our Portsmouth-built boat, as good as it was, no matter how much we could beat on, cajole and coax, went nineteen knots. It was a clear night with a bright moon with 97% illumination." Soon the men aboard the *Archerfish* realized the large enemy ship was taking on the shape of an aircraft carrier rather than of a tanker.

The *Shinano* adopted a zigzag course. When Abe changed his direction, ninety degrees, Enright concluded that the carrier was heading for the Inland Sea. All eighty-one submariners had been at their battle stations since the initial target detection. The officer of the deck was exuberant. "We can do it!" he said, "*Archerfish* needs this one! They can't see us—I know it!"

The chase continued for hours as the *Archerfish* maneuvered for a favorable position from which to fire her torpedoes. The sub's radioman transmitted a coded message twice to headquarters about the *Archerfish*'s pursuit of a carrier.

"Keep after him, Joe," Lockwood radioed back. "Your picture is on the piano."

"We dove then," Enright said, "and didn't know about it [Lockwood's advice] for months. The sub could not receive messages while submerged."[101]

It was 3:05 A.M., November 29. The *Archerfish* had won the race to pull ahead of the *Shinano*, which had dropped back because of its zigzag course. At 3:16 A.M. the carrier zigged again and headed in the direction of the *Archerfish*. "I couldn't believe it," Enright said. "The target was coming down with the whole starboard bow to shoot at. At 1400 yards we were ready to shoot."

The carrier was approaching so closely that Enright noticed through the periscope that the warship's smokestacks were leaning over twenty degrees to one side. The designers building the vessel originally as a battleship had the stacks vertical. Upon its conversion to a carrier, the stacks were tilted to one side to allow room for a flight deck. Enright drew a sketch of the carrier on a piece of paper and showed it to his officers. No one could identify the huge carrier, different from any ship in Enright's recognition book.

The time was now 3:17 A.M. and the sub had perfect position. The boat's log reads: "Started firing all bow tubes . . . 0317-47. Heard and observed first hit just inside stern near props and rudder. Large ball of fire climbed his side. 0317-57. Second hit observed and heard . . . Four more properly timed hits . . . breaking up noises started immediately."[102]

The *Archerfish* dove deep. A nineteen-year-old quartermaster, Enright's assistant on the periscope, timed the elapsed seconds. "We hit the bastard," the quartermaster exclaimed, jumping up and down. "We hit the bastard."[103]

Four of the six torpedoes fired had penetrated the *Shinano*'s hull. The huge ship listed ten degrees starboard immediately. Three torpedoes entered the firerooms and one went into the amidship compartment, resulting in a tremendous explosion with considerable noise continuing on for thirty-five minutes. The men on the *Archerfish* could hear loud crunching noises even through the sub's hull.

The enemy escort destroyers made a half-hearted effort to sink the *Archerfish*, dropping fourteen depth charges in twenty minutes. The closest exploded 300 yards away. At 6:10 A.M. the sub made her first observation at periscope depth. "Nothing in sight," the log reported. "1000 [10:00 A.M.]. Large and distant single explosion. Origin indefinite. Our target by all rights should have been down long ago." That evening Enright sent to Pearl Harbor his weather report and information on the attack, believing he had sunk a 28,000-ton *Hayataka* type carrier.

The belated Thanksgiving festivities for the jubilant crew the next day were a great celebration. The cooks prepared a soup-to-nuts banquet. Enright carved the turkey at the wardroom table. Everyone ate dressing, yams, creamed onions and peas, fresh rolls and pies, strawberry short-cake with whipped cream, all washed down with drinking water with ice cubes.[104]

Two weeks later the *Archerfish* returned to Guam. One of Lockwood's intelligence officers met the boat and questioned Enright about his patrol. The intelligence staff had never heard of this carrier and hesitated to support the claim.

"Will you settle for a cruiser?"

"No, I saw a carrier."

"You can claim a cruiser."

"OK, OK, a cruiser."

Then Enright remembered the sketch he had drawn of his target. He made inquiries and retrieved it. The quartermaster had picked up the discarded sketch from the sub's floor.

"Why did you save that?" Enright asked.

"The Navy has trained me not to throw anything away."[105]

This evidence helped justify the claim as the *Archerfish* received credit for sinking a 28,000-ton carrier, later increased to 59,000 tons. After the war a more complete and accurate account of the *Shinano* and her last hours emerged. Japanese sources and other authorities listed the *Shinano*'s full-load displacement at about 70,500 tons.

Despite the damage incurred by his carrier from the four torpedoes, Captain Abe believed his architects had built an unsinkable ship. He ordered the ship to continue its voyage at eighteen knots over rough seas. Damage control parties below soon realized that the carrier was in serious trouble. Counter-flooding measures failed. At 6:00 A.M. the *Shinano* lost all power.

Chaos broke out among an almost completely untrained crew, Japanese navy yard workers and civilian technicians aboard the doomed vessel. Discipline broke down and at dawn many civilians started abandoning ship.

Abe finally accepted the reality that his ship was sinking. With Abe's permission a junior officer removed the emperor's portrait, wrapped it carefully, and transferred it by line to one of the escort destroyers alongside. About half the crew transferred to the waiting destroyers as *Shinano*'s end drew near. Between 10:00 and 11:00 A.M. on November 29, 1944, about twenty hours after the beginning of her maiden voyage and seven hours after her torpedoing, the *Shinano* sank stern down with Captain Abe and more than 400 men aboard.[106]

The loss of the supercarrier *Shinano* broke the heart of the Imperial Japanese Navy. Conducting a top-secret investigation, the Japanese made only five copies of their report and destroyed all five before the American occupation. "The *Shinano* was indeed," wrote one Japanese historian, "a child of misfortune."

The *Archerfish* had sunk the largest ship in any war in any ocean. Enright received the Navy Cross and Legion of Merit. After the military capitulation of Japan, in the summer of 1945, the *Archerfish* entered Tokyo Bay. Within forty-eight hours the sub would be present at the official surrender ceremonies scheduled for September 2. With some free time until that occasion, Enright and his men walked around Yokosuka and viewed the dry dock in which the *Shinano* was built. They took pride in knowing that their sinking of this giant Japanese ship hastened the end of the war.[107]

Victory!

V-J Day, victory in Japan, finally occurred on Tuesday, August 14, 1945. Admiral Thomas Withers immediately granted a two-day holiday at the Yard. "The Portsmouth Navy Yard," he stated, "with its military and civilian personnel has made a major contribution towards victory ... The submarines from Portsmouth inflicted vital damage on the enemy ...." On August 17 Withers announced that the Yard would revert to a five-day work week. "The midnight shift," rigger Fred White said, "just went home and never came back."

In a poem called "Victory," Yard worker Reginald H. Thorpe wrote in part:

> The Junkers who prepared a war
> The Empire of the Rising Sun
> Are finished and will rise no more
> To conquer us. Our job is done.[108]

At Ofuna prison camp near Yokohama, Japan, American and British prisoners of war greeted their liberators. Among them was Commander Richard H. O'Kane, who had barely survived his long captivity. A native of Durham, New Hampshire, and the son of a university professor, O'Kane had skippered EB's *USS Tang* to the most outstanding record of the war with twenty-four confirmed sinkings on five patrols.

"We had no interpreters," O'Kane said, "to acquaint us with the Japanese rules of conduct at Ofuna. Men were given 10 full swings with the baseball bats for whistling or singing. Camp rules were not in writing and each guard interpreted them to suit his purpose, often sadistically mauling the prisoners for amusement." O'Kane later reported to the Yard hospital to regain his health. The next year he received the congressional Medal of Honor.[109]

Submariners in the United States celebrated the end of the war with parties and dancing in the streets. Many Naval Academy officers and midshipmen were attending summer classes at the Submarine School at New London. Such students were receiving an accelerated

Complement of Pampanito, *veterans of successful patrols in the Pacific, appear in dress uniform at the close of World War II. PA.*

program at the Academy with summer schools and cruises to graduate as a three-year class. Midshipman Sam Francis was at the base recreation building, shooting a game of pool for a few minutes of relaxation. A friend ran into the pool room, and exclaimed, "The Japanese have surrendered; the war is over."

Francis looked up and said, "You've ruined my shot."[110]

On September 2, 1945, Japanese officials surrendered aboard the American battleship *USS Missouri* in Tokyo Bay. Admiral Lockwood observed the ceremonies. A short distance away there was one American sub tender and twelve subs, six tied to either side. Among them were Portsmouth boats *Archerfish, Pilotfish, Razorback, Runner II, Segundo, Sea Cat,* and *Tigrone.*

Lockwood was proud of his boys. The American submarine force sapped and ultimately crippled the Japanese effort. During their years on patrol in the Pacific, American skippers sank 1334 enemy vessels displacing 5.3 million tons. When the war began, there were about 122,000 Japanese merchant marine personnel. At war's end submarine attacks had killed 16,200 and wounded or "otherwise incapacitated" about 53,400. The American submariners, representing less than two percent of the U.S. Navy, accounted for 55 percent of Japan's maritime losses. Since Japan was dependent on imports of fuel and raw material to maintain her war machine, such heavy losses in ships, manpower, cargoes of petroleum, rubber, coal, fish and foodstuffs hastened defeat.

American submarine losses from all causes (including training) amounted to fifty-two boats, with the deaths of about 375 officers and 3131 enlisted men of the 16,000 submariners who engaged in war patrols. To those in the navy, these lost boats are considered "still on patrol." In August 1945 the U. S. Navy had 260 boats in commission with many more under construction when the conflict ended.

The vigilance of U. S. Navy submarines at sea saved many lives. During the war American subs devoted 3272 submarine-days on life-guarding status and rescued 504 airmen.[111]

Portsmouth boats saw action from the beginning to the end of World War II, from the *Dolphin* firing back at Pearl Harbor to the *Archerfish* and other subs standing by in Tokyo Bay. In assessing the role of those submariners on Portsmouth submarines as well as those built elsewhere, Admiral Lockwood wrote:

> Whether Regulars or Reserves, the lads who fought in submarines, who served in tenders or bases, or who composed the relief crews were part of a splendid team of fighting men. . . .
> No one can deny that they won their spurs during World War II.
> They were no supermen, nor were they endowed with any supernatural qualities of heroism. They were merely topnotch American lads, well trained, well treated, well armed and provided with superb ships.[112]

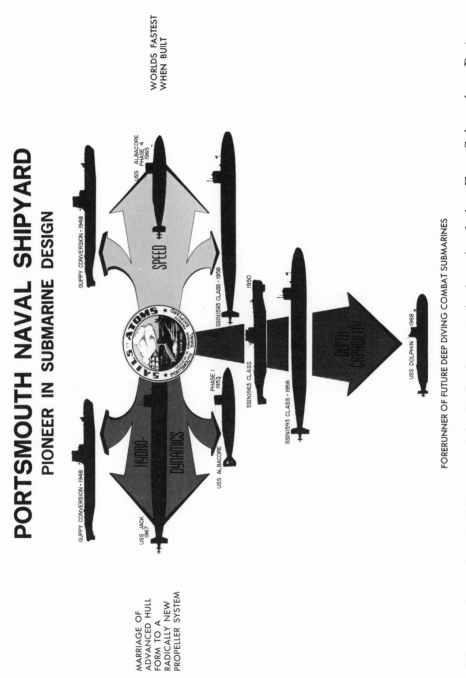

Diagram shows the role of Portsmouth in the development of submarine design. From Submarines, Portsmouth Naval Shipyard published by the Portsmouth-Kittery Armed Services Committee.

IV *Entering the Nuclear Age, 1945-1971*

The Post-War Adjustment

AFTER WORLD WAR II, the Yard built new classes of submarines and harnessed nuclear power for propulsion. It was a period of many Portsmouth-first inventions, the implementation of rigid construction and testing regulations after the *Thresher* disaster, and the rescinding of a closure order. With the commissioning of the *Sand Lance*, the last Portsmouth-built boat, the Yard became the leading repair and overhaul facility for American submarines.

On Sunday, September 9, 1945, 25,000 people watched Portsmouth's V-J parade and victory celebration, which featured a float from the Yard. A huge trailer carried a superstructure replica of a submarine. Sailors manned her conning tower. Battle flags of Pacific engagements and banners from each shop fluttered in the breeze. The war was over.[1]

Peace meant fewer contracts and jobs and a reduced payroll in an area where the Yard was the predominant employer. The transition was painful. By October 1, the Yard had only one working shift. A delegation of workers led by inside machine shop foreman Bart Dalla Mura left that fall on the first of many trips through the years to Washington to appeal for more work. The Yard had to fight for every navy contract.

"The Navy Department [of the Truman administration] was adamant about layoffs," Dalla Mura said. "I rounded up all the representatives and senators from the New England states I could get, all except Connecticut which was our competitor. Vermont didn't help us. Margaret Chase Smith [senator from Maine] was unconvinced."

"We have Bath, Maine," she said, referring to the Bath Iron Works.

"We don't compete with Bath's destroyers," Dalla Mura said. "We build subs at the Yard."

Senator Styles Bridges of New Hampshire, a Republican stalwart in Washington since 1937, was receptive. "Bridges was the best friend the Yard ever had," Dalla Mura said. "His senate offices had four rooms. There were ten thousand [model] elephants in his offices ranging from a few inches to the size of a real elephant one could mount. Bridges arranged for our committee to call him directly on the floor of the Senate whenever we needed help." However, Bridges could not halt the trend by himself. "The Navy [Department] had all the guns out and stood its ground," Dalla Mura said, "and there was a layoff."

The navy announced, nevertheless, that the Yard would be retained as a leading submarine repair, construction and design base.[2]

The "reduction in force" policy shrank the 1945 V-J Day total of about 14,000 employees to 4,047 by 1950. "I got my graduation certificate from the apprentice school and the papers laying me off on the same day," said one worker. The Yard's status was changed by navy directive in late 1945 to become the Portsmouth Naval Shipyard as a component of the newly formed naval base. The billet of shipyard commander was assigned to an officer competent in the design, construction and repair of submarines.[3]

Despite layoffs at the shipyard, submarine activities still continued with the local naval reserve. "After V-J Day, the guys at the discharge stations manned a desk at the end of the line urging the boys to sign up 'to keep their rates.'" said John Rowe, the officer-in-charge of the local naval reserve unit. "Thousands did. The Yard maintained a number of 'dead' submarines with the propellers taken off, which could submerge but could not get underway. After weekly drills on the subs and classroom work, the petty officers and sailors regained or got their sea legs on small surface ships during weekend and two-week annual cruises, usually to Puerto Rico or Cuba." The Electric Boat *Greenling* served as a reserve training submarine.[4]

The World War II vintage Portsmouth submarines became subject to the whims of peacetime dictates. Portsmouth boats found themselves at Bikini Atoll in the Pacific in 1946, so the American government could test the vulnerability of warships to atomic attack. The navy assembled a flotilla of sixty-seven ships, including several captured German and Japanese vessels, and moored them at Bikini. Among the eight submarines were Portsmouth-built *Searaven*, *Apogon*, *Parche* and *Pilotfish*. Some of the subs were on the surface while others were submerged by remote control to predetermined depths.

On July 1, 1946, the atomic air burst of Test Able sank a number of surface ships, but all the submarines survived the attack. The *Parche* was undamaged and later became a trainer. After repositioning the subs with six submerged to various depths, the navy suspended a bomb beneath a landing craft for an underwater explosion.

On July 25 Test Baker detonated a powerful blast which sank all six submerged submarines. The *Apogon* remained on the bottom. Crews raised the other subs, checked the damage and towed them back to the West Coast. The Bikini tests proved that submerged submarines could survive air blasts, but the navy needed more durable submarines for the future.[5]

Historic Cruises

Other Portsmouth boats received better assignments. Many embarked on voyages that made nautical history.

On May 15, 1947, the *Sea Robin* left Balboa, Panama Canal Zone for a fifty-five-day, 12,500-mile voyage around Cape Horn, South America en route to Portsmouth. The objectives of the cruise were cold-weather training and surveying for the Navy Hydrographic Office to correct unreliable nautical charts.

On June 1, the *Sea Robin* became the first submarine in history to round Cape Horn. After seventeen hours of darkness, the sun rose at 8:30 A.M., when the crew went topside to record the event with their cameras. For a few moments the men stood on deck with the wind blowing at gale force. They sensed immediately the reasoning behind the old sailor's warning, "Don't spit to wind'ard at Cape Horn." The nasty weather sent the amateur photographers scurrying below to steaming coffeepots.

Persistent storms, dense fogs and heavy seas made surface travel rough going. Once the boat hit a whale. When the *Sea Robin* submerged to calmer waters, everyone was happy except the baker. As air pressure was built up in the *Sea Robin* prior to diving, to assure all openings were closed, the sub's baker observed that the compression caused his batch of rising dough to fall as flat as a pancake. He told the skipper that if he wasn't given ample warning, he would be serving the men hardtack!

After cruising in sub-Antarctic waters and avoiding icebergs, the *Sea Robin* completed her rough-weather tests. The boat then swung northward to the Falkland Islands, the first visit by any American warship to Port Stanley in fifty years. On July 8 the *Sea Robin* arrived at Portsmouth, completing her historic voyage. A crew member quickly painted a Cape Horn "hash mark" on the conning tower.[6]

After making other extended cruises, the *Sea Robin* became a trainer out of New London. In the 1960s she joined the exclusive Ten Grander Club, joining the Portsmouth-built *Spikefish*, *Sarda*, and *Toro*, when she recorded her 10,000th dive. Earning the nickname "Bobbin Robin," she dove a record 12,920 times during her career.[7]

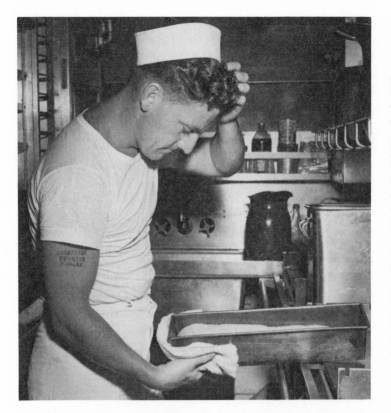

(left) Sea Robin baker takes a rueful glance at collapsed bread dough. When air pressure built up in boat prior to a dive to assure all openings were closed, rising batch fell flat. (below) Crewman paints a Cape Horn hash mark on Sea Robin's conning tower fairwater. Note campaign ribbons. Stars indicate successful war patrols. NGS.

CAPE HORN

(left) "Patsy," English springer spaniel mascot, goes down the hatch of Sea Robin. During dives, Patsy took her stand in the control room. The rest of the time she stuck close to cook. (below) Sailor checks off June 1, 1947 on calendar, the day Sea Robin reached Cape Horn. Stationed at bow tubes, he stood farthest forward to be the first submariner around the Horn. Photograph by Willard R. Culver ©1948, NGS.

Other Portsmouth boats embarked on noteworthy cruises. The *Sennet* accompanied the third Antarctic expedition, Operation Highjump, led by Admiral Richard E. Byrd, in 1946-1947. As the first American submarine to operate in Antarctic waters, the *Sennet* proved unsuitable for this operation because the ice made subs vulnerable to possible damage.

The *Pickerel (SS524)* engaged in a record-shattering voyage. Having a complex building history, she was laid down and launched without christening at the Boston Naval Shipyard in 1944 and then brought to Portsmouth for outfitting and completion. In 1949 the boat was christened and commissioned at the Portsmouth Naval Shipyard. In 1950 the snorkel-equipped *Pickerel* traveled completely submerged from Hong Kong to Pearl Harbor in twenty-one days, probably the longest distance ever traveled by a submerged diesel-electric submarine. The Navy described the 5200-mile voyage as "just a routine run." Later that same year the *Pickerel* spent four months in the Korean war zone, being one of the first submarines to enter the Korean conflict.

In 1958 the *Gudgeon (SS567)* became the first submarine to circumnavigate the globe. She traveled some 23,111 miles in returning to her Pearl Harbor home port. As she approached the dock, a celebration erupted. A helicopter dropped thirty pounds of exotic orchid blossoms on the crew while a navy band played "Around the World in Eighty Days." Two navy tugboats sprayed water high in the air while whistles blew all over the harbor.[8]

The *Archerfish* shifted to peacetime duties. After the torpedo tubes of the *Archerfish* were removed, she was refitted to carry highly sensitive electronic equipment for hydrographic and oceanographic work. Homeported at Pearl Harbor and staffed with an all-bachelor crew, this submarine spent sixty-five percent of her time at sea surveying vast areas of the ocean. After the war she traveled more than 369,000 miles in all oceans on her special scientific assignment. There was always a waiting list of bachelors who wanted to join the crew. Once a bevy of Playboy nightclub bunnies came aboard the *Archerfish* at San Diego in an attempt to alter the crew's disinclination toward matrimony.[9]

The *Redfish* also courted peacetime adventure. In 1952 she left San Diego en route to the Arctic Ocean. Her job was to test a newly invented fathometer to determine whether a submarine could penetrate beneath the Arctic ice. Off the coast of Alaska the *Redfish* submerged to pass through the Bering Strait. After surfacing, she proceeded to the ice-covered Beaufort Sea. If her electric batteries failed while she was under the ice, every man aboard faced certain death, locked in a crystalline tomb. On August 23, 1952, while the fathometer measured the amount of

Postwar view of the Archerfish (SS311), *the sub which sank Japanese aircraft carrier* Shinano *in 1944. After the war* Archerfish *was refitted with electronic equipment (center on superstructure) for hydrographic and oceanographic work. PA.*

water between the sub and the ice ceiling, the *Redfish* cruised under the ice for twenty miles in eight hours and then surfaced in open water. This was the first time a submarine had sailed beneath the Arctic ice.

Two years later the *Redfish*, receiving a more glamorous assignment, became a movie star in Walt Disney's "Twenty Thousand Leagues Under the Sea." Hollywood directors recognized a good actress, and in 1958 they cast her again, in "Run Silent, Run Deep," based on Edward L. Beach's novel of the same name. Camera crews filmed the boat on speed runs off the coast of San Diego. Since the *Redfish* had been stripped of her deck guns long before, the filmmakers mounted one on the boat's deck for authenticity.

In 1961 the *Redfish* appeared in her last film, "Battle of Bloody Beach," a war drama with Audie Murphy in the leading role. However, the nation's most decorated soldier of World War II met his match with the old sub. "It's all very interesting down there," Murphy said, "but not quite roomy enough for me."[10]

During the late 1940s and throughout the 1950s, many Portsmouth subs were turned over to NATO allies, including the well-known *Bang (SS385), Ronquil (SS396), Picuda (SS382), and Thornback (SS418).*

When Electric Boat's *Lapon (SS260)* arrived at Portsmouth in 1956, workmen spent almost a year overhauling and modernizing the sub for the Greek government. Sam Francis, the boat's skipper, spent almost four months training the Greek crew. "We had a skeleton crew," Francis said, "trained ourselves, and then trained them." Fluent in Greek, the bilingual Francis experienced no difficulty communicating with the Greek officers. "They all spoke English," Francis said. On August 10, 1957, in ceremonies at the Yard the *Lapon* was officially transferred to the Greek Royal Navy and renamed the *Poseidon.*[11]

While earning membership in the Ten Grander club, the *Toro (SS422)* was involved in a remarkable incident just forty miles east of Portland, Maine, during May of 1954. During antisubmarine warfare exercises a Brunswick Naval Air Station pilot scored a practice "hit" on the *Toro.* Flying his bomber at 225 miles per hour, the pilot spotted *Toro's* periscope 100 feet below. The periscope, or "eye," measuring three and a half inches in diameter, extended a foot and a half out of the water. The pilot took aim and dropped a thirteen-pound practice bomb.

The *Toro's* skipper watched the bomber through his periscope and swung it forward to locate the "splash" in the water. But the bomb struck the periscope directly. "Everything went black," the skipper said. Astounded at such accuracy, he had the top of the periscope cut from the twisted wreckage and mounted on a plaque. In October he presented the plaque, suitably inscribed, to the pilot, who became the first and only navy pilot to receive the "Order of the Busted Periscope." It has never been awarded again.[12]

"We had fun," said "Legs" Legare, one of the post-war diesel submarine skippers. "Nuclear power was just another way of generating steam. The diesel force became a training ground for the nuclear subs."[13]

GUPPYs and Snorkels Combine for the Tang Class

New and improved diesel submarines soon evolved to become capable of increased submergence time, depth and underwater speed. Portsmouth led the way in these developments. The Yard pioneered the concept of the GUPPY program, completing the first GUPPY conversion of the Portsmouth boat *Odax* in 1947. (GUPPY is an acronym devised from "Greater Underwater Propulsive Power" with the Y added for euphony). This adaptation included both greater battery power and a streamlined hull. Workmen removed anything which resisted the smooth flow of water by stripping non-essential deck fittings or recessing them. They also enclosed the conning tower and periscope within a "sail" to further reduce friction.[14]

During the war, each fleet submarine contained 252 battery cells. The improved GUPPY battery contained 504 cells which delivered 600 volts, thereby increasing underwater speed and endurance. Subs could

Portsmouth-built Odax, *first boat to receive a GUPPY conversion, pioneered at the Navy Yard in 1951. GUPPY overhauls extended life of fleet boats with streamlined outer hulls and increased battery capacities. PM.*

Post-World War II view of USS Tigrone, *sporting radar, scanners, antennae and sophisticated detection and communications equipment. KHNM.*

now travel at submerged speeds of sixteen to eighteen knots. Other improvements included better sonar (derived from *sound navigation and ranging*) for detecting submerged objects, radar, and radio equipment.[15]

At the same time the Yard experimented with adapting the German snorkel to American subs. The need to enlarge the German snorkel prototype to accommodate the bigger American boats required much trial-and-error development. In 1947 the Yard fitted a snorkel, the first on a fleet boat, on the Portsmouth-built *Irex*.

The almost simultaneous perfection of the snorkel and the first GUPPY conversions resulted in the two programs being combined in the new GUPPY II design. This coincidence extended the useful life of the fleet submarines for many years and prevented early obsolescence of the older boats.

On May 21, 1948, the first launching in two and a half years occurred at the Yard (since the end of the war, the *Volador* had remained on the building ways because peace had suspended construction). In contrast to the war years, security at her launching was relaxed. The *Volador* slid down the ways in the presence of many spectators and workmen. On the sponsor's stand was Andy McKee, who became, after his retirement from the navy, the design director and assistant general manager of Electric Boat.

The long delay in the *Volador*'s construction worked to her advantage. When work was resumed during the winter of 1947-1948, she was equipped with a "GUPPY-snorkel" to make her among the most modern in the fleet. Of the fifty-three GUPPY conversions, the Yard successfully completed over twenty. These boats remained in front-line service until the 1970s.[16]

The outbreak of the Korean conflict in June of 1950 triggered a long boom of design and construction at the Yard. "The Yard was hiring engineers in the 1950s," said Russell Van Billiard, an ordnance system engineer who worked in the design division. "It usually takes three or five years from blank paper to the boat's building and launching. Those were for me the most exciting and happiest years at the Yard, to watch an idea evolve to welded steel."

The new boat the Yard was building was the *Tang*, the prototype of a new class named for Richard H. O'Kane's legendary boat. "The *Tang* class was essentially developed," Van Billiard said, "from our own operations in the war and lifted as well from the German subs. With this outgrowth of German technology we made the *Tang's* hull a little thicker so she could go below 400 feet" (the U. S. Navy has restricted depths below 400 feet as classified information).[17]

Tang, launched on June 19, 1951, was the first post-war sub built at

Tang in floating drydock (YFD-82) flooded down. Tang was the first post-war sub built at the Yard to incorporate latest design and technological changes. PA.

the Yard. Mrs. Richard H. O'Kane christened the new boat and her daughter Marcia was matron of honor.

The *Tang* eventually lived up to the reputation of her predecessor. Early problems with the diesels of this class prompted a jingle among submariners:

> *Trigger, Tang, Darter* and *Trout,*
> Always in, never out.

After correcting the usual bugs associated with a new class, with many boats named after World War II subs, the *Tang* class received new power plants which drove the subs at a submerged speed of seventeen knots. As an attack submarine *Tang* engaged on a cold weather training cruise in 1959 and tested a newly developed snorkel de-icer system.[18]

The revived spirit of innovation associated with the *Tang* continued during the following year with the laying of the keel of the *USS Albacore (AGSS 569)*. On March 21, 1952, a keel-laying ceremony took place in the building ways or "big shed" for this experimental submarine. About 300,000 mandays would be required to build her.

On Friday morning, October 17, virtually everyone in the Shipyard took a brief break for a special occasion. Commander-in-Chief Harry S. Truman was in the area. Stumping for the Democratic ticket, the president found time during his whirlwind swing to visit the Yard. Riding in an open-car motorcade in ideal weather, Truman arrived at the main gate. Thousands of workers lined the streets of the base to greet the president. After a tour by naval officials, the president and his party experienced an interruption of their tight schedule. Shipyard fire engines, speeding to a blaze, broke through the presidential motorcade. The firemen, in spic-and-span dress blues, had been waiting for Truman to pass in review when the alarm sounded. They extinguished a minor fire, but missed the ceremony. At the Mall the president received a twenty-one-gun salute. He inspected the marine guard of honor and read the plaque on the *Sailfish* superstructure.

The visit lasted twenty-five minutes; no president has appeared at the Yard since. When the excitement was over, workmen went back to their shops and building ways to resume work on the *Albacore*, designed to be the world's fastest submerged submarine.[19]

The Revolutionary Albacore

One of the most important submarines in United States naval history, the *Albacore* has few equals. She was intended to be, in the words of naval designer Eugene Allmendinger who worked on her throughout her career, "a full-scale floating hydrodynamics laboratory." The *Albacore* was a familiar sight at the Yard during the '50s and '60s as she underwent four conversions. As the fastest, quietest and most maneuverable underwater boat of her day, the *Albacore* ruled beneath the waves as a harbinger of the future. Every American sub since that time has benefited from the *Albacore*'s legacy.

In 1948 Rear Admiral Charles B. Momsen and other veteran submariners visualized a radically new hull designed for speed. Before then submarine design had become a tug-of-war of compromises among various bureaus. As Momsen said:

> I felt that the Bureau of Ships had in the past been so restricted in their design studies by contradictory instructions concerning characteristics that it was impossible for them to produce the best submarines. It was almost like stuffing a turkey. First, they designed a hull and then every person in the Department began to stuff it from both ends. In the old days, design became a four ring circus. The Bureaus of Ordnance, Engineering, Navigation and Construction and Repair all vied with one another to get their own pet projects included.

Yard mobile crane holds in suspension complete bow of **Albacore** *prior to installing component to hull of boat. UNH.*

Yard employees examine quarter scale model of **Dolphin** *prior to construction. Maximum hull diameter of completed boat measured over 27 feet. UNH.*

Momsen managed to circumvent competing departments. The Bureau of Ships approved his idea of designing the *Albacore* on the sole basis of submerged performance. The boat would be powered with a single propeller. "Because of better speed characteristics of the submarine," Momsen said, "it is fair to predict that when better power plants are available, submarines will be able to make more than fifty knots while submerged."[20]

In 1949 the best American naval minds and laboratories went to work to design the perfect submarine hull form. Engineers and scientists conducted the testing at the David W. Taylor Experimental Model Basin at Carderock, Maryland, on the Potomac River northwest of Washington. Since 1937 the Model Basin was pre-eminent in this field. Howell Russell, a Model Basin engineer at this time, said:

> Through the use of small models and accurate testing facilities, they were able to predict the performance of full-scale ships. The place built hundreds of models, at least one for every class or modification, of beautiful clear mahogany or pine. At one time there were over 3000 different ship and propeller models. It cost about $20,000 to $30,000 to build each model, nothing except the basic hull, no superstructure, no gingerbread. There were four or five parameters of models and we selected the best one. Then we took the models to the towing tanks for test runs.

For the *Albacore* the designers built a series of models, ranging in length from seven to seventy-five feet. After selecting the best form, they built two new models, one as a single-screw vessel and the other with twin screws, used by conventional subs. At Langley Aeronautical Laboratory, Langley Air Force Base, Virginia, the two models were tested in a wind tunnel to calculate drag and lift. The navy ultimately adopted the single-screw design as the best for the *Albacore*.

At the Portsmouth Naval Shipyard the *Albacore* began with plans, models and literally miles of blueprints. Workmen built additional scale models and wooden mock-up forms to insure that all equipment components would fit into the crowded hull. Everything, including the puppet sailor, "Little Joe," was one-quarter actual size.[21]

During 1952-1953 the *Albacore* evolved. Her stubby hull was shaped like a fish for maximum speed with a cod's head and a mackerel's tail. A separate maneuverable dorsal rudder was attached to the rear of the sail in the same position as a fin on a fish. "The fleet boats," Allmendinger said, "spent eighty percent of their time on the surface and twenty percent below." The navy sought to reverse this. "The *Albacore*," Allmendinger continued, "was not at all happy on the surface. With the hull developed along mathematical lines, the *Albacore* had an easy hull to

Launching of the John Adams *(SSBN620) on January 12, 1963, showing distinctive whale-like hull design. Note sign at top of building ways offering a challenge to rival yard in California. PA.*

drive when submerged but not on the surface." As an experimental sub the *Albacore* would undergo four conversions of rebuilt sterns, repositioning of diving planes and other configurations to achieve the most efficient form. Forgoing any weapons systems or torpedo tubes, the boat was fitted with pancake General Electric diesel engines and a GUPPY

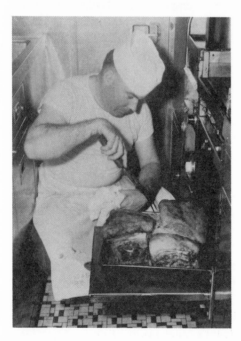

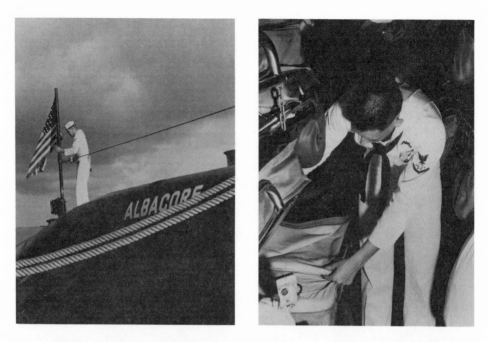

Duty routine aboard the **Albacore** *included (clockwise) flag-raising; straightening up bunk; relaxing in reading room; and turning roast in galley. UNH.*

battery. Among the Yard workmen, the $20 million *Albacore* was affectionately known as the "pregnant whale," because of her short length and large diameter.[22]

On launch day, August 1, 1953, Vice Admiral Edward L. Cochrane (Ret.), whose experience in design extended back for more than forty years, observed the *Albacore*'s hull with special interest. "Gee whiz," he remarked to others in the reviewing stand, "it's taken a long time to come back to John Holland's design." The Holland submarine purchased by the navy in 1900 possessed almost exactly the same lines as the *Albacore*.[23]

After commissioning in December 1953, the *Albacore* was ready for sea trials. In most respects she surpassed scientific expectations. The *Albacore* easily exceeded twenty knots submerged to earn the nickname, "the world's fastest submarine." However, speed was not her only asset. The *Albacore* maneuvered extremely well through tight turns, dives and overshoots, the last referring to the quickness of response to commands. "Our turning rate," said one skipper, "is faster than a jet plane's." The control room even resembled the cockpit of a jet plane, because the diving officer controlled the course and depth with a single stick. This steering arrangement was the first single-pilot console on an American submarine.[24]

During 1955-1956 the *Albacore* underwent conversion of her stern, according to plan. A program of extensive noise reduction was also undertaken to make the *Albacore* one of the quietest subs in the navy. Workmen mounted major equipment systems on special rubber pads to reduce machinery noises that would otherwise be conducted through the hull into the water.

The invention of the Portsmouth test tank in 1953 assured the reliability of each steel section in the *Albacore*'s hull. This tank, about thirty feet across and fifty feet long, applied pressure and then removed it to determine the stress fatigue of the metal. In a few months of constant hydrostatic pressure testing, the tank could simulate the use of a sub's lifetime and proceed to as much as five times the sub's projected length of service. If a crack appeared in the steel hull section, the Yard engineers continued testing to trace the crack's history. The information compiled by the Portsmouth test tank not only assured safety but also led to further improvements in sub design. New steel alloys for sub hulls continued to be tested through the 1970s.[25]

In her third conversion and overhaul during 1960, the *Albacore*'s appearance changed again. An "X" configuration of the stern diving planes and rudders replaced the existing cruciform arrangement. Workmen also installed ten dive brakes around the periphery of the hull. By extending these brakes, naval designers hoped to stop the *Albacore* at

Invented in 1953 to measure stress fatigue of hulls, Portsmouth test tank led to safety and improvements in design. UNH.

high speed during submerged runs. "This idea didn't prove feasible," said Frederick Smith, the sub's engineering officer. "The tremendous speed of the boat popped them."

To address this problem, the submariners on the *Albacore* experimented with a parachute of a C-47, obtained from Newington's Pease Air Force Base. They reinforced the chute which, upon release, acted as a drag sea anchor. This ingenious idea technically worked. Stored and rigged in a large can, the chute expanded, slowed the boat and headed her in a positive up angle. Because the chute invariably tangled in the sail, this experiment was abandoned after a half dozen trials.

More farfetched ideas arose in navy circles at this time. One invention, "Combination Submarine and Aircraft and Method of Maneuvering the Same," was actually patented in 1955 by the navy's Bureau of Aeronautics. The flying sub, complete with skis for water landings, would use propeller drive under water and jet power in flight. This fantasy, however, remained on paper.[26]

During a test run in 1962 the *Albacore* undertook an emergency

Albacore *"broaching" or breaking water during high speed surfacing exercise. Note water streaming out of vents. UNH.*

mission at sea. While operating 110 miles south of Long Island, New York, the *Albacore* surfaced for a routine battery charge. A distressed pigeon landed on her deck. A sailor caught the bird and brought it below for food and water. Since the bird had an identification tag, the skipper brought the pigeon back to Portsmouth. It was identified as a gray banded homer from Trenton, New Jersey. Upon release the pigeon fluttered up to a television antenna on a roof to get its bearings, and then flew southwest toward New Jersey.[27]

The fourth and final conversion of the *Albacore* occurred during 1963-1964. Modifications further improved the sub's performance. Inventing another Portsmouth-first device, the Yard installed an emergency recovery unit, featuring a new main ballast tank blow system. Workmen also placed a new silver-zinc battery in her hull. "The battery contained $10 million worth of silver," said Frederick "Pete" Smith, who was responsible for its performance. "It gave out 16,000 amps per hour, the largest capacity in the world. When the battery was broken up and the silver given back to the Treasury Department, the navy made money

Albacore *at dockside, displaying her famous whale-shaped hull. This is the as-built configuration with bow places and cruciform stern. UNH.*

on the silver content as it was worth more then than when obtained."[28]

The officers and men aboard the *Albacore* enjoyed one of the most sought-after assignments in the navy. "My shipmates were the most enlightened and finest people I ever met," said one crew member. "There was a fantastic education in subs which equaled a college degree. The men were mentally quick and alert. You were given six months to qualify. If not, you were out."

The *Albacore*'s crew undertook special drills, known as "blackout" and "bailout." In the event that the *Albacore* lost power, these drills would save the boat. The lights were systematically shut off as the crews searched out the systems in blackout darkness. Upon the restoration of the systems for surfacing, the simulated bailout completed the drill. Time and experience attuned the crew to the personality of each machine. They reacted almost instinctively when anything seemed about to go wrong. The automatic shut-down of a machine at the end of its cycle in the middle of the night was enough to awaken Pete Smith.

Lando W. Zech, Jr., one of the *Albacore*'s skippers, became known later in his career as the "sailor's admiral" for his inspired leadership. Zech often invited the wives and children of his crew aboard when the

Albacore was in Portsmouth. "You can handle this someday," Zech said to a little boy, pointing out the machinery. Zech was right—the sailor's son later enlisted in the navy.[29]

On September 1, 1972, the *Albacore* was decommissioned at the Yard in traditional naval ceremonies. She had served almost twenty years in her remarkable career. An admiral delivering the principal address at the occasion referred to the *Albacore* as "the submarine which gave its body to science."

The *Albacore* was later towed to the Philadelphia Naval Base to become a member of the Naval Inactive Ship Maintenance Detachment. There she remained for more than a decade until her return to Portsmouth as a tourist attraction.[30]

The Seadragon *Breathes Fire Under the North Pole*

The Portsmouth Naval Shipyard followed Electric Boat in the race to construct nuclear-powered submarines. Once committed, the Yard produced many outstanding boats.

On January 12, 1950, Captain Hyman G. Rickover, Chief of the Naval Reactors Branch of the Atomic Energy Commission, arrived at the Yard. In conference with the Yard commander, Rickover proposed that Portsmouth supply designers and constructors to build an atomic submarine reactor at Arco, Idaho. These Portsmouth personnel, Rickover insisted, would report directly to him.

The Commander balked, saying that Portsmouth could not take the job because funds were low. The Yard was already heavily involved with the GUPPY conversions as well as leading the development of the new *Tang* class.

"Do you mind if I use your phone?" Rickover asked.

"Not at all."

Without hesitation Rickover reached over the desk and placed a call to the manager of the Electric Boat Company in Groton, Connecticut.

"Do you want to get ready to build the Navy's first atomic-powered submarine? I can't get the Navy Yard interested."

The answer from Groton was affirmative.

"Thanks. I'll be down there tonight."

The navy's preliminary research in nuclear propulsion for submarines dated back to 1939. After the war, interest increased. Many naval officers saw the nuclear reactor as the perfect propulsion plant for a submarine. The heat produced by fission in uranium atoms could produce steam to drive turbines. No combustion occurred in this atomic reaction, so no air was required. In theory, submariners had found the perfect propulsion plant for their boats.[31]

In fairness to the Portsmouth shipyard commander, the superiority of the concept of using nuclear power for submarines was totally unproven in 1950. Because of Portsmouth's preoccupation with the GUPPY and *Tang* project, the Yard saw her competitor, Electric Boat, accept the challenge. EB built the world's first three nuclear submarines during the early 1950s.

On January 24, 1956, the Portsmouth Shipyard joined the nuclear club by laying the keel for the *Swordfish (SSN579)*, the first atomic-powered submarine constructed in a government-owned yard. It was, nevertheless, a Rickover-directed project. "With the building of nuclear submarines at the Yard," Wilma "Bill" Letch, long-time machinist, said, "It was an organization within an organization. Crews, engineers and men reported to and were responsible to Rickover and not to the Portsmouth Yard. Rickover had his own inspectors on the job, and everything had to be recorded. Failure to report the slightest incident resulted in firing."

After the controversy about authority was resolved, the work went on. Special emphasis was placed on safety so that the project could be accomplished without adverse effects on health. Construction of the *Swordfish* would require two and a half years before launching and commissioning.[32]

On Monday, June 25, 1956, the routine in the Yard halted momentarily as news spread about the passing of a tough sailor whose name was synonymous with the old navy of steam and diesels. The daily personnel report of the United States Naval Hospital, Portsmouth, New Hampshire, carried the following item:

"KING, Ernest Joseph   FADM   USN   Discharged by Death"

In frail health following a stroke in 1947, Admiral King had spent every summer thereafter at the Portsmouth Naval Hospital to escape the Washington heat.

A marine guard stood at attention at the Mall and the flag flew at half-mast that afternoon as a hearse passed by, bearing the remains of the architect of naval victory in World War II. Historians credited King with lifting the navy "off its back" after Pearl Harbor, just when nuclear power in turn was transforming the navy in the 1950s.[33]

Launched in mid-1957 and commissioned the next year, the *Swordfish* steamed to Pearl Harbor, her home port. In 1960 she became the first nuclear-powered sub to cruise in the Western Pacific.

The *Seadragon*, the second Portsmouth nuclear sub, lived up to her pugnacious name. The last of four subs of the *Skate* class, the *Seadragon* was an Electric Boat design, a small and simple boat designed for

Launching of the USS Seadragon *in 1958, Portsmouth's second nuclear submarine. PNSY.*

mass production if necessary. "The *Seadragon* was cannibalized for the *Swordfish*," said Jack Sousae, navy superintendent of construction. "We were months behind schedule, but we made up the difference."[34]

Launched in 1958, the *Seadragon* left for sea trials on October 5,

1959. Aboard the boat was Admiral Hyman Rickover, who personally rode initial sea trials for each of his nuclear subs. The Yard workmen became accustomed to his familiar figure. Rickover always appeared hatless in a floppy civilian coat as he inspected the various compartments. A perfectionist, Rickover attended to business, politely asking civilian employees questions on his inspection tours. He did not spend all his time in the officers' wardroom.

Beyond the Isles of Shoals, the *Seadragon* was scheduled for four hours of maximum speed on the surface before diving for four hours of maximum speed underwater. "After three hours and forty-five minutes on the surface," said Sousae, "there was a tremendous crash. The sub had hit a whale, evidently lying asleep on the surface. The propeller was bent." A crew member picked up whale flesh after the accident.

Inside the control room the radioman suggested sending the message, "Whacked whale, warped wheel." Rickover and George Steele, skipper of the boat, decided in favor of a more dignified message. The cruise was over; the *Seadragon* turned back with a deformed propeller shaft and bent propeller. Upon entering the Piscataqua channel, Rickover spoke over the public address system. "I think you've got a whale of a ship here," he said, in about the only comical statement anyone in the navy ever heard him make. The crew groaned.[35]

After this inauspicious maiden voyage, the *Seadragon* prepared for a historic mission: to make a transit of the Northwest Passage. She would then continue to the North Pole. The sub would explore the practically unchartered Arctic basin for a month, operating thousands of miles from other American ships, before ultimately docking at Pearl Harbor. The navy wanted to gather information for defense against possible enemy missile submarines. "The only way to track enemy subs up there," said skipper George Steele, "is with our own submarines."

The Yard installed $500,000 worth of under-ice equipment in addition to the same amount allotted for normal shakedown cruise repairs. Shipyard engineers developed TV cameras to calculate the thickness of ice, measured by the degree of light coming through it. They were also aware that Arctic water is denser than water in more temperate ocean zones and freezes at twenty-eight degrees F. to produce additional pressure on the hull. To compensate, they placed special equipment on deck to break the ice if the *Seadragon* needed to surface.

The crew was excited about the trip, adopting the unofficial slogan of "Under the Ice to Paradise." Skipper Steele, however, was firm on one point. His communications officer had a pet skunk, "Flower," which if it made the trip would be the first "pole cat" at the North Pole. Steele ruled against Flower's boarding as skunks are inclined to be aromatically temperamental.[36]

On August 1, 1960, the *Seadragon* sailed northward. Eight days later she entered Baffin Bay, which lay between Baffin Island and Greenland, an area known to be a breeding ground for icebergs. The *Seadragon* became the first sub in history to dive under icebergs. One iceberg required a dive of more than 300 feet to clear it. The civilian scientists aboard studied and measured eleven icebergs from their unique vantage points.

On August 15, the *Seadragon* entered Parry Channel and proceeded westward through the various sounds surrounding the islands of the Canadian archipelago. For three days the submerged sub navigated through shallow Barrow Strait, a little known and poorly surveyed bottleneck. Negotiating this difficult passage without incident, the *Seadragon* made navigational fixes with radar and surfaced several times in surprisingly ice-free water. Several islands were discovered to be as much as five miles away from the positions shown on the existing nautical charts. Then the sub entered the deeper McClure Strait and finally the Arctic Basin. The *Seadragon* had made the first submerged transit of the Northwest Passage. Her voyage established the feasibility of this route for American subs.

Arriving at the North Pole on August 25, the *Seadragon* found a polynya, an area of open water in the sea ice. She surfaced. A SCUBA team with special electronic "ice suits" operated under the ice. In twenty-eight degrees F. air a party of Seadragonites rowed a life raft to a nearby ice cake. There they laid out a baseball diamond and played the first baseball game at the top of the world. It was an unusual game. When a batter hit a home run it would land on the next day, owing to the international dateline time zones. A runner leaving home plate at full speed would arrive at first base twelve hours later.

On September 14, the *Seadragon* arrived at Pearl Harbor amidst the aloha spirit generated by dancing Hawaiian hula girls at the dock. Since leaving Portsmouth, the sub had traveled 11,231 miles, 10,415 of which were underwater or under ice.[37]

Two years later, from her Pearl Harbor homeport, the *Seadragon* returned to Arctic waters for a rendezvous with EB's *Skate (SSN578)* under the ice pack. In a secret operation the two subs participated in hide-and-seek war games, using each other as targets. On August 2, 1962, they surfaced through a polynya at the North Pole. In a news conference a few days later, President John F. Kennedy commented on the "historic rendezvous" and congratulated "all of those involved in this exceptional technical feat." This operation marked the beginning of multi-sub cruises under the ice pack and the development of under-ice antisubmarine tactics.[38]

Electric Boat's Skate (SSN-578) *and Portsmouth's* Seadragon (SSN-584)
(left to right) at historic rendezvous at North Pole in August 1962. UNH.

Accompanied by tugs, the nuclear-powered Abraham Lincoln *was
Portsmouth's first Polaris submarine. PM.*

Polaris Subs Operate out of Holy Loch, Scotland

Launched on May 14, 1960, the *Abraham Lincoln (SSBN602)* was Portsmouth's first Polaris sub and the fifth ballistic missile submarine. Longer than a football field, the *Abraham Lincoln* displaced 6030 tons. The nuclear-powered sub of the *George Washington* class was outfitted with advanced navigational aids. Her navigator could determine the boat's position while submerged, completely independent of the earth's atmosphere.

Earlier submarines were named for marine creatures. Breaking with tradition in view of the strategic importance of the Polaris weapons system, the navy named fleet ballistic missile subs for famous Americans, starting with the *George Washington* as the lead boat of the new class. The *Abraham Lincoln* was the first navy ship to bear the full name of the Civil War president.[39]

The submerged *Abraham Lincoln* served as a launching pad for sixteen missiles. Housed in a missile room, nicknamed "Sherwood Forest" since the tubes resembled giant trees, the missiles had a range of 1,200 miles.

Assigned two full crews, the "Blue" and the "Gold," the *Lincoln* went on patrol with one crew aboard while the other crew remained in its home port of New London, undergoing refresher training and breaking in new crew members. Those on patrol cruised submerged and maintained radio silence for the duration of their two-month mission. The endurance of the submarine was limited only by the stamina of her crew.

The boat's routine was usually a ten-to twelve-hour day. To distinguish between day and night, the boat was "rigged for red" at night time. The cooks served four meals a day, breakfast, lunch, dinner, and a soupdown in mid-afternoon. Some of the most enticing menu items were chicken Isabella, baked Alaska, shrimp Newburg, beef Stroganoff, and lasagna; the standard favorites were roast beef and steak.

It was originally thought that boredom would plague the crews on these long patrols, but this did not prove to be true. The long hours of work coupled with recreational facilities including bicycles, rowing machines, a well-stocked library and Harvard University extension courses kept everyone busy. "Movie call" at least once a day, bingo and singalong nights also enlivened the cruise. The Armed Forces Radio Service delivered daily news broadcasts and "familygrams," brief, personal messages from kin and friends. A "babygram" announced new arrivals; the new dad could pass out cigars but would have to wait to see the new heir and future submariner. "What other career," said one skipper, "offers a honeymoon every six months?"[40]

Black profile of submarine (left center) alongside tender Holland *at Holy Loch, Scotland. UNH.*

On July 17, 1961, the *Abraham Lincoln* left the Yard for patrol duty and assignment to the submarine squadron operating from the tender *Proteus* stationed at Holy Loch, Scotland. This base in the territorial waters of the United Kingdom is directly under the control of the U. S. Navy. The *Proteus* had arrived that March at Holy Loch, an arm of the Firth of Clyde, about forty miles west of Glasgow. Setting up shop in this strait, the *Proteus* was warmly received by the local residents with invitations to dances and parties, but elicited strong protests from some factions of the British people, and, predictably, the Soviet Union. On a two-year rotation, the *Proteus* was later relieved by the *Hunley*, a new tender named for the Confederate submarine built the century before.

The Portsmouth Naval Shipyard played a vital role in this advanced base, which placed American Polaris submarines near the North Sea and thousands of miles closer to Soviet waters. After a multi-section dry dock was towed across the Atlantic and assembled at Holy Loch, the Yard designed and built an all-weather shelter for use by Polaris submarines. The shelter protected workmen on stormy days.[41]

During the fall of 1963 the Yard received a special assignment, winning a $1 million competitive bid to overhaul the *Sam Houston (SSN-609)*, a Newport News-built Polaris sub at Holy Loch. It was economically as well as strategically advisable to overhaul and refit subs in Scotland rather than return the boats to American yards.

Donald Marion, a Yard electronics technician, headed the first Tiger Team to perform the work. "I hand-picked thirty boys from four different shops: welders, chippers, and pipefitters," Marion said. "All were volunteers and we were allotted two weeks to do the job. I had a layout on the work and we were ready to go on a moment's notice. We were flown over there, thirty men plus five tons of equipment. The mission was top secret and confidential."

After flying to London with a connecting flight to Glasgow, the team traveled by railroad to Greenock and then boarded a ferry across the Firth of Clyde to Dunoon. There they lived at a Scottish hotel. At 7:00 A.M. taxis were waiting at the door to take the men dockside to a U.S. Navy launch for a ride to the floating dry dock.

"Time was of the essence," Marion said. "We worked one twelve-hour shift a day, cut holes in the hulls and within four hours the hull had to be re-sealed to restore its watertight integrity. Experienced welders, chippers, and technicians pulled the cables through the hulls. We worked in oil-skins as the weather was miserable, rainy and cold."

The Tiger Team completed the job for under $500,000, saving the American government an equal amount. Such routine overhaul had never been done before outside the Portsmouth Shipyard. "The boys were happy as larks," Marion said. "They loved it and considered it the highlight of their careers at the Yard. We had a night in London as well — unofficially." The *Sam Houston* was ready to resume her North Sea patrols at a fraction of the time and money it would have required if the boat had returned to the United States.[42]

Work on new Portsmouth subs was under way at the Yard. On May 12, 1964 a "triple-header" in submarine construction occasioned one of the biggest events in Yard history. The *John Adams*, the Yard's second fleet ballistic missile submarine, was placed in commission. Named for two presidents, John Adams and his son John Quincy Adams, the boat received the nickname "Big John" in navy circles. Workmen then conducted the keel laying ceremony of the *Grayling*, a nuclear-powered boat which carried on the name of the famous World War II sub. The last event was the launching of the *Nathanael Greene* in late morning to take advantage of the incoming tide. The boat was named for the famed Revolutionary War general. Members of the *Lafayette* class and sister subs, the *Adams* and the *Greene* were the heaviest and largest boats ever built at the Portsmouth Naval Shipyard. Each displaced 7250 tons surfaced and 8250 tons submerged.[43]

The *John Adams* and *Nathanael Greene* eventually served at Holy

Inspectors check over missile tubes of John Adams (SSBN620). *Top covers of "silos" open on end at left. "Big John" carries sixteen missiles and is active today (1984). UNH.*

Loch on rotation with other Polaris submarines. In the 1960s Howell Russell left the David W. Taylor Model Basin on temporary assignment to install sonar equipment on EB's *George Washington*. In preparation for the job Russell had a tent made at the Portsmouth Shipyard's Sail Shop to insure his protection against the weather.

"Holy Loch is sheltered, isolated, and acts as a wind tunnel," Russell said. At the end of a particularly windy day at Holy Loch, Russell left his tent and stepped aboard the Navy launch to go ashore for the night.

"Is that your tent?" the launch sailor asked.

"Yes."

"Can you give me confidential information? The boys have a betting pool as to what time during the night it will blow over."

Russell remained noncommittal. The next morning the wind was blowing at 100 knots and continued for four days. All outside work on the *Hunley* and *George Washington* was suspended. When Russell finally returned, he saw that all the staging had blown down, but the tent remained upright.

As Russell completed his work, the commanding officer of the *Hunley* stopped by. "When you leave," he said to Russell, "I want that tent." Russell left it, and upon his return a year later, the tent was still standing and in use.[44]

Coordinated through the fleet support type desk at the Yard, Portsmouth Tiger Teams still head for Holy Loch whenever necessary. "Tiger Teams might be two people for a week or thirty for a month," said Russell Van Billiard, present incumbent of the fleet support type desk of the Yard. "The Holy Loch submarine squadron performs most of their own repair work. But if things get complicated they come to us for help and we respond. No two are the same."[45]

Thresher

The modern submarine most intimately associated with the Yard was the *Thresher (SSN593)*. She was designed, built, launched, commissioned, and overhauled at the Yard as the lead boat of the new *Thresher* class, the world's most advanced class of nuclear attack submarines.

"The *Thresher* had radically new equipment," said Russell Van Billiard, one of the engineers who worked on her. "The big difference was depth. The reactor plant was the same. The entire bow was sonar, and the torpedo room was located amidships with two torpedo tubes on each side. This idea is kept to this day."

The $45 million *Thresher* incorporated many innovations. Like the *Albacore*, she had a teardrop-shaped hull and was bred for speed and maneuverability. Built with the commercially developed HY-80 (High Yield-80) steel, her hull could withstand extreme sea pressure, some 80,000 pounds per square inch (the tensile steel of the older boats could withstand only half that amount). The new HY steel required a whole new system of welding techniques and testing. This superior hull enabled the *Thresher* to dive deeper than any American sub had before.

Another *Thresher* improvement was her built-in silence from bow to stern since the boat was designed from the start to be quiet. With many concepts developed by the Yard's noise reduction program, workmen reduced the sub's operating noise by building and installing quieter machinery. "Silence is a virtue" became a motto for the *Thresher* and her class.

The launching of the *Thresher* on July 9, 1960, also cast tradition aside. According to plan, the sub hit the water bow first because of her special buoyancy distribution and new design.[46]

Typical of the experience of a lead submarine of a new class, the *Thresher* needed modifications to eliminate bugs. "The propulsion plant was mounted on rubber," said engineer Russell Van Billiard, "so it could move back and forth. Designed to slide and give and take, the rubber

Breaking precedent with earlier submarine launchings, Thresher
(SSN593) hits water bow first during 1960 ceremonies. UNH.

[pads] could keep the noise within a confined place." The noise thus never
radiated to the hull where it would escape into the water to allow detection
by the enemy. "Comparing the noise made by the *Threshers* against the
Skipjacks [older nuclear boats]," said one submariner, "is like comparing
a new Cadillac to an old Model-A Ford."

Commissioned in 1961, the *Thresher* participated in nuclear submarine exercises along the Atlantic coast. The boat was the pride of the
Yard. The local seacoast community also was proud of the Yard's recent
achievement. On March 24, 1962, many of the Yard's naval officers and
top civilian personnel attended the dedication of the *USS Thresher* Room
at Valle's Steak House, a popular eating place in Kittery.[47]

After a nine-month overhaul at the Yard, the *Thresher* was ready
to go to sea in April 1963.

"It was the Admiral's [Rickover's] policy," said Jack Sousae, a staff
officer at Sublant [Submarine Headquarters, Atlantic Fleet, New
London], "to oversee the operation on a major overhaul. The inspecting
officer would report to Rickover personally and would board the sub

ready for sea trials. It was my turn to rotate."

Sousae contacted Wesley Harvey, the *Thresher* skipper. "Wes Harvey assured me that the sub was ready to go on schedule in a week," Sousae said. "All that was remaining to be done were a few nuts and bolts and window dressing. On Friday Bob Krag [a new staff Sublant officer] arrived. He was young and saw his future in nuclear submarines. But he had a conference pending in Washington, and didn't know if he could make it [the sea trials]."

On Saturday Sousae and Krag conferred off and on by telephone as to who would make the trials. Sousae had his bags packed and planned to leave New London on Sunday for the drive up to the Yard. Just as he was leaving his house for some Saturday afternoon errands, the telephone rang. It was Krag. "The conference is postponed," Krag said. "I've got *Thresher*."

Sam Francis was another officer at New London engaged in submarine research for the squadron. For his own edification, he hoped to go on the trials. Francis called up Harvey the day before the cruise.

"Gee, I've never been on one," Francis said.

"No, Sam, I've got 129 people aboard. You'd have to sleep in the passageways."

"Well, I only go first class. I'll ride you next time."[48]

Back in the Yard, hydraulics specialist Bob Harford boarded the *Thresher* with a suitcase holding a three-day supply of underwear and toilet articles. Harford had worked on the *Thresher* throughout her career and had accompanied her on earlier trials. The navy paid extra money for such service, and more workers than were needed always volunteered. Shipyard workers performed a variety of duties and rarely obtained much sleep on these short cruises. Harford was used to sleeping on air mattresses placed on plywood platforms, built for the occasion, in the torpedo rooms. The sea and air pressure varied according to depth and often the mattresses would go flat and the occupant ended up sleeping on the plywood.

"Frank Palmer was ill with a heavy cold," Harford said. "I was taking his place on these trials. As a civilian, Frank took a physical before a cruise. The navy didn't want heavy colds, or sinus congestions aboard." Otherwise the whole crew would be affected within such closed quarters. While Harford was standing on the deck, Franklin Palmer boarded the *Thresher*. "The dispensary says I'm all right," Palmer said to Harford, "and I can make the trip."

Bumped from the cruise, Harford picked up his suitcase and left. "I was disappointed." he said.[49]

On the morning of Tuesday, April 9, 1963 the *Thresher* left Berth

Memorial services for Thresher *crew being conducted from* Squalus
/Sailfish *superstructure at the Mall during April 1963. UNH.*

11 for two days of trials. The next day, Wednesday, April 10, the *Thresher*
failed to surface from a dive 220 miles east of Cape Cod. She sank with all
hands in 8400 feet of water.

Upon hearing the news of the *Thresher's* disappearance, many
American submariners around the world broke into tears and cried
unashamedly. "We have lost respect for the sea," said one officer. "The sea
is a cruel taskmaster."

A memorial service, the largest of its kind at the Yard, was held at
the Mall on Friday, April 12. At the approximate time the service was
ending, a plane left Pease Air Force Base carrying Dean Axene, the
Thresher's first skipper. Flying over the spot where the boat had disappeared, he dropped a floral replica on the waters.[50]

The Yard sent letters of sympathy to the relatives of the men lost at
sea. Ethel D. Stadtmuller, mother of Sperry Gyroscope engineer Donald
Stadtmuller, responded to this kindness. "For the last few months," she
wrote, "my son enjoyed many pleasant moments with a great many of the

navy men and always spoke very highly of their treatment of him."
Stadtmuller had made a number of trips on the boat.

The parents of Robert Prescott, a Yard marine engineer, expressed
similar sentiments. "We shall always believe," Mr. and Mrs. Ithel Prescott
wrote, "that when the *Thresher* left the Portsmouth Naval Shipyard that
it was as safe as human hands could make it .... If you were personally
acquainted with Robert, you know that he was very exacting and
conscientious in his work, and no report was ever signed by him that he
didn't think was correct."[51]

A *Thresher* memorial fund established a trust for relief and
educational assistance for the 149 dependent children of the navy and
civilian personnel lost at sea. A carillon, known as the Thresher Bells, was
installed at the Portsmouth Shipyard Chapel (shortly thereafter renamed
the Thresher Memorial Chapel) to ring out daily in memory of the men.[52]

The Thresher Memorial Chapel stands atop a knoll partly forested
with a grove of Maine pine. This simple, white, colonial-style church
looks over the Piscataqua as it winds to the sea. On the right side of the
main door a bronze plaque reads:

IN MEMORY OF
OUR DEPARTED SHIPMATES
WHO STILL SAIL
A MIGHTY SHIP
U.S.S. THRESHER SSN593
3 AUGUST 1961-10 APRIL 1963

A Closure Order Threatens the Shipyard

The *Thresher* incident prompted implementation of stricter safety
standards and procedures throughout American submarine yards.
Portsmouth remained in the forefront in inaugurating necessary reforms.
Concurrently during this period the administration of President Lyndon
B. Johnson subjected all government shipyards and military bases to a
stringent review and evaluation based on economic considerations.
Receiving one of the many closure orders issued in late 1964, the
Portsmouth Naval Shipyard strove to reverse this decision. Otherwise
the Portsmouth facility would be shut down within ten years.

The navy inquiry into the *Thresher*'s sinking did not ascribe an
official reason for the sub's loss. Whatever the cause might have been, the
navy was determined to correct any possible deficiencies. Depth limita-
tions on deep-diving subs went immediately into effect. Studies tested a
sub's ability to recover from flooding as well as the necessary technology
to recover from such conditions. Navy engineers collected "at sea" data—

real data from actual facts, as contrasted with hypothetical calculations.

Extensive welding tests, new techniques of inspecting pipe joints, and quality control on materials were now Yard policy. An emergency blow system pioneered the adoption of the "panic button," a single button which could blow water out of the ballast tanks for surfacing during emergencies. A quality and reliability assurance department, established in 1966 as the outgrowth of a 1963 Yard directive, emphasized inspection and monitoring of all phases of workmanship. The result was, as the common phrase asserted, that "every sub is now safer because of the *Thresher*."[53]

After the *Thresher* failure, "the paperwork increased," said group superintendent machinist Wilma "Bill" Letch. "Everything was recorded down to the smallest item." Emphasis on safety extended to a single bolt. "One doesn't go to a local hardware store for a Japanese bolt," said Percy Whitney, superintendent of the foundry at that time, "when you know nothing about what's in it. A Washington congressman may be alarmed at a hearing about a $70 bolt. He has to be reeducated. Before the nuclear days, my superiors trusted me and took my word as to what was in the bolt without any questions. After nuclear, you have a flow of paper with the bolt. Each bolt has a pedigree, and with all the paper I could tell more about the casting than I knew about myself. It's hard to get perfection. To go from 90 percent to 99 percent, you have more rejections. If you want 99.5 percent, you pay more money to obtain bolts with more specifications."

This watchdog attitude extended throughout every aspect of the Yard's operations in the post-*Thresher* era with inspectors on top of inspectors. "There are builders trials," said designer Philip Hoyt. "There are tests and specifications from the Yard itself. Finally there are acceptance tests by someone else, teams from Washington. There are checklists as long as one's arm."[54]

After delays to institute a most comprehensive safety policy, the navy resumed construction on sister submarines in the *Thresher* class. The design was not affected. The resulting *Thresher-Permit* class (the *Permit* was the second one and built at California's Mare Island Naval Shipyard) eventually numbered fourteen submarines.

Portsmouth contributed two boats, the *Jack* and the *Tinosa*. Striving to embody the *Albacore*'s famed whale-like hull in the new class, naval designers also incorporated military features on the *Jack* and *Tinosa*. Such modifications represented a less than exact duplication of the *Albacore*'s ideal hydrodynamic form. But all the *Thresher-Permit* boats as well as subsequent American submarine classes approached as closely as possible the classic lines of the *Albacore* model. The *Jack* and the *Tinosa* also featured engineering innovations to reduce operating noises and to improve both power efficiency and controllability.[55]

Resuming construction, the Yard anticipated more contracts. In April 1964 the Yard Commander invited President Lyndon B. Johnson to attend the May 12th *Adams-Greene-Grayling* triple-header, billed as the biggest event in the Yard's history. The president declined.

On a sunny Friday afternoon, April 17, another visitor arrived. Secretary of Defense Robert S. McNamara, accompanied by the secretary of the navy and an official party, landed by helicopter at the marine barracks parade grounds. As he held his bulging briefcase, McNamara declared in a prepared statement that "the cost of ship construction in naval yards is greater than comparable work in private shipyards." In a brief press conference at the parade grounds, McNamara reiterated his determination "to reduce those costs."

After a private briefing with the Yard officers, McNamara met with union officials and then with civic leaders at the Officers' Club. "Portsmouth has a hell of a way to go," he said. After a quick tour of the Yard, the secretary and his party returned to their helicopter.[56]

An ominous air of uncertainty about the Yard's status accompanied McNamara's visit. A shipyards policy board had convened in December 1963 to undertake a comprehensive study. Heading this special board, McNamara had been touring shipyards around the country since early 1964 to obtain, in his own words, "firsthand evidence." He often visited two facilities in one day, touring San Francisco and Mare Island Shipyards on January 17, and the Boston and Portsmouth Shipyards on April 17.

During the summer and fall the people of Portsmouth, civilian and military alike, waited uneasily. On November 18, McNamara announced in general terms the planned closure of unnamed defense installations. Everyone braced for the news. On a cold dreary Thursday, November 19, 1964, New Hampshire Senator Thomas McIntyre and Governor John King held a press conference at the Rockingham Hotel in downtown Portsmouth.

McIntyre provided the unofficial information that the Yard, which had 7274 employees at the time, would be closed over a ten-year, phasing-out period. "LOCAL SHIPYARD TO CLOSE" announced the huge headline of the *Portsmouth Herald*. The reaction of Maine and New Hampshire officials was bitter. "If this is President Johnson's idea of efficiency," said the Portsmouth mayor, "McNamara should be made secretary of agriculture. All in all, it looks like a bleak Christmas."[57]

That same afternoon, at 3:00 P.M., Captain William C. Hushing, the Yard commander, received the official news via courier from

Washington. The next day he informed employees at a meeting on the Mall that "the situation looked good for the next six months at least." On November 20, McNamara, nicknamed "Mac the Knife" for his cutbacks, announced that his decision to shut down ninety-five "obsolete and surplus" military bases and plants was "absolutely, unequivocally, without qualification irrevocable." In response to anguished cries of congressmen, governors and mayors around the country, McNamara asserted "The only thing that might [change my mind] would be some new evidence, and the chances of that are damned small."

On Monday morning, November 23, Hushing again spoke to the workers at the Mall. "Our product must be of such high quality," he said, "such timeliness, and at such a cost, that the customer will clamor for what we have to offer. I urge every employee to become more intolerant of waste and to give a full day's work every day. Adopt an attitude that we are doing our best individually and as a team."[58]

During the winter of 1964–1965, area citizens and supporters of the Yard assessed the future. Their great friend in the United States Senate was gone. Styles Bridges, regarded by many political insiders as one of the most powerful men in Washington, had died in 1961. "We depended too much on Bridges," was a common sentiment around the Yard.

To fill this void in leadership, a group of citizens, acting independently of the Yard, raised $60,000 and formed the Greater Portsmouth (later changed to Portsmouth-Kittery) Armed Services Committee. The group decided to maintain a paid representative in Washington, a policy first employed by the supporters of the Mare Island Naval Shipyard, Vallejo, California, another submarine yard. The Mare Island approach had proved very successful for the West Coast base.

On February 25, 1965, the Committee hired Rear Admiral Joshua W. Cooper (Ret.) as its lobbyist. An Annapolis graduate with thirty-six years in the navy before his retirement, Cooper lived in Alexandria, Virginia, across the Potomac from Washington, and would man a "listening post" for Yard interests.

As "the man in Washington," Cooper was charged with presenting the facts to the congressmen and senators of Massachusetts, New Hampshire and Maine, and issuing a report every January. He briefed Congress on matters relating to military construction. "Before Cooper, no one might have known or presented the facts," said Russell Van Billiard, a member of the committee which hired Cooper. "Now Congress invited and expected this briefing. With three states to account for, it is a job in itself."[59]

Outer hull sections for Dolphin, *experimental deep-diving submarine. UNH.*

The Experimental "Triple Nickel" Dolphin

On December 19, 1964, a month to the day after McNamara's order, workmen laid the keel of the *Dolphin*, an experimental boat in the tradition of the *Albacore*. Despite the Yard's unsettled status, designers and builders strove to produce another great sub.

The *Dolphin* was a Portsmouth-designed boat from the start. As early as 1959, the chief of naval operations issued instructions to the Portsmouth design engineers to develop a deep-diving noncombat submarine with special abilities for acoustic and oceanographic research. The Yard engaged in developing and testing many components. A system known as Project Glaucus evolved for prooftesting. It was named for a legendary fisherman who lived about 400 B.C. in the Greek town of Athedon, noted for the passion of its citizens for diving.

The pressure hull represented a most significant technical achievement. Shaped as a cylinder capped at its ends with hemispheres, the *Dolphin*'s design was as simple as possible. Whereas virtually all other subs had two hatches, the *Dolphin* had only one, which afforded greater strength. Since the boat was designed to go deep, the one-hatch concept kept irregularities in the hull to a minimum and created a safer boat.

In May 1963, after the *Thresher* incident, all construction work came to a standstill while a review group studied some forty *Dolphin* design features. Such testing involved magnetic particle, ultrasonic, and X-ray inspections.

The *Dolphin* ultimately cost $40 million and was built to dive well below 400 feet. About half of the size of a conventional sub, she would be propelled on the surface by diesels and submerged under electric power from silver zinc batteries. The *Dolphin's* hull number, 555, taken from a block of numbers cancelled late in World War II, prompted the nickname, "Triple Nickel."[60]

"Work on the *Dolphin* in the late 1960s occupied much of the time of design division personnel," said Chief Design Engineer Philip Hoyt. "Designing the *Dolphin* represented a special challenge. We started with space diagrams and developed different arrangement drawings and mock-ups to provide options in locating power plant components, control areas and living quarters for maximum utility of space. Livability took a back seat in favor of features more important to the mission of the submarine. There were many trade-offs necessary to develop the arrangement considered to provide the optimum operational capability. I believe the end product justified the care we took."

The testing of the *Dolphin* also received top priority. "Testing goes on all during construction," Hoyt said, "with emphasis on X-ray, ultra-sonic and magnetic particle testing of all hull and pipe joint welds. In addition, each component is operated as soon as possible after it is installed and as part of the whole system test to insure satisfactory performance. So testing begins on the first day of the job on the submarine and is carried through daily to the end."

All 259 employees working on the *Dolphin* as a project team received distinctive buttons identifying them as permanent members of the team. They worked on a computerized submarine safety monitoring system, another experimental feature. The computer could take over the sub to return the boat and crew back to the surface in the event of an emergency.[61]

As work on the *Dolphin* continued through the 1960s, the Yard struggled to provide the best possible construction and repair program. However, this effort was hampered. The Yard was due to close within ten years. Appropriations and funds for Public Works projects were curtailed or in short supply. "The steam, oil, compressed air and electrical lines needed modernization," said Arthur Castelazo, the public works officer. "The power plant needed improvements to meet the growing demands of the ship repair program." The portal cranes operated over two sections with different rail gauges, and the need to standardize all crane service was evident. "A sewer system was installed as a result of ecological pressures," said Castelazo. "Up to that time [the late 1960s] the raw sewage was dumped directly into the river. Now sewage is treated as part of the town of Kittery system." The Yard managed to acquire some cranes and engines as a result of the closing of the Boston and Brooklyn Naval Shipyards. However, closure hung over the Yard like smog.[62]

Sometimes problem solving had little to do with money. The Polaris submarines under construction or repair at the Yard needed to test the alignment of their navigational systems. The answer to this multimillion-dollar question was the installation of a twenty-five-watt bulb. James Barker Smith, owner of the Wentworth-by-the-Sea Hotel in New Castle, agreed to install a light on the hotel's roof for the navy. A white light turned out to be too bright for the powerful Polaris system which sights on stars. A low-wattage red light proved satisfactory. The air force also assisted the navy's alignment check by placing a second light atop the water tower of nearby Pease Air Force Base.[63]

For years submarines had arrived at the Yard with urgent repair demands. This created an uneasy situation, because often little advance notice was given. Once the boat arrived, the question around the Yard was, "What is going to be ripped out?" In 1966 Shipyard Commander Hushing and several senior engineers tackled this perennial problem. Their solution was another Portsmouth-first concept.

The answer to the confusion about repairs was the development of the PERA (Planning and Engineering for Repairs and Alterations) system. Established in 1967, PERA provided a timetable that allowed standard repairs to be scheduled in advance.

The Yard also developed a system of procedures to be followed to repair and service the boats in the most efficient manner. Under this program the planning, procurement, and supply details were coordinated nationally for all shipyards. Standardized lists, time allotments, and improved techniques and procedures common to and available to all shipyards streamlined the repair process. Now the Portsmouth Shipyard could reasonably predict how often specific components should be serviced.

With the PERA program, the Yard was able to schedule repairs months or years in advance. When a commanding officer of a submarine met with the appropriate type desk officer to review the work to be accomplished, the major portion of his work list was already established, components and material had been procured, and drawings and job orders were ready to be issued. This idea saved so much time and money that American shipyards, public and private, adopted the Portsmouth PERA concept in repairing all classifications of ships.[64]

The commitment to excellence and economy was evident in the *Dolphin* when she was launched on June 8, 1968. The assistant secretary of the navy for research and development noted that the reusing of ship's names was never more appropriate since the new *Dolphin* was carrying on the tradition of the famous World War II sub which fought back at Pearl Harbor. As a boat capable of independent operations which did not require the aid of a mother ship, the new *Dolphin*, the speaker said, "will help lead to what could become the Deep Fleet of the twenty-first century."[65]

Commissioned in August of that year, the *Dolphin* was successful from the start. She exceeded everyone's most optimistic predictions on her trials and assignments. Following the example of the *Albacore*, the stubby deep-diving boat was modified in time to new configurations. A torpedo system was installed in 1970. Later that year she was transferred to San Diego, which has remained her home port. Involved in all aspects of naval technology, the *Dolphin* engaged in the deepest launching of a torpedo. This last completely designed Portsmouth boat, because of her continuing contributions to research and development, will significantly determine the design of sonars, weapons, and submarines into the 1990s. Making the 555 a winning number, the *Dolphin* is truly a "pioneer of inner space."[66]

The Sand Lance *Closes the Construction Era*

At noon on January 15, 1965 the building ways of the Yard were the scene of the keel laying of the *Sand Lance* (SSN 660). The lengthening shadow of the closure order caused participants and observers alike to believe that the *Sand Lance* represented the last submarine construction at the historic Yard less than fifty years after the same ceremony was held for the *L-8*. After the welding was completed on the symbolic first arc of the *Sand Lance*, the officer-in-charge spoke the traditional words, "Keel well and truly laid" to Yard Commander Hushing.

It was a special occasion. Hushing urged the Yard to make a showing with the 660. "Let's work together as a team—do better than we have ever done before," he said, adding that Portsmouth's performance on this sub would be carefully watched by people outside the local area. The *Sand Lance* was one of thirty-seven submarines of the *Sturgeon* class, an EB design. This nuclear attack class represented an improved and slightly larger model of the *Thresher-Permit* design.[67]

On May 20, 1966, Vice President Hubert H. Humphrey visited the Yard. He cheerfully donned a hard hat similar to those worn by Yard workers and said there might be a job open for him at Portsmouth.

"Submarines built and overhauled at Portsmouth," he told 5000 workers and military personnel assembled at the Mall, "are not ships of war but instruments of peace. Your government is keenly interested in your future and the Shipyard." However, Humphrey did not comment further on this apparent reference to the closure order. He took the traditional tour of the Yard and viewed the *Sand Lance* under construction at the building ways.[68]

Dissatisfied with Humphrey's lack of commitment, Yard promoters seized another opportunity only three months later to press their case. The Navy League, a civilian arm of the U.S. Navy since 1902, was especially adamant to save the Yard.

On Saturday, August 20, 1966, President Lyndon B. Johnson and his party landed at Grenier Field, Manchester, New Hampshire, on a speechmaking swing through New England. This was billed as a "nonpolitical" tour. Navy League members from the coastal area traveled to Manchester to attend a Navy League hotel luncheon with Johnson as guest speaker, but league members who had hoped to learn something about the situation at the Yard were disappointed. The president's speech dealt entirely with the war in Viet Nam and made no official pronouncement on the phaseout order.

Speculation among league members then held that Johnson would board Air Force #1 and land at Pease Air Force Base. The *USS Northampton*, a guided-missile heavy cruiser, had been docked at the Portsmouth Shipyard for a few days, waiting to pick up the president for his voyage along the Maine coast (ultimately Johnson planned to confer with Canadian Prime Minister Lester Pearson at Campobello Island, New Brunswick). The rumor that Johnson was going to Portsmouth touched off reports that the president wanted a personal look at the Yard, where he could observe first-hand that the facility was capable of improved production. Navy leaguers and area political figures hoped that Johnson would drop the phaseout order.

The Yard swung into action in anticipation of the president's arrival. On short notice a boarding walkway and platform of proper height were needed to enable the president and his party to board the *Northampton*. As a construction and repair facility for submarines, the Yard was not normally equipped to handle large ships and had no such equipment.

A group superintendent was assigned the responsibility of building a boarding structure using appropriate shop materials, in time for the president's arrival. He tackled his job vigorously to meet this emergency.

The workers prepared a platform on four posts with a stairway with guard rails. A brow would then span the distance to the ship's deck.

The boarding structure was made of iron pipe and bolted together, then painted and left to dry with very little time. Fred White, the group superintendent, spent much time and effort in adhering to rigid specifications. On the afternoon before the president's expected arrival on August 20, the special structure was ready.

The preparations were somewhat invalidated when the Yard was informed that Johnson would board the ship in Portland, Maine, fifty miles to the north. The president spent only ninety minutes in New Hampshire. Following his Navy League luncheon in Manchester, he was airborne, not to Pease Air Force Base but for stops at Burlington, Vermont, and Brunswick and Lewiston, Maine. This change in schedule indicated that Johnson's plane would finally land at the end of a long day at Portland airport, whereupon he would motor to Portland's municipal pier for boarding the *Northampton*. The Portsmouth Shipyard contacted the Portland Port Authority concerning this change and learned that the Authority had no such boarding structure.

Faced with this news, the Yard decided to transport the structure to Portland. It seems certain that Johnson himself and none of his party knew anything of the frantic efforts made on their behalf.

The structure was disassembled and loaded onto a truck for a nighttime drive on the Maine Turnpike. En route, the truck broke down. A second truck was sent immediately. The valuable cargo finally reached Portland harbor and was reassembled for use at 8:00 A.M. on Saturday, August 20. That evening the president and his party boarded the *Northampton* for their overnight cruise to Canada. After its brief and only use at Portland harbor, the structure was disassembled and transported back to the Yard.[69]

The boarding structure had saved the president's trip. The ordeal of the Yard workers and navy officials was over.

The rest of the 1960s remained an anxious time for the Yard. With increasing realization that submarine construction had ended, the Yard became primarily involved with nuclear submarine overhaul and repair work. Work on fifteen submarines actually increased employment to 8400 in 1968.

This new role brought mixed feelings. "It is harder to overhaul and repair subs in many ways," said one employee, "than it is to build them." Veteran submariners were concerned with Portsmouth leaving the design field. "You shouldn't have one guy [Electric Boat] doing all the design," said one skipper. "He would become too set in his ways. With two yards, you get the latest designs."[70]

The *Sand Lance* was ready for launching on November 11, 1969. Senator Tom McIntyre of New Hampshire was the principal speaker at

Scene at 1969 christening of the Sand Lance (SSN660), *the last Portsmouth-built boat. As his wife breaks bottle on bow, Senator Tom McIntyre winces to avoid spray of champagne. McIntyre's daughter and Shipyard Commander Donald H. Kern stand by. PA.*

the ceremony. "This particular launch has a certain sadness to it," he said, "for this *Sand Lance* may have the dubious distinction of being the last submarine ever built at this yard."

As his wife prepared to christen the boat at 11:42 A.M., McIntyre kept his remarks brief. He recalled an earlier, almost botched, launching which warned against long speeches. "In 1943," McIntyre said, "Mrs. Franklin D. Roosevelt, sponsor of the aircraft carrier *Yorktown*, abruptly interrupted the opening remarks of the master of ceremonies to take a desperate—but accurate—swing at the ship's bow as it prematurely slid down the building ways, earning the *Yorktown* the nickname 'Eager Ship,'" The *Yorktown* keynote speaker was so shaken by the incident he was unable to complete his speech.

As McIntyre concluded his remarks, his wife christened the boat on time, smashing the bottle on the first swing. As the *Sand Lance* slid down to the Piscataqua, Yard designers and workers realized an era was over. "When the *Sand Lance* was launched," said one employee, "there

Launching of Sand Lance, *Portsmouth's 134th submarine, in 1969,
signaled end of construction era at Yard. PM.*

was nothing more in store, plans or otherwise."

Frederick "Pete" Smith, the officer in charge of the launching,
stayed aboard the *Sand Lance*, bedecked with red, white and blue bunting
as she slid into the tide-swollen waters. Navy tugs escorted the new boat
into dry dock. After the dewatering of the dock, the *Sand Lance* finally
lay on blocks. These post-christening activities consumed five hours. "I
missed the party," Smith said, referring to the food and drinks at the
reception held for the dignitaries and Yard personnel. The last post-
launch party was over.[71]

As workers were completing the *Sand Lance* during the next two
years, the plaguing question about the Yard's status loomed larger every
day. Although Robert McNamara had resigned in 1969 with the end of
the Johnson administration, the closure order still stood. President
Richard M. Nixon did not rescind the McNamara order. At stake were
7500 jobs and $80 million in payrolls and procurement.

The Yard Commander in 1970 parried all questions of a Maine
newspaperman about the closing of the Yard. "Look," he said, "I am a
naval officer. My job is to carry out whatever orders the Navy Department
gives me. And the order which stands now is that Kittery closes in 1974."[72]

Rumors and counter-rumors filled the air. Finally on Wednesday,
March 24, 1971, the Yard received its reprieve and extension of life. In
Washington, D.C., New Hampshire's Representative Louis Wyman,
Senator Norris Cotton and Maine's Senator Margaret Chase Smith

received identical hand-delivered letters from couriers from President Nixon. The letter on White House stationery initialed by Nixon stated:

> I have delayed answering your questions on the future of the Portsmouth Naval Shipyard until the review I requested was completed.
>
> Now, on the basis of that review and the recommendations made to me, I am pleased to inform you that the McNamara order closing the yard in 1974 will be rescinded.

"SHIPYARD WILL STAY OPEN" announced a banner *Portsmouth Herald* headline. Statements of rejoicing and relief from local politicians, Yard workers and area citizens filled the *Herald*'s columns for days. The newspaper editorialized, "The next time Wyman goes to the Yard they ought to call him an ambassador or something and give him 19 guns." The Yard was once again a full-fledged member of the naval shipyard family, with a modernization program in store.[73]

On September 25, 1971, the *Sand Lance* was commissioned at the Yard. The nuclear-attack submarine, equipped with the most advanced sonar and fire-control system, had required six and a half years to complete. Shortly thereafter the sub left on a shakedown cruise to the Caribbean, but she did not return to Portsmouth. The *Sand Lance* was assigned to Submarine Squadron Four, homeported at Charleston, South Carolina. Portsmouth had contributed her last and 134th boat to the fleet.[74]

The future of the American submarine is bright and unlimited. Ahead is a scientific frontier of Arctic technology, acoustics, and automatic control and guidance. A whole new field where computers direct submarines by remote control will eventually come into its own. Eventually there will be an automatic submarine, underwater or under ice, for military research and industrial needs. The Yard will repair and overhaul these boats. "From Sails to Atoms," the present motto of the Yard, might be amended in time to "From Sails to Automation."[75]

There was no finer hour in the history of the Yard than the 1914–1971 submarine construction period. The 134 Portsmouth-built boats during those fifty-seven years helped to win two world wars and to pioneer breakthroughs in marine science and technology. "Portsmouth is synonymous with submarines," a local saying, is also a well-deserved national compliment.

"Well done," the United States Navy's traditional words of praise for an excellent job, has been heard many times at the Portsmouth Naval Shipyard. Its submarines have ruled the Kingdom beneath the waves, their "keels well and truly laid."

Aerial view of 278-acre Seavey's Island, home of the Portsmouth Naval Shipyard, looking toward mouth of the Piscataqua. Bridges connect Kittery, Maine to Yard while New Castle, New Hampshire appears in right rear. PA.

Epilogue: "Beaching the Whale," 1971 – 1984

TWO NOTEWORTHY EVENTS marked 1984 in the Portsmouth area: a continuous nuclear sub repair workload at the Yard, and the arrival of the *USS Albacore*, to become a major tourist attraction.

The Portsmouth Naval Shipyard in the 1980s looks more like a prosperous business corporation than a military base. "We know we've got plenty of work," said one Yard official. In 1983 the Yard employed almost 9000 civilians, who received more than $216 million in paychecks.

Its new role as a service facility has been successful. In 1983 it completed three comprehensive overhauls and began work on two other boats. Shipyard workers also performed four extended refits at New London and Holy Loch, which involved from 200 to 300 workers. They also handled forty voyage repairs at these facilities.

"After *Thresher*," said shipyarder John Shea, "the navy crews gave the Yard workers a funny look. The feeling is now that the crews would rather have their subs overhauled here than any place else."[1]

This spirit has radiated to Washington officialdom. Assistant Secretary of the Navy James Goodrich visited the Yard in 1983. "In the 1970's the [Portsmouth] Shipyard suffered from low productivity," he said. "It contrasted poorly with its sister shipyards. Today its performance is outstanding. You have nothing to worry about; the Shipyard is going to be around for a long time."[2]

This new-found confidence was reflected in a dedication speech at the Mall by Shipyard Commander Joseph F. Yurso on July 6, 1983, when he praised Admiral Rickover, whose career had intertwined with the Yard for more than thirty years. "It is particularly fitting," Yurso said, "that in this historic navy shipyard, where the memory of such famous navy leaders as Captain John Paul Jones, Admiral David Farragut, and

Commodore Isaac Hull are a part of our tradition, the name of Admiral Hyman G. Rickover will be permanently placed on public view as a tribute to his major contributions to the navy and the country."

A bronze likeness of the admiral mounted on a granite block, located a short distance from the *Sailfish* memorial, is inscribed "Father of the Nuclear Navy." To Jack Sousae, who worked with Rickover during the early nuclear ship days, Rickover's accomplishments superseded the controversies and stormy relationships associated with his long naval service. "He took an idea," Sousae said, "advanced it to the state of art, and proved it could be done. He will go down in history with the Fultons and Eli Whitneys."[3]

On Saturday, October 1, 1983, the Yard commissioned its first submarine in fourteen years. The impressive ceremonies at dockside recalled earlier boom times. The *USS Portsmouth (SSN-707)*, named in honor of towns in New Hampshire and Virginia, brought James Goodrich back for another supportive speech. The $600 million *Portsmouth*, an Electric Boat-built sub, displaces 6090 tons surfaced and is 360 feet long. A member of the *Los Angeles* class nuclear-powered attack submarines, the *Portsmouth* was one of the few submarines not commissioned in the shipyard in which she was built.[4]

The renaissance of the Yard coincided almost simultaneously with the revitalization of the historic city of Portsmouth as a tourist attraction. The Tall Ships celebration in Portsmouth during the summer of 1981, together with the continuing Strawbery Banke living museum, brought many visitors to town. Assistant Mayor William Keefe, a key booster to bringing the Tall Ships to the Piscataqua, decided to push for another project. Keefe said,

> I was on the city council while working as a security guard at the Portsmouth Savings Bank. One day a man from Philadelphia came into the bank and happened to mention to me that the *Albacore* was in mothballs at the Philadelphia Navy Yard. "That boat, such a fine looking craft," the man said, "ought to be returned to Portsmouth."
>
> I thought about that conversation that night without deciding anything. But the next morning I got a committee together to work to bring the *Albacore* back home.

During the early winter of 1981–1982 Keefe initiated the "Bring the *Albacore* back to Portsmouth" movement. At the time it was generally considered an implausible scheme, a wild idea with little chance of success.[5]

However, the "Bring Back the *Albacore*" committee, formed in 1982 by maritime enthusiasts and area businessmen, gained momentum.

The selection of the *Albacore*, Portsmouth's 1950s experimental submarine, was an excellent choice for an educational exhibit in a projected museum complex. The first objective of the committee was to obtain release of the boat from the navy.

During May of 1983 Committee Chairman Joseph G. Sawtelle traveled to Washington to persuade navy officials to release the *Albacore* to Portsmouth in the fall. The committee also arranged for the lease of ten acres of land south of Market Street Extension from the Maine-New Hampshire Interstate Bridge Authority. On this site, overlooking the Piscataqua River on the New Hampshire side, the committee planned to place the boat and to erect a museum building with parking for 240 automobiles.

Eugene Allmendinger, one of the *Albacore*'s original designers, was an early backer of this program and worked to fit a cradle for the boat. "Beaching the whale," Allmendinger predicted, would be an enormously complex feat of engineering.

Congressman Norman D'Amours, representing New Hampshire's navy yard district, submitted bill HR 3980 for the sub's release (theoretically any group from any state could have claimed the *Albacore* with a competitive offer). Following D'Amours' testimony before the House Armed Services sub-committee, both houses of Congress passed the bill. On Monday, November 7, 1983, President Ronald W. Reagan signed the bill for the boat's release, making front-page headlines in New Hampshire's newspapers.[6]

Larger battles loomed in the future. Now the Portsmouth Submarine Memorial Association (as the committee was renamed) had to sell the idea to the seacoast area and to the public at large. The project had no public funding; money had to come from private contributions. Allmendinger predicted it would cost from $600,000 to $1 million to move the sub to dry land at its Albacore Park site. The entire complex, including the museum building, was estimated at $1.6 million. "Capt. Ahab's battle with Moby-Dick," wrote a *Portsmouth Herald* reporter, "may not have been much tougher than the job Portsmouth faces in moving a black mechanical whale up the Piscataqua River."

The first part of the move was comparatively easy; the Army Corps of Transportation offered to tow the sub as a training exercise from Philadelphia to Portsmouth free of charge except for fuel costs and incidental traveling expenses. The real cost of the move, however, was transporting and lifting the sub from the Piscataqua to the Albacore Park site. This engineering operation involved dredging a canal from the river to the Park. In the way were two obstacles: the Boston & Maine railroad trestle and the Market Street Extension. City, state and federal

The Albacore Comes Home—Sunday April 29, 1984

On April 29, 1984, Albacore *returned to the mouth of Portsmouth Harbor for her last trip up river. The modern submarine contrasts with Fort Constitution in the background, site of a military installation for more than 350 years. Jean Sawtelle photograph.*

officials granted approval to cut across these transportation arteries.

To make the public aware of these financial and technological challenges, Allmendinger and others gave slide lecture presentations to local civic groups. Press releases appeared regularly in area newspapers.[7]

After years of planning and work, association officers and members finally realized their reward. On Sunday, April 29, 1984, the *Albacore* returned. Towed by the army tugboat *Okinawa* of the 1175th Army Transportation Unit of Pedericktown, New Jersey, the *Albacore* approached Portsmouth harbor at 7:00 A.M. The tugboat then waited for the incoming tide.

Frederick "Pete" Smith, a retired *Albacore* engineer, had taken his lobster boat out that spring morning to meet his old submarine. Upon seeing the sub approach with the numbers 569 on the side of her sail,

Smith was thrilled. "It'll be another hundred years before they catch up with all they learned from her," Smith said. Praising the *Albacore*'s teardrop hull design, he added, "Even the Russians are building them that way today."[8]

At the mouth of the Piscataqua, a Portsmouth Navigation Company tug joined the *Albacore* and her escort. When the tide turned, the two tugs accompanied the submarine up river. At 11 A.M. the *Albacore* arrived at Berth 7, adjacent to the Naval Reserve Center at the Yard. The navy provided berthing for the submarine until her transfer to the park.

The legendary *Albacore* continues to symbolize the Piscataqua's naval technology and power.[9]

The majority of the 134 submarines listed in the following appendix were authorized and built during the twelve-year presidency of Franklin D. Roosevelt. During the summer of 1940, Commander-in-Chief Roosevelt (facing camera from right rear seat of limousine) toured the booming Portsmouth Navy Yard. PA.

Appendix

*Submarines Built at the Portsmouth Naval Shipyard,
Portsmouth, New Hampshire, 1914 – 1971*

This composite list is based on the following official and semi-official sources:

Alden, John, *The Fleet Submarine in the U.S. Navy: A Design and Construction History.* (1979), Appendix #8, pp. 248-275.

Cradle of American Shipbuilding. (1978), pp. 79-83.

Dictionary of American Naval Fighting Ships. 8 Volumes, (1959-1981).

Jane's Fighting Ships, 1983-84. (1983), pp. 630, 633-645.

Submarine Data Report, Primary Sort Hull Number. n. p.: 1982. Computer Printout Sheet List of Active Submarines. Copy, Shea Collection.

Submarines of the U.S. Navy, Support Ships, Rescue [Ships]. n. p.: ca. 1982. Computer Printout Sheet List of All Submarines, Active and Inactive. Copies, Copley and Shea Collections.

Legend

COM.	—	Year of First Commission
DECOM.	—	Year of Last Commission
ST	—	Year Stricken from Naval Register
FATE OF HULL	—	Final Disposition of Hull and Year
SS	—	Submarine
#R	—	Radar Picket
##G	—	Guided Missile
*N	—	Nuclear Propulsion
**B	—	Ballistic Missile Submarine
***AG	—	Research Submarine
N/A	—	Not Available. Information not recorded in standard sources or in other lists.

	HULL NO.	NAME	COM.	DECOM.	ST	FATE OF HULL
1.	SS48	L-8	1917	1922	1925	SOLD, 1925, SCRAP
2.	SS62	O-1	1918	1931	1938	SOLD, 1938, SCRAP
3.	SS107	S-3	1919	1936	1937	SCRAP, 1937
4.	SS109	S-4	1910	1933	1936	SUNK, 1927, REFLOATED and REBUILT as TEST SUB, SCUTTLED, 1936
5.	SS110	S-5	1920		1921	SUNK, 1920
6.	SS111	S-6	1920	1936	1937	N/A
7.	SS112	S-7	1920	1936	1937	N/A
8.	SS113	S-8	1920	1937	1937	N/A
9.	SS114	S-9	1921	1936	1937	N/A
10.	SS115	S-10	1922	1936	1936	SOLD, 1936, SCRAP
11.	SS116	S-11	1923	1945	1945	SOLD, 1945, SCRAP
12.	SS117	S-12	1923	1945	1945	SOLD, 1945, SCRAP
13.	SS118	S-13	1923	1945	1945	SOLD, 1945, SCRAP
14.	SS163	BARRACUDA (SF-4, B-1, V-1)	1924	1924	1945	SOLD, 1945, SCRAP
15.	SS164	BASS (SF-5, B-2, V-2)	1925	1945	1945	SOLD, 1945, SCRAP
16.	SS165	BONITA (SF-5, B-3, V-3)	1926	1945	1945	SOLD, 1945, SCRAP
17.	SS166	ARGONAUT (V-4, A-1, SF-7, SM-1, APS-1)	1928			WAR LOSS, 1943
18.	SS167	NARWHAL (V-5, N-1, SF-8, SC-1)	1930	1945	1945	SOLD, 1945, SCRAP
19.	SS169	DOLPHIN (V-7, D-1, SF-10, SC-3)	1932	1945	1946	SOLD, 1946, SCRAP

	HULL NO.	NAME	COM.	DECOM.	ST	FATE OF HULL
20.	SS170	CACHALOT (V-8, C-1, SF-11, SC-4)	1933	1945	1947	SOLD, 1947, SCRAP
21.	SS172	PORPOISE (P-1)	1935	1945	1956	SOLD, 1957, SCRAP
22.	SS173	PIKE (P-2)	1935	1945	1956	SOLD, 1957, SCRAP
23.	SS179	PLUNGER (P-8)	1936	1945	1956	SOLD, 1957, SCRAP
24.	SS180	POLLACK (P-9)	1937	1945	1946	SOLD, 1947, SCRAP
25.	SS185	SNAPPER (S-4)	1937	1946	1948	SOLD, 1948, SCRAP
26.	SS186	STINGRAY (S-5)	1938	1946	1946	SOLD, 1947, SCRAP
27.	SS191	SCULPIN (S-10)	1939			WAR LOSS, 1943
28.	SS192	SQUALUS (S-11)	1939			SUNK, 1939
		SAILFISH (S-11)	1940	1946	1946	SUPERSTRUCTURE, WAR MEMORIAL, 1946. Portsmouth Naval Shipyard; HULL SOLD, 1948, SCRAP
29.	SS196	SEARAVEN (S-15)	1939	1946		SUNK, A-BOMB TEST, 1948
30.	SS197	SEAWOLF (S-16)	1939			WAR LOSS, 1944
31.	SS201	TRITON	1940			WAR LOSS, 1943
32.	SS202	TROUT	1940			WAR LOSS, 1944
33.	SS205	MARLIN	1941	1945	N/A	SOLD, 1946, SCRAP
34.	SS209	GRAYLING	1941			WAR LOSS, 1943
35.	SS210	GRENADIER	1941			WAR LOSS, 1943
36.	SS228	DRUM	1941	1946	1948	WAR MEMORIAL, Mobile, Alabama
37.	SS229	FLYING FISH	1941	1954	1958	SOLD, 1959, SCRAP
38.	SS230	FINBACK	1942	1950	1958	SOLD, 1959, SCRAP
39.	SS231	HADDOCK	1942	1947	1960	SOLD, 1960, SCRAP
40.	SS232	HALIBUT	1942	1946	1947	SOLD, 1947, SCRAP

	HULL NO.	NAME	COM.	DECOM.	ST	FATE OF HULL
41.	SS233	HERRING	1942			WAR LOSS, 1944
42.	SS234	KINGFISH	1942	1946	1960	SOLD, 1960, SCRAP
43.	SS235	SHAD	1942	1960	1960	SOLD, 1960, SCRAP
44.	SS275	RUNNER	1942			WAR LOSS, 1943
45.	SS276	SAWFISH	1942	1960	1960	SCRAP, 1960
46.	SS277	SCAMP	1942			WAR LOSS, 1944
47.	SS278	SCORPION	1942			WAR LOSS, 1944
48.	SS279	SNOOK	1942			WAR LOSS, 1945
49.	SS280	STEELHEAD	1942	1960	1960	SCRAP, 1960
50.	SS285	BALAO	1943	1963	1963	TARGET, 1963
51.	SS286	BILLFISH	1943	1946	1968	SCRAP, 1971
52.	SS287	BOWFIN	1943	1960	1971	WAR MEMORIAL, 1979 Pearl Harbor, Hawaii
53.	SS288	CABRILLA	1943	1946	1968	SCRAP, 1971
54.	SS289	CAPELIN	1943			WAR LOSS, 1943
55.	SS290	CISCO	1943			WAR LOSS, 1943
56.	SS291	CREVALLE	1943	1968	1968	SCRAP, 1971
	SS298	LIONFISH (Began at Cramp Shipyard, Philadelphia, Completed at Portsmouth Navy Yard)	1944	1953	1971	WAR MEMORIAL, Fall River, Massachusetts
	SS299	MANTA (Began at Cramp Shipyard, Philadelphia, Completed at Portsmouth Navy Yard)	1944	1955	1967	TARGET, 1969
57.	SS308	APOGON	1943	1946	1947	SUNK, 1946 Bikini Atomic Bomb Tests

	HULL NO.	NAME	COM.	DECOM.	ST	FATE OF HULL
58.	SS309	*ASPRO*	1943	1946	1962	TARGET, 1961
59.	SS310	*BATFISH*	1943	1960	1969	WAR MEMORIAL, Muskogee, Oklahoma
60.	SS311	*ARCHERFISH*	1943	1968	1968	TARGET, 1968
61.	SS312	*BURRFISH*	1943	1961	1969	TARGET
62.	SS381	*SAND LANCE*	1943	1963	1972	SOLD, 1972 to Brazil
63.	SS382	*PICUDA*	1943	1972	1974	N/A
64.	SS383	*PAMPANITO*	1943	1945	1971	WAR MEMORIAL, San Francisco, California.
65.	SS384	*PARCHE*	1943	1947	1968	SCRAP, 1970
66.	SS385	*BANG*	1943	1972	1974	N/A
67.	SS386	*PILOTFISH*	1943	1946	1947	SUNK, 1946, Bikini Tests; RAISED AND SUNK, Eniwetok, 1948
68.	SS387	*PINTADO*	1944	1946	1967	SOLD, 1969, SCRAP
69.	SS388	*PIPEFISH*	1944	1946	1967	SOLD, 1969, SCRAP
70.	SS389	*PIRANHA*	1944	1946	1967	SOLD, 1970, SCRAP
71.	SS390	*PLAICE*	1944	1963	1973	LOAN, 1963 to Brazil; MEMORIAL, 1973 Santos, Brazil
72.	SS391	*POMFRET*	1944	1971	1973	LOAN, 1971 to Turkey
73.	SS392	*STERLET*	1944	1968	1968	TARGET, 1969
74.	SS393	*QUEENFISH*	1944	1963	1963	TARGET, 1963
75.	SS394	*RAZORBACK*	1944	1970	1970	SOLD, 1970 to Turkey
76.	SS395	*REDFISH*	1944	1965	1968	TARGET, 1969
77.	SS396	*RONQUIL*	1944	1971	1971	SOLD, 1971, to Spain
78.	SS397	*SCABBARDFISH*	1944	1965	1976	LOAN, 1965 to Greece

	HULL NO.	NAME	COM.	DECOM.	ST	FATE OF HULL
79.	SS398	SEGUNDO	1944	1970	1970	TARGET, 1970
80.	SS399	SEA CAT	1944	1968	1968	SCRAP, 1973
81.	SS400	SEA DEVIL	1944	1964	1964	TARGET, 1964
82.	SS401	SEA DOG	1944	1960	1968	SOLD, 1973, SCRAP
83.	SS402	SEA FOX	1944	1970	1970	SOLD, 1970 to Turkey
84.	SS403	ATULE	1944	1969	1973	N/A
85.	SS404	SPIKEFISH	1944	1963	1963	TARGET, 1964
86.	SS405	SEA OWL	1944	1969	1969	SCRAP, 1969
87.	SS406	SEA POACHER	1944	1969	1973	SOLD, 1974 to Peru
88.	SS407	SEA ROBIN	1944	1970	1970	SCRAP, 1971
89.	SS408	SENNET	1944	1968	1968	SCRAP, 1973
90.	SS409	PIPER	1944	1967	1970	SCRAP, 1971
91.	SS410	THREADFIN	1944	1972	1973	SOLD, 1972 to Turkey
92.	SS417	TENCH	1944	1969	1973	SOLD, 1973 to Peru
93.	SS418	THORNBACK	1944	1971	1973	SOLD, 1973 to Turkey
94.	SS419	TIGRONE	1944	1975	1975	TARGET, 1975
95.	SS420	TIRANTE	1944	1973	1973	SCRAP, 1974
96.	SS421	TRUTTA	1944	1972	1972	LOAN, 1972, to Turkey
97.	SS422	TORO	1944	1963	1963	SCRAP, 1965
98.	SS423	TORSK	1944	1971	1971	WAR MEMORIAL, Baltimore, Maryland
99.	SS424	QUILLBACK	1944	1953	1973	SCRAP, 1973
100.	SS475	ARGONAUT	1945	1968	1968	SCRAP, 1977
101.	SS476	RUNNER	1945	1969	1971	SCRAP, 1971
102.	SS477	CONGER	1945	1964	1964	SCRAP, 1964
103.	SS478	CUTLASS	1945	1963	1963	SCRAP, 1973

	HULL NO.	NAME	COM.	DECOM.	ST	FATE OF HULL
104.	SS479	DIABLO	1945	1964	1964	LOAN, 1964 to Pakistan. SUNK in War with India, 1971
105.	SS480	MEDREGAL	1945	1970	1970	SCRAP, 1972
106.	SS481	REQUIN	1945	1968	1971	WAR MEMORIAL, Tampa, Florida
107.	SS482	IREX	1945	1969	1969	SCRAP, 1971
108.	SS483	SEA LEOPARD	1945	1973	1973	LOAN, 1973 to Brazil
109.	SS484	ODAX	1945	1972	1972	N/A
110.	SS485	SIRAGO	1945	1972	1972	SCRAP, 1972
111.	SS486	POMODON	1945	1970	1970	SCRAP, 1972
112.	SS487	REMORA	1946	1973	1973	LOAN, 1973 to Greece
113.	SS488	SARDA	1946	1964	1964	SCRAP, 1965
114.	SS489	SPINAX	1946	1969	1969	SCRAP, 1972
115.	SS490	VOLADOR	1948	1972	1977	SOLD, 1977, to Italy
	SS524	PICKEREL	1949	1972	1977	SOLD, 1977, to Italy
		(Built and Launched at the Boston Naval Shipyard, 1944; Commissioned at the Portsmouth Naval Shipyard, 1949)				
116.	AGSS555	DOLPHIN	1968		1987	ACTIVE
117.	SS563	TANG	1951	1980	1987	SOLD, Turkey, 1987
118.	SS565	WAHOO	1952	1980	1983	SCRAP SALE, 1985
119.	SS567	GUDGEON	1952	1983	1987	SOLD, Turkey, 1987
120.	AGSS569***	ALBACORE	1953	1972	1980	WAR MEMORIAL, 1984 Portsmouth, New Hampshire

HULL NO.	NAME	COM.	DECOM.	ST	FATE OF HULL
121.	SSR572#	SAILFISH	1956	1978	1978	PUGET
122.	SSR573	SALMON	1956	1977	1977	SUNK, 1993
123.	SSG577##	GROWLER	1958	1964	1980	NEW YORK,1988
124.	SSN579*	SWORDFISH	1958	1989	1989	SCRAP, 1995
125.	SSN580	BARBEL	1959	1989	1990	SCRAP SALE, 1992
126.	SSN584	SEADRAGON	1959	1984	1986	SCRAP, 1995
127.	SSN593	THRESHER	1961		1963	LOST AT SEA, 1963
128.	SSBN602**	ABRAHAM LINCOLN	1961	1981	1982	SCRAP, 1994
129.	SSN605	JACK	1967	1990	1990	SCRAP, 1992
130.	SSN606	TINOSA	1964	1992	1992	SCRAP, 1993
131.	SSBN620**	JOHN ADAMS	1964	1989	1989	SCRAP, 1996
132.	SSBN636	NATHANAEL GREENE	1964	1986	1987	PUGET
133.	SSN646	GRAYLING	1969	1997	1997	SCRAP, 1998
134.	SSN660	SAND LANCE	1971	1998	1998	SCRAP, 1999

Notes

Notes for Preface

1. *Cradle*, p. 3; Hoyt interview.
2. *Portsmouth Herald*, November 28, December 1, 1980.
3. Holman, pp. 465–469 with quotation on p. 469.
4. Shea interview.

Notes for Chapter I

1. The early years of the Portsmouth Naval Shipyard are well chronicled in the following sources listed in order of publication: Fentress (1876); Preble (1892); Sullivan (1904); *Portsmouth Herald*, June 11, 1970; and *Cradle* (1978). An excellent unpublished source covering the years 1878–1930 is Boyd, "Continuation" (1930).
2. Petition, March 1816, Langdon Papers.
3. Boyd, "Continuation," unpaginated sheet.
4. U.S. House of Representatives, *Proceedings*, p. 1264; *Portsmouth Chronicle*, April 11 1878; Boyd, "Continuation," p. 4.
5. Sullivan, pp. 66–73.
6. Boyd, "Continuation," p. 21; Domina, pp. 1–17.
7. *Ibid.*, p. 25.
8. *Ibid.*, pp. 28–30; *Cradle*, p. 40.
9. Brown, p. 36; Whitehouse, p. 10; Blair, p. 23.
10. Polmar, *American Submarine*, pp. 3–10.
11. Blair, pp. 28–35.
12. Alden, *Fleet Submarine*, pp. 2–6; Barnes, pp. 14–26; Polmar, *American Submarine*, pp. 13–19, 33.
13. Barnes, pp. 40–41; Blair, p. 33.
14. Blair, p. 30.
15. Daniels, p. 333.
16. *Ibid.*, p. 334.
17. Cronon, pp. 23–24. There are unfortunately no Daniels diaries for the key years of 1914 and 1916.
18. *Portsmouth Herald*, February 26, 1914, and June 23, 1938, Hartford's obituary.

19. *Ibid.*, March 5, 9, 11, 1914. A search of the Gallinger, Chandler, George H. Moses, and James O. Lyford Papers, New Hampshire Historical Society, does not disclose additional information on this 1914 lobbying effort.
20. *Ibid.*, March 18, 1914; *Annual Reports of the Navy Department for the Fiscal Year 1914*, pp. 253–254.
21. *Statutes*, p. 414.
22. *Portsmouth Herald*, December 30, 1914.
23. *Ibid.*, January 18, 1915; Boyd, "Continuation," p. 30.
24. *Ibid*, January 18, 1915; *Dictionary*, 4:2–3; Polmar, *American Submarine*, pp. 17–19.
25. *Ibid.*, February 24, 1915.
26. *Cradle*, pp. 47, 76; Boyd, "Continuation," p. 30.
27. *Life Buoy*, October 1918.
28. *Portsmouth Herald*, April 7, 23, 1917; *Periscope*, May 2, 1952.
29. *Ibid.*; White interview.
30. *Portsmouth Herald*, April 24, 1917.
31. *Ibid.*
32. Boyd, *Extracts*, entry for May 24, 1917.
33. Burtner interview.
34. *Portsmouth Herald*, October 4, 1917.
35. *Dictionary*, 4: 2–3; Blair, p. 44.
36. *Life Buoy*, November and December 1918; *Portsmouth Herald*, April 4, November 21, 1917.
37. Burtner interview.
38. *Ibid.*
39. *Portsmouth Herald*, September 1, 5, 1917.
40. Lockwood and Adamson, *Tragedy at Honda*, p. 171; Morrison, pp. 65–66.
41. *Life Buoy*, November and December 1918.
42. *Ibid.*, July and August 1918.
43. *Portsmouth Herald*, November 12, 13, 1918; Letch interview.

Notes for Chapter II

1. Letch interview; *Cradle*, p. 76.
2. Morrison, pp. 109, 286; Boyd, "Continuation," pp. 33, 37; Polmar, *American Submarine*, pp. 33-35.
3. Boyd, *Extracts*, entries of December 12, 17, and 21, 1918.
4. *Life Buoy*, September, 1919; Blair, p. 47; Polmar, *American Submarine*, p. 35. Material on the Portsmouth Compressor is based on: White interview; *Annual Reports of the Navy Department for the Fiscal Year 1920*, pp. 649–650; *Navy Day: October 27, 1923*, pp. 19-20.
5. Barnes, pp. 80–83; Bauman, pp. 30–31; Lockwood, *Down to the Sea in Subs*, pp. 122–125.
6. *Portsmouth Herald*, February 7, 1921; Typed notes, Wilson Collection.
7. *Portsmouth Herald*, May 24, 1939, June 11, 1970; *Periscope*, February 2, 1962; Smith, pp. 44–45; White interview; Lockwood, *Down to the Sea in Subs*, p. 159.
8. Smith, pp. 44–45; Boyd, "Continuation," p. 42.

9. *Portsmouth Herald*, June 11, 1970; Lockwood and Adamson, *Hell at 50 Fathoms*; pp. 141–144; Barnes, pp. 86–88.

10. King and Whitehill, pp. 195–204.

11. Lockwood and Adamson, *Hell at 50 Fathoms*, pp. 144–182.

12. *Ibid.*, pp. 183–189, with quotation on p. 186.

13. Allmendinger interview; Alden, *Fleet Submarine*.

14. Boyd, "Continuation," p. 37.

15. Alden, "Andrew Irwin McKee, " pp. 49–50; Lockwood, *Down to the Sea in Subs*, p. 158.

16. Polmar, *American Submarine*, pp. 39 – 41; Alden, *Fleet Submarine*, pp. 25–26; McKee, pp. 352–353.

17. *Ibid.*

18. Blair, p. 57; Alden, *Fleet Submarine*, pp. 28–32.

19. Alden, "Andrew Irwin McKee, " p. 52; Alden, *Fleet Submarine*, pp. 36–37.

20. "Extracts...1929–1964," p. 8; Blair, pp. 63–64.

21. *Periscope*, February 20, 1959.

22. *Portsmouth Herald*, March 10, 11, 1936; White and Ford interviews; "Extracts...1929–1964," p. 13.

23. Alden, *Fleet Submarine*, pp. 45–46.

24. *Portsmouth Herald*, July 23, 1936, August 24, December 15, 1937; *Submarines: Portsmouth Naval Shipyard*. Blair, p. 64, holds that EB's *Shark*, built in 1933–1936, represents the first sub with an all-welded hull.

25. Alden, *Fleet Submarine*, p. 48.

26. *Ibid.*; Blair, p. 65.

27. *Ibid.*, pp. 65–66.

28. Evans interview.

29. Material on the *Squalus* is voluminous. See full-length book studies by Barrows; Maas; articles by Estaver; McKay; Portsmouth Scrapbooks; unpublished paper by Learnard; book chapter by Stafford; *Portland Press Herald*, June 6, 1979; McLees Collection. For the log of the last voyage of the *Squalus*, see *Navy Times*, pp. 169–173.

30. McLees interview.

31. *Ibid.*

32. Shea and Evans interviews; Blair, p. 67.

33. Andrew I. McKee, U.S. Navy Yard, Portsmouth, New Hampshire, to R.S. Edwards, Submarine Base, New London, Connecticut, October 4, 1939, *Sailfish* folder, Submarine Museum and Library.

34. *Portsmouth Herald*, February 2, 1940; Evans interview.

35. "Extracts...1929...1964," p. 20; *Portsmouth Herald*, May 14, 15, 1940; McLees interview.

36. *Ibid.*, August 21, 1940; Evans and Gray interviews.

37. Alden, *Fleet Submarine*, p. 57; *Cradle*, p. 76.

38. *Portsmouth Herald*, August 9, 10, 1940.

39. *Ibid.*, August 15, 1940; Alden, *Fleet Submarine*, p. 74; *Submarines*, p. 19.

40. *Portsmouth Herald*, September 7, 9, 1940.

41. "Activities 1939-1945," Chapter #1, pp. 1-4; Chapter #2, pp. 1-2, Navy Yard folder, Portsmouth Public Library.

42. *Portsmouth Herald*, March 20, 1941.

43. *Ibid.*, October 3, 1941; White interview.

44. Bongartz, pp. 56-58, 100-102; Grigore, pp. 15-17; *Surcouf* folder, Portsmouth Naval Shipyard.
45. Letch, Burke, Hoyt and White interviews.
46. *Surcouf* folder; *Portsmouth Herald*, October 3, 1941.
47. *Ibid.*, June 21, 23, July 10, September 18, 1941; White interview.
48. Evans interview.
49. *Ibid.*; Whitehill, pp. 146, 160.

Notes for Chapter III

1. Roscoe, pp. 7-8; Blair, pp. 82-85, 97-98.
2. Hermenau interview.
3. *Ibid.*; *Portsmouth Herald*, December 5, 1982.
4. *Ibid.*
5. Hatch, pp. 3-5; Legare interview.
6. *Ibid.*
7. Roscoe, pp. 10-11; Blair, pp. 106-107.
8. "Yard Activities, 1939-1945," p. 2, Portsmouth Public Library file; *Portsmouth Herald*, July 19, August 15, 1945, June 11, 1970; Davis, pp. 933-939; Palfrey interview.
9. *Portsmouth Herald*, December 8, 15, 1941.
10. *Ibid.* December 27, 29, 1941; January 12, 1942; *Cradle*, pp. 58-59.
11. *Ibid.*, January 15, 1942.
12. *Ibid.*, January 8, April 18, 1942; Bongartz, p. 102; Grigore, pp. 15-17.
13. *Ibid.*, April 27, 1942; *Surcouf* file, *Periscope* office; Roscoe, p. 86; Bongartz, pp. 57, 102; Burke and Shea interviews.
14. Burke interview.
15. Evans interview.
16. Alden, *Fleet Submarine*, pp. 101-105; Alden, "Andrew Irvin McKee," pp. 54-56.
17. *Portsmouth Herald*, October 28, 1942.
18. *Periscope*, July 3, 1953.
19. *Portsmouth Herald*, January 4, 11, December 11, 1943; White and Lawrence interviews.
20. Harford interview.
21. Palfrey interview.
22. *Cradle*, p. 58; *Portsmouth Herald*, August 13, 17, 1942; *Periscope*, November 29, 1945; "Activities 1939-1945," Portsmouth Public Library file.
23. Palfrey and Beane interviews.
24. White interview.
25. "Activities 1939-1945," Portsmouth Public Library file; *Cradle*, p. 59; Alden, *Fleet Submarine*, pp. 113-114.
26. *Ibid.*
27. *Portsmouth Herald*, July 21, 1942.
28. *Ibid.*, October 27, 28, 1943.
29. Harford and MacIsaac interviews; *Periscope*, March 16, 1984.
30. *Portsmouth Herald*, January 28, 1944; Alden, *Fleet Submarine*, p. 117; White interview.

31. *Ibid.*, pp. 86, 99, 108–109, 271; "Extracts...1929...1964," pp. 34–39.
32. *Portsmouth Herald*, October 1, 1943.
33. *Ibid.*, April 13, 1945.
34. Gray, pp. 1–30; "Extracts...1929...1964," pp. 38–39; *Cradle*, p. 59.
35. *Portsmouth Herald*, May 16, 17, 1945, November 14, 1982; *Periscope*, June 9, 1945, Gray, p. 26.
36. *Ibid.*, May 17, 1975; Gray, pp. 26–27.
37. *Ibid.*, July 2, 1945, May 17, 1975, November 14, 1982.
38. *Ibid.*, April 17, 1976; "Extracts...1929...1964," p. 39.
39. *Ibid.*, September 18, 20, 24, 1945, April 24, August 18, 1953, May 15, June 26, 1954; Gallery, pp. 312–326.
40. Polmar, *American Submarine*, pp. 57, 69; *Dictionary*, 3: frontispiece, 140–142.
41. Lockwood, *Sink 'Em All*, pp. 13–14, 17; MacIsaac interview
42. *Ibid.*; Kitchen, p. 55.
43. Blair; pp. 107–109, 263–265; Roscoe, pp. 17–18, 184–186; *Dictionary*, 3:319–320; 6:458–459; Francis and McLees interviews.
44. Poss interview.
45. Enright interview; *Portsmouth Herald*, November 21, 1982.
46. Wheeler, p. 45.
47. *Periscope*, February 20, 1959.
48. Woodbury, pp. 106, 114–118; Sousae and MacIsaac interviews.
49. *Ibid.;* Gray interview.
50. Roscoe, p. 17; McLees and MacIsaac interviews.
51. *Ibid.*, Barfield and Hermenau interviews.
52. Wheeler, p. 75; Legare interview.
53. *Ibid.*, p. 45; MacIsaac interview.
54. McLees interview; Lockwood, *Sink 'Em All*, p. 17.
55. "History of USS *Sailfish* (*SS 192*) (ex-*Squalus*)," Ships' Histories Section; Blair, pp. 141–142; McLees interview.
56. *Ibid.*, p. 339.
57. *Ibid.*, p. 463; Roscoe, pp. 232, 549; Gray interview.
58. *Ibid.*
59. *Portsmouth Herald*, April 11, 1945.
60. Roscoe, pp. 296–298, which reprints the *Sailfish* log, December 2–3, 1943; Blair, pp. 527–530.
61. *Portsmouth Herald*, April 11, 1945; "*Sailfish* ship's history."
62. *Ibid.*; Gray interview.
63. *Portsmouth Herald*, August 27, 1945.
64. "*Sailfish* ship's history," p. 11; Blair p. 818.
65. *Portsmouth Herald*, September 21, 26, October 5, 20, 27, 30, 1945; *Periscope*, October 10, 1945; Gray interview.
66. *Portsmouth Herald*, October 29, 1945.
67. *Ibid.*, November 1, 2, 16, 1945.
68. *Ibid.*, December 14, 1945, January 12, 16, 1946.
69. *Ibid.*, November 9, 12, 1946, May 4, 1948; *Periscope*, August 19, 1946, May 29, 1969; Gray interview; Alden, *Fleet Submarine*, p. 251.
70. Blair, p. 508; Roscoe, pp. 508–522.
71. "*USS Trout* Second War Patrol Log," p. 2.
72. Dettbarn, pp. 51–57; Cross, pp. 22, 56, 58, 60; Blair, pp. 206–208.

73. Blair, pp. 207–208.
74. *Ibid.*, pp. 394–396; Palmer, pp. 16–19; Roscoe, pp. 219–221.
75. Poss interview.
76. *Ibid.*; Polmar, *American Submarine*, p. 68.
77. Blair, pp. 494–495; McLees interview.
78. *Ibid.*, pp. 624–625; Roscoe, pp. 516, 533; Hoyt, *Submarines at War*, p. 247; McLees interview.
79. *Ibid.*
80. Mueller, pp. 69–70; Roscoe, pp. 340, 352; Blair, pp. 509, 702.
81. Barfield and MacIsaac interviews.
82. *Ibid.;* Roscoe, pp. 353–354.
83. "History of the *U.S.S. Redfish (SS 395),*" U.S. Navy Ship Biographies; Barfield interview.
84. "1st [*Redfish*] Patrol," 4 pp. typescript, MacIsaac collection; Blair, p. 706.
85. *Ibid.*, "Second Patrol," "History of the *U.S.S. Redfish (SS 395).*
86. *Ibid.*, MacIsaac interview.
87. Mueller, p. 72.
88. *Redfish* log.
89. MacIsaac interview.
90. Sousae interview.
91. "*U.S.S. Redfish (SS 395)* Damage Due to Depth Charging," pp. 65–69 in *Redfish* log, MacIsaac collection; MacIsaac interview.
92. *Ibid.*
93. *Ibid.*; *Redfish* log.
94. MacIsaac interview; "Extracts…1929…1964," p. 37; Blair, p. 803.
95. "History of the U.S.S. *Redfish (SS 395),*" p. 3.
96. *Portsmouth Herald*, May 29, June 1, 1943; "History of USS *Archerfish (SS 311),*" Ships' histories section.
97. "Captain Joseph F. Enright, U.S. Navy," Biographies Branch; Enright interview; Blair, pp. 515, 568.
98. "*Archerfish*, Report of Fifth War Patrol," pp. 1–14; Enright, pt. 1, p. 14–15.
99. *Ibid.*, Moore, pp. 142–146; Underbrink, pp. 81–83; Enright interview.
100. *Ibid.*, *Archerfish* log, pp. 8–10.
101. *Ibid.*; Beach, pp. 136–137.
102. *Archerfish* log, pp. 9–10.
103. *Ibid.*; Enright, pt. 2, pp. 18–19, 38.
104. *Ibid.*, pp. 38–41.
105. *Ibid.*; Enright interview.
106. Underbrink, pp. 86–87; Moore, pp. 148–149.
107. *Ibid.*; Enright, pt. 2, pp. 40–45.
108. *Portsmouth Herald*, August 15, 17, 1945; White interview.
109. *Ibid.*, February 9, 1943, May 18, 1944, August 31, October 5, 1945; Lockwood *Sink 'Em All*, p. 364; O'Kane, *Clear the Bridge.*
110. McLees, Gray and Francis interviews.
111. Roscoe, pp. 474, 490–494; Lockwood, *Sink 'Em All*, pp. 361–363; Blair, pp. 877–879; Polmar, *American Submarine*, pp. 69–71.
112. Lockwood, framed written statement, Submarine Museum and Library.

Notes for Chapter IV

1. *Portsmouth Herald*, September 6, 10, 1945.
2. *Ibid.*, September 26–28, 1945; Dalla Mura interview.
3. *Cradle*, pp. 60, 76, 86–87; Furer, pp. 540–543; *Periscope*, September 13, 1946; May 31, September 1, 1949; Burke and Russell interviews.
4. *Periscope*, October 24, 1947; Rowe interview.
5. Polmar, *American Submarine*, pp. 75–77; Alden, *Fleet Submarine*, pp. 129–130.
6. Stimson, pp. 129–144; *Periscope*, July 25, 1947; December 23, 1964; July 29, 1966.
7. *Ibid.*, November 23, 1960; clipping in Somers Collection.
8. Polmar, *American Submarine*, p. 77; *Periscope*, April 15, 1949; April 21, 1950; April 18, 1958.
9. Alden, *Fleet Submarine*, pp. 138, 179; *Periscope*, January 13, 1967; clipping in Somers Collection.
10. Mueller, pp. 72–73; *Periscope*, April 14, 1961.
11. Alden, *Fleet Submarine*, pp. 196, 246–247; *Periscope*, August 24, 1956; April 13, July 26, August 9, 23, 1957; Francis interview.
12. *Periscope*, November 5, 1954.
13. Legare interview.
14. *Cradle*, pp. 60–61; Polmar, *American Submarine*, pp. 81–82; Alden, *Fleet Submarine*, pp. 130–134; *Periscope*, March 4, 1948.
15. *Ibid.*; Andrews, "Submarine against Submarine," pp. 44–45; Ford and White interviews.
16. Alden, *Fleet Submarine*, pp. 131–133; *Periscope*, May 17, 26, 1948.
17. Van Billiard interview; *Periscope*, July 25, 1947; June 15, November 2, 1951; November 2, 1954; *Dictionary*, 7:39.
18. *Ibid.*; Polmar, *American Submarine*, pp. 92–93, 97; *Portsmouth Herald*, June 20, 1951; Smith interview.
19. *Periscope*, March 21, October 23, 1952; *Portsmouth Herald*, October 17–18, 1952.
20. *Periscope*, June 23, 1950; December 5, 1953; "History of the *Albacore*," typescript, *Albacore* file, Ships' Histories Section: Allmendinger interview; Momsen speech, typescript, Taylor Model Basin archives.
21. *Ibid.*; For the David W. Taylor Experimental Model Basin, see Saunders, 46:307–324; 48:173–209; 49:10–46 and Mumma, 49:47–61. Russell interview; Alden, "Portsmouth Naval Shipyard (Pictorial)," p. 96.
22. Allmendinger, Hoyt and Letch interviews.
23. *Ibid.*
24. *Ibid.*; Merriman, pp. 20–21; Ryan, pp. 25–29; Soule, pp. 82–85, 226, 228.
25. Soule, p. 23; *Periscope*, November 21, 1955; Russell, White and Van Billiard interviews.
26. *Periscope*, November 4, 1955, November 23, 1960; Russell and Smith interviews.
27. *Ibid.*, August 31, 1962.
28. *Ibid.*, March 1, 1963; February 14, September 25, 1964; March 26, 1965; Smith interview.
29. *Ibid.*; McConnell interview.
30. *Periscope*, September 15, 1972.

31. Blair, *Atomic Submarine*, pp. 140–142; Polmar and Allen, pp. 146–147; Polmar, *American Submarine*, pp. 109–111.

32. *Periscope*, January 24, 1956; January 18, August 23, September 6, 1957; Sousae and Letch interviews.

33. *Ibid.*, June 29, 1956; Whitehill, p. 144.

34. Steele, *Seadragon; Periscope*, August 1, 1958; June 12, September 12, 1959; Van Billiard and Sousae interviews.

35. *Ibid.*; Harford interview; Polmar and Allen, p. 683.

36. *Periscope*, May 13, August 5, 1960; Steele, pp. 65-71; Marion and Woods interviews.

37. *Ibid.*, September 2, 30, 1960; March 8, 1968; Rees, pp. 106-107; Strong, pp. 59–64; Polmar, *Atomic Submarines, pp. 132–136.*

38. *Ibid.*, pp. 136–139; *Periscope*, August 31, 1962.

39. "Extracts," p. 72; *Periscope*, March 11, May 13, 1960; March 3, 1961.

40. *Ibid.*, July 28, 1961; April 19, May 3, 17, 1968; Steele and Gimpel, pp. 74-85; Polmar, *Atomic Submarines*, pp. 220–247.

41. *Periscope*, July 28, 1961; March 15, April 5, December 6, 1963; January 24, 1964; Polmar, *Atomic Submarines*, pp. 238–239, 243.

42. Marion interview.

43. *Periscope*, May 1, 8, 15, 22, 1964; *Portsmouth Herald*, May 12, 1964; *Dictionary*, 3:523; 5:21.

44. Russell interview.

45. Van Billiard interview.

46. Materials on the *Thresher* are voluminous. For books see Polmar, *Death of the Thresher;* Bentley, *The Thresher Disaster;* and *United States Ship Thresher (SSN 593): In Memoriam, April 10, 1963.* For articles, consult Andrews "Searching for *Thresher;"* Grenfell; Pritchett; and Wakelin. *Thresher* Scrapbook, Portsmouth Public Library; *Thresher* file, *Periscope* office; Polmar and Allen, pp. 370-373, 423-445; *Periscope*, October 16, 1959; July 8, 1960; March 30, 1962; Woods, Hoyt and Van Billiard interviews.

47. *Ibid.*; Polmar, *Atomic Submarines*, p. 153.

48. Sousae and Francis interviews.

49. Harford interview.

50. *Periscope*, April 17, May 24, 1963; Jones and Johnston interviews.

51. Ethel D. Stadtmuller, Roslyn, New York, to Leslie R. Rowe, Portsmouth Naval Shipyard, April 30, 1963; Mr. and Mrs. Ithel Prescott, Sanford, Maine, to Charles J. Palmer, Portsmouth Naval Shipyard, May 28, 1963, *Thresher* file, *Periscope* office.

52. *Periscope*, August 23, 1963; June 5, 1964; *Cradle*, pp. 64-65; *United States Ship Thresher*, pp. 127–128.

53. Jones, Francis, Johnston and Van Billiard interviews; Polmar, *American Submarine*, pp. 145, 147; *Periscope*, August 12, 1966.

54. Letch, Whitney and Hoyt interviews.

55. Polmar, *American Submarine*, pp. 142, 147; *Cradle*, p. 65; *Periscope*, November 20, 1959; March 24, April 7, 1967; June 12, 1970; Allmendinger, Russell and Van Billiard interviews.

56. *Ibid.*, April 3, 17, 24, May 8, 1964; *Portsmouth Herald*, June 11, 1970.

57. *Periscope*, December 1, 1964; *Portsmouth Herald*, November 19–23, 1964.

58. *Ibid.*, with Hushing quotation, *Portsmouth Herald*, November 23, 1964.

59. *Portsmouth Herald*, February 23-24, 1965; Van Billiard interview; Cooper, "Fundamentals."

60. *Periscope*, March 10, September 22, 1967; January 30, 1970; Van Billiard and Smith interviews.
61. Hoyt interview; *Periscope*, March 15, 1963; September 22, October 20, 1967; *Dolphin* news release, August 14, 1968, *Dolphin* file, *Periscope* office.
62. Castelazo interview.
63. *Periscope*, May 21, 1965.
64. Hoyt interview; Cooper, "Fundamentals."
65. *Periscope*, March 10, 1961; June 7, 21, 1968 with quotation in last issue.
66. *Ibid.*, February 7, May 29, September 19, 1969; January 30, 1970, with quotation; January 22, 1971; "Welcome Aboard *USS Dolphin*," *Dolphin* file, Ships' Histories Branch; Van Billiard interview.
67. *Periscope*, January 15, 29, 1965.
68. *Ibid.*, June 3, 1966.
69. *Portsmouth Herald*, August 20, 22, 1966; *New York Times*, August 20–23, 1966; Castelazo and White interviews.
70. *Cradle*, pp. 71, 84–85; *Periscope*, December 2, 1966; Jones and Johnston interviews.
71. *Ibid.*, November 10, 21, 1969; *Portsmouth Herald*, November 12, 1969; Johnston, Van Billiard and Smith interviews.
72. *Maine Sunday Telegram*, April 12, 1970 with quotation; April 19, 26, 1970.
73. *Portsmouth Herald*, March 24–25, 30, 1971, the latter with facsimile of Nixon letter; *Periscope*, April 2, 1971.
74. *Periscope*, September 17, October 1, 1971; *Portsmouth Herald*, September 27, 1971; Van Billiard interview. If the *Squalus* and *Sailfish* are counted as two boats, the total number of Portsmouth-built submarines is 135 boats. If the count includes *Lionfish* and *Manta*, begun at Cramp Shipyard, Philadelphia, Pennsylvania, and the *Pickerel* begun at Boston Naval Shipyard, with all three completed at Portsmouth, the grand total is 138 boats.
75. Allmendinger interview.

Notes for Epilogue

1. *Cradle*, pp. 71–75; *Progress 1983*, March 23, 1983; *Portsmouth Herald*, January 20, 1983, February 19, 1984; Shea and Van Billiard interviews.
2. *Portsmouth Herald*, March 20, 1983.
3. *Periscope*, July 22, 1983; Sousae interview.
4. *USS Portsmouth SSN 707 Commissioning 1 October 1983* program; *Portsmouth Herald*, January 20, September 18, 25, 1983; *Rockingham Gazette*, September 28, 1983.
5. Keefe interview; *Portsmouth Herald*, September 21, 1983, May 1, 1984.
6. *Portsmouth Herald*, May 4, September 20–21, October 6, 19, November 8, 1983; *Foster's Daily Democrat*, November 8, 1983; Allmendinger interview.
7. *Portsmouth Herald*, February 17, 23, March 23, 1984; Allmendinger speech, February 19, 1984, Portsmouth, New Hampshire.
8. *Portsmouth Herald*, April 18, 24, 30, May 1, 1984; *Foster's Daily Democrat*, April 30, 1984; *Rockingham Gazette*, May 9, 1984.
9. *Ibid.*; *Periscope*, May 11, 1984; *Portsmouth Herald*, May 7, 1984.

Symbols used in captions for sources of photographs

JPCC — Joseph P. Copley Collection, New Castle, New Hampshire.
KHNM — Kittery Historical and Naval Museum, Kittery, Maine.
NGS — National Geographic Society, Washington, D.C.
PA — Piscataqua History Club Collection, Portsmouth Athenaeum, Portsmouth, New Hampshire.
PH — *Portsmouth Herald*, Portsmouth, New Hampshire.
PM — Peabody Museum, Salem, Massachusetts.
PNSY — Portsmouth Naval Shipyard, Portsmouth, New Hampshire.
SB — Strawbery Banke, Portsmouth, New Hampshire.
UNHMS University of New Hampshire Media Services Department, Dimond Library, Durham, New Hampshire.
USNI — United States Naval Institute, Annapolis, Maryland. From Theodore Roscoe's *United States Submarine Operations in World War II*. Copyright © 1949.

Bibliography

Published sources on the general subject of American submarines constitute a vast literature; by contrast, books, pamphlets, and articles geared specifically to the Portsmouth Naval Shipyard and its submarines are relatively few and usually brief. As a result I have relied heavily on local newspapers and interviews, sources rarely consulted by earlier writers on this subject.

I have approached this subject as history, not as technology. My bibliography reflects this emphasis. For those who seek scientific information, excellent technical articles on American submarines appear in the multi-volumed *United States Naval Institute Proceedings*, and *The Society of Naval Architects and Marine Engineers Transactions*. John D. Alden's monograph, *The Fleet Submarine in the U.S. Navy: A Design and Construction History* (1979), is a definitive treatment of the subject replete with graphs, drawings and tables.

Glossaries of submarine terms appear in Richard H. O'Kane's *Clear the Bridge!* (1977), George P. Steele and Herbert J. Gimpel's *Nuclear Submarine Skippers and What They Do* (1962), and Arch Whitehouse's *Subs and Submariners* (1961).

Some readers may be interested in a more detailed account of some of the 134 Portsmouth subs. For a published ship's history, one should refer to the eight-volume *Dictionary of American Naval Fighting Ships*, readily available in the reference section of most libraries or through inter-library loan.

For access to unpublished materials on any Portsmouth sub, one should contact the Naval Historical Center, whose files are open to the general public. Upon request, the Center will photocopy and mail specified materials for a nominal fee. For this service, visit or write:

> Naval Historical Center
> Department of the Navy
> Washington Navy Yard
> Washington, D.C. 20372

Pictures of all Portsmouth submarines are also available for $5.35 per photograph. For a black and white, 8″ x 10″ glossy photo of an individual sub, contact:

> Still Picture Branch
> National Archives (NNSP)
> 7th and Pennsylvania Avenue N.W.
> Washington, D.C. 20408

In the preparation of this book I have consulted the following:

Books

Alden, John D., *The Fleet Submarine in the U.S. Navy: A Design and Construction History.* Annapolis, Maryland: Naval Institute Press, 1979.

Bagnasco, Ermino, *Submarines of World War II.* Annapolis, Maryland: Naval Institute Press, 1977.

Barnes, Robert Hatfield, *United States Submarines.* New Haven: H.F. Morse Associates, Inc., 1944.

Barrows, Nat A., *Blow All Ballast! The Story of the Squalus.* New York: Dodd, Mead & Company, 1940.

Beach, Edward L., *Submarine!* New York: Henry Holt and Company, 1946.

Bentley, John, *The Thresher Disaster: The Most Tragic Dive in Submarine History.* Garden City, New York: Doubleday & Company, Inc., 1974, 1975.

Blair, Clay, Jr., *The Atomic Submarine and Admiral Rickover.* New York: Henry Holt and Company, 1954.

        , *Silent Victory: The U.S. Submarine War Against Japan.* Philadelphia and New York: J.B. Lippincott Company, 1975.

Boyd, David F., *Extracts from the Daily Log Book: U.S. Navy Yard, Portsmouth, New Hampshire, October 15, 1819 - December 17, 1929.* Portsmouth, N.H.: United States Naval Prison, 1931.

Burns. Thomas S., *The Secret War for the Ocean Depths: Soviet-American Rivalry for Mastery of the Seas.* New York: Rawson Associates Publishers, Inc., 1978.

Cronon, E. David, ed., *The Cabinet Diaries of Josephus Daniels: 1913 - 1921.* Lincoln: University of Nebraska Press, 1963.

Daniels, Josephus, *The Wilson Era: Years of Peace, 1910–1917.* Chapel Hill: The University of North Carolina Press, 1944.

Fentress, Walter E. H., *Centennial History of the United States Navy Yard, at Portsmouth, N.H.* Portsmouth, N.H.: O.M. Knight, 1876.

Frank, Gerald and James D. Horan with J.M. Eckberg, *U.S.S. Seawolf: Submarine Raider of the Pacific.* New York: G. P. Putnam's Sons, 1945.

Furer, Julius Augustus, *Administration of the Navy Department in World War II.* Washington: [Government Printing Office?], 1959.

Gallery, Daniel V., *Twenty Million Tons Under the Sea.* Chicago: Henry Regnery Company, 1956.

Gray, Charlie, *Surrender at Sea: A Compilation of the Stories of the Surrender of the Nazi Submarines as Presented Over WHEB, Portsmouth, New Hampshire.* [Portsmouth]: WHEB, Inc., and Colonial Laundry, 1945.

Grider, George as told to Lydel Sims, *Warfish*. Boston and Toronto: Little, Brown and Company, 1959.

Harris-Warren, H.B., *Dive! The Story of an Atomic Submarine*. New York: Harper & Brothers, 1960.

Hatch, Alden, *Heroes of Annapolis*. New York: Julian Messner, Inc., 1943.

Hewlett, Richard and Francis Duncan, *Nuclear Navy 1946-1962*. Chicago and New York: The University of Chicago Press, 1974.

Holman, Hugh C., ed., *The Thomas Wolfe Reader*. New York: Charles Scribner's Sons, 1962.

Holmes, W. J., *Undersea Victory: The Influence of Submarine Operations on the War in the Pacific*. Garden City, New York: Doubleday & Company, Inc., 1966.

Hoyt, Edwin P., *Bowfin: The Story of One of America's Fabled Fleet Submarines in World War II*. New York: Van Nostrand Reinhold Company, 1983.

   , *Submarines at War: The History of the American Silent Service*. New York: Stein and Day, 1983.

Icenhower, Joseph B., compl., *Submarines in Combat*. New York: Franklin Watts, Inc., 1964.

King, Ernest J. and Walter Muir Whitehill, *Fleet Admiral King: A Naval Record*. New York: W. W. Norton & Company, Inc., 1952.

Lockwood, Charles A., *Down to the Sea in Subs*. New York: W. W. Norton & Company, Inc., 1967.

   , *Sink 'Em All: Submarine Warfare in the Pacific*. New York: E. P. Dutton & Co., Inc., 1951.

Lockwood, Charles A. and Hans Christian Adamson, *Hell at 50 Fathoms*. Philadelphia and New York: Chilton Co., 1962.

   , *Tragedy at Honda*. Philadelphia and New York: Chilton Co., 1960.

   , *Zoomies, Subs and Zeroes*. New York: Greenberg, 1956.

Maas, Peter, *The Rescuer*. New York, Evanston and London: Harper & Row, 1967.

Middleton, Drew, *Submarine: The Ultimate Naval Weapon — Its Past, Present and Future*. Chicago: Playboy Press, 1976.

Moore, John, ed., *Jane's Fighting Ships, 1983-1984*. London: Jane's Publishing Company Limited, 1983.

Morrison, Joseph L., *Josephus Daniels: The Small-d Democrat*. Chapel Hill: The University of North Carolina Press, 1966.

Naval History Division, Navy Department, Office of the Chief of Naval Operations, *Dictionary of American Naval Fighting Ships*. Washington: Government Printing Office, 1959-1981. 8 vols. James L. Mooney and Richard T. Speer, eds., vols. 7-8.

   , *U.S. Submarine Losses in World War II*. Washington: Government Printing Office, 1963.

Navy Day: October 27, 1923, Navy Yard, Portsmouth, New Hampshire. n. p.: ca. 1923.

Navy Times, *They Fought Under the Sea: The Saga of the Submarine.* Harrisburg, Pennsylvania: The Stackpole Company, and Washington, D.C.: The Army Times Publishing Company, 1962.

O'Kane, Richard H., *Clear the Bridge! The War Patrols of the U.S.S. Tang.* Chicago: Rand McNally & Company, 1977.

Polmar, Norman, *Atomic Submarines.* Princeton, New Jersey: D. Van Nostrand Co., Inc., 1963.

_____, *Death of the Thresher.* Philadelphia and New York: Chilton Books, 1964.

_____, *The American Submarine.* Annapolis, Maryland: The Nautical & Aviation Publishing Company of America, 1981.

_____, *The Ships and Aircraft of the U.S. Fleet.* Annapolis, Maryland: Naval Institute Press, 1981.

Polmar, Norman and Thomas B. Allen, *Rickover.* New York: Simon and Schuster, 1982.

Portsmouth Naval Shipyard, *Cradle of American Shipbuilding.* Portsmouth, New Hampshire: Portsmouth Naval Shipyard, 1978.

_____, *Submarines, Portsmouth Naval Shipyard.* n.p.: ca. 1967.

Pratt, Fletcher, *The Compact History of the U.S. Navy.* New York: Hawthorn Books, 1957.

Preble, Geo. Henry, *History of the United States Navy-Yard, Portsmouth, N.H.* Washington: Government Printing Office, 1892.

Rees, Ed, *The Seas and the Subs.* New York: Duell, Sloan & Pearce, 1961.

Roscoe, Theodore, *United States Submarine Operations in World War II.* Annapolis, Maryland: United States Naval Institute, 1949.

Rush, Charles W., *The Complete Book of Submarines.* New York: The World Publishing Co., 1958.

Staff, Deputy Commander Submarine Force, U.S. Atlantic Fleet, *United States Ship Thresher (SSN593): In Memoriam, April 10, 1963.* n.p.: 1964.

Stafford, Edward Peary, *The Far and the Deep.* New York: G. P. Putnam's Sons, 1967.

Steele, George P., *Seadragon: Northwest Under the Ice.* New York: E. P. Dutton & Co., Inc., 1962.

Steele, George P. and Herbert J. Gimpel. *Nuclear Submarine Skippers and What They Do.* New York: Franklin Watts, Inc., 1962.

USS Portsmouth SSN707 Commissioning 1 October 1983. n.p.: [1983].

Wheeler, Keith, *War Under the Pacific.* Chicago: Time-Life Books, 1980.

Whitehill, Walter Muir, *Analecta Biographica: A Handful of New England Portraits.* Brattleboro, Vermont: The Stephen Greene Press, 1969.

Whitehouse, Arch, *Subs and Submariners.* Garden City, New York: Doubleday & Co., 1961.

Woodbury, David O., *What You Should Know about Submarine Warfare.* New York: W. W. Norton & Company, Inc., 1942.

Unpublished Reports and Proceedings

Cooper Joshua W., "Fundamentals of the Situation pertaining to Portsmouth-Kittery Naval Shipyard," n.p.: Portsmouth-Kittery Armed Services Committee, Inc., 1973. 14 pages. (Typewritten.) Copy at Langdon Library, Newington, New Hampshire.

Public Documents

United States Government, *Annual Reports of the Navy Department for the Fiscal Year 1914, 1920, 1922*. Washington: Government Printing Office, 1915, 1921, 1923.

, *The Statutes at Large of the United States of America from March 1913 to March 1915* ... Washington: Government Printing Office, 1915.

United States House of Representatives, *The Proceedings and Debates of Forty-fourth Congress, 2d Sess*. Washington: Government Printing Office, 1876.

Articles

Alden, John D., "Andrew Irwin McKee: Naval Constructor," *United States Naval Institute Proceedings* 105 (June 1979): 49–57.

, "Portsmouth Naval Shipyard (Pictorial)." *United States Naval Institute Proceedings* 90 (November 1964): 86–105.

Allmendinger, Eugene, "Submersibles: Past-Present-Future." *Oceanus: The Magazine of Marine Science and Policy* 25 (Spring 1982): 18–29.

Andrews, Frank A., "Searching for *Thresher*." *United States Naval Institute Proceedings* 90 (May 1964): 68–77.

, "Submarine against Submarine." In *Naval Review*. Frank Uhling, Jr., ed. Annapolis, Maryland: United States Naval Institute, 1965. pp. 43–57.

Bauman, Richard, "The Incredible Rescue." *The Retired Officer* 39 (August 1983): 30–31.

Bongartz, Roy, "Found: One Supersub." *Argosy* (January 1967): 56–58, 100–102. Copy in Somers Collection.

Brown, Allan D., "Torpedoes and Torpedo Boats." *Harper's New Monthly Magazine* 55 (June–November 1882): 36–47.

Cross, Farrell, "W.W. II's Great Goldbrick Escape." pp. 22, 56, 58, 60. Copy in Somers Collection.

Davis, H.F.D., "Building U.S. Submarines in World War II." *United States Naval Institute Proceedings* 72 (July 1946): 933–939.

Dettbarn, John L., "Gold Ballast: War Patrol of *USS Trout*." *United States Naval Institute Proceedings* 86 (January 1960): 51–57.

Enright, Joseph F., "The Short Life and Sudden Death of the *Shinano*." Part 1, *The American Legion Magazine* 107 (August 1979): 14–15, 40–45. Part 2, 107 (September 1979): 18–19, 38–45.

Estaver, Paul E., "The Nineteenth Dive." Part 1, *New Hampshire Profiles* 8 (August 1959): 18–19, 36, 38–39. Part 2, 8 (September 1959): 28–29, 34.

Gray, Charles W. , "Down to the Sea." *New Hampshire Profiles* 17(June 1968): 28–31.

Grenfell, E. W., "*USS Thresher* (SSN-593) 3 August 1961–10 April 1963." *United States Naval Institute Proceedings* 90 (March 1964): 37–47.

Grigore, Julius, "World War II Sea Tragedy That Made No Headlines." *The Panama Canal Review* (August 1967): 15–17. Copy in Somers Collection.

Keach, Donald L., "Down to *Thresher* by Bathyscaph." *National Geographic* 125 (June 1964): 764–777.

Kitchen, Ruben P., *"The U.S.S. Clamagore's (SS-343)* Final Berth." In *Sea Classics: U.S. Submarines at War 1941-45.* Ed Schnepf, ed. Canoga Park, Calif.: Challenge Publications, Inc., Winter 1983, pp. 50-55.

McKay, Ernest, "The *Squalus* Tragedy: 35 Years Ago This Month." *New Hampshire Profiles* 23 (May 1974): 22–27.

McKee, Andrew Irwin, "Development of Submarines in the United States." *Historical Transactions, 1893-1943* (New York: The Society of Naval and Marine Engineers, 1945): 344–355. Copy in Shea Collection.

Merriman, David D., "*USS Albacore*: Forerunner of Today's Submarines." *Sea Classics* 80 (January 1980): 18–29.

Meyer, J. J., Jr., "Our Nation's Shipyards." *United States Naval Institute Proceedings* 90 (November 1964): 34–45.

Moore, Lynn Lucius, "*Shinano*: The Jinx Carrier." *United States Naval Institute Proceedings* 79 (February 1953): 142–149.

Mueller, William Behr, "The *USS Redfish*: War Hero and Movie Star." In *Sea Classics: U.S. Submarines at War 1941-45,* Ed Schnepf, ed. Canoga Park, Calif.: Challenge Publications, Inc., Winter 1983, pp. 68–73.

Mumma, Albert G., "The Variable-Pressure Water Tunnels at the David W. Taylor Model Basin." In *The Society of Naval Architects and Marine Engineers Transactions* 49 (1941). New York: The Society of Naval Architects and Marine Engineers, 1942, pp. 47–61.

Palmer, Robert W., "The Sinking of the *USS Grenadier SS210*." *Polaris* 27 (April 1983): 16–19.

Pritchett, Richard, "The Only Man Who Didn't Go Down with the *Thresher*." *Yankee* 42 (April 1978): 76–77, 119–121.

Ryan, Cornelius, "I Rode The World's Fastest Sub." *Collier's* 135 (April 1, 1955): 25-29.

Saunders, Harold E., "The David W. Taylor Basin." In *The Society of Naval Architects and Marine Engineers Transactions* 46, 48–49 (1938, 1940–1941). New York: The Society of Naval Architects and Marine Engineers, 1942. 3 parts. part 1, 46:307–324; part 2, 48: 173–209; part 3, 49: 10–46.

Smith, Carl T., "Three Locomotives and a Submarine." *New Hampshire Profiles* 15 (February 1966): 44–55.

Soule, Gardner, "Fastest Sub Points Way to Undersea Liners." *Popular Science* (December 1956): 82–85, 226, 228. Copy in Somers Collection.

Stimson, Paul C., "'Round the Horn by Submarine." *National Geographic* 93 (January 1948): 129-144.

Strong, James T., "The Opening of the Arctic Ocean." *United States Naval Institute Proceedings* 87 (October 1961): 58-65. Copy in Somers Collection.

Sullivan, Timothy P., "The Portsmouth Navy Yard, The New Dry Dock, and Henderson's Point." *The Granite Monthly* 36 (February 1904): 64-88.

Underbrink, Robert L., "Your Island is Moving at 20 Knots!" *United States Naval Institute Proceedings* 95 (September 1969): 81-87.

Van Saun, A., "Attack Submarine: The Hidden Persuader." *United States Naval Institute Proceedings* 108 (June 1982): 100-103.

Wakelin, James H., Jr., "*Thresher*: Lesson and Challenge." *National Geographic* 125 (June 1964): 759-763.

Newspapers

Foster's Daily Democrat (Dover, New Hampshire).

Life Buoy (Industrial Department, Portsmouth Navy Yard, Portsmouth, New Hampshire).

Maine Sunday Telegram (Portland, Maine).

New York Times.

Periscope (Portsmouth Naval Shipyard, Portsmouth, New Hampshire).

Portland Press Herald (Portland, Maine).

Portsmouth Chronicle.

Portsmouth Herald.

Progress 1983 (Supplement to *Exeter News-Letter, The Hampton Union* & *Rockingham Gazette*, Exeter, New Hampshire).

Rockingham Gazette (Exeter, New Hampshire).

Manuscript Collections

Boyd, David F., Captain, U.S.N., "Continuation of Preble's History of the United States Navy Yard, Covering the Years 1878 - 1930." 45 pp. with various appendices. (Typewritten.) Copy at the Maine Room, Rice Public Library, Kittery, Maine.

Copley, Joseph P., Collection. Typescripts, photo albums, documents and related materials pertaining to the Portsmouth Naval Shipyard and its submarines. New Castle, New Hampshire.

David W. Taylor Model Basin, Collection. Documents, speeches, press releases, articles and miscellaneous items. Navy Laboratories Archives Record Collection 7-1; Records of the Experimental Model Basin 1899-1939; and Records of David Taylor Model Basin, 1939 - 1967. David W. Taylor Naval Ship Research and Development Center, Bethesda, Maryland.

Domina, Walter E., "A History of the U.S.N. Prison and Disciplinary Command: The Castle, 1908 - 1974." 17 pp. typescript with 34 attached photographs.

Delivered as a speech before the Piscataqua History Club, Portsmouth, New Hampshire, January 21, 1971. Joseph P. Copley copy.

"Extracts from the Daily Log From December 17, 1929 to August 18, 1964, Portsmouth Naval Shipyard, Portsmouth, New Hampshire." 75 pp. typescript. Joseph P. Copley copy.

Hoyt, Philip, Collection. Lists, speeches, documents and pamphlets, pertaining to the Portsmouth Naval Shipyard, Portsmouth, New Hampshire. Rye, New Hampshire.

Langdon, John, John Langdon Papers, New Hampshire Historical Society, Concord, New Hampshire.

Learnard, Arthur N., "The Sinking of the *U.S.S. Squalus* on May 23rd, 1939." 24 pp. typescript (1968). Office of the *Periscope* and Public Affairs, Portsmouth Naval Shipyard, Portsmouth, New Hampshire.

Lockwood, Charles A., Statement. Framed manuscript on display. Submarine Museum and Library, United States Submarine Base, Groton, Connecticut.

MacIsaac, Daniel R., Collection. Newspaper clippings, documents, reports, typescripts and materials mostly relating to the *USS Redfish*. Kittery, Maine.

McLees, Gerald C., Collection. Newspaper clippings, documents, letters and materials relating to McLees's naval career and the *USS Squalus*. Portsmouth, New Hampshire.

Portsmouth Naval Shipyard, Collection. Individual folders for each submarine and for Shipyard events containing documents, launching and commissioning programs, incoming original letters, copies of outgoing correspondence, clippings, press releases, photographs and circulars. Office of the *Periscope* and Public Affairs, Building #86, Portsmouth Naval Shipyard, Portsmouth, New Hampshire.

Portsmouth Public Library, Portsmouth Room, Collection. Navy Yard Scrapbooks, folders, photographs and related materials. Portsmouth Public Library, Portsmouth, New Hampshire.

Shea, John, Collection. Pamphlets, articles, computer print-out sheets and related materials on the Portsmouth Naval Shipyard and American submarines. Rye, New Hampshire.

Somers, Chester L., Collection. Extensive materials on all aspects of submarines and submariners, American and foreign. Books, files, clippings, correspondence, photographs and memorabilia. Lowell, Massachusetts.

Submarine Museum and Library, Collection. Exhibits, World War II submarine war logs, books, files, maps, manuscripts and memorabilia. Submarine Museum and Library, United States Submarine Base, Groton, Connecticut.

United States Navy, Naval History Division, Collection. Ships' histories, file material on each individual United States naval ship. Washington Navy Yard, Washington, D.C.

Wilson, Thomas C., Piscataqua History Club Collection. Scrapbooks, photo albums, correspondence, books, pamphlets and related materials. Portsmouth Athenaeum, Portsmouth, New Hampshire.

Interviews

Allmendinger, Eugene. Durham, New Hampshire, March 18, 1983. (United States Navy, 1943 - 1945; Portsmouth Naval Shipyard, 1946 - 1950, naval architect; United States Naval Academy, teacher; University of New Hampshire, 1958-1983, Director of Marine Operations and Associate Professor of Naval Architecture; Portsmouth Submarine Memorial Association, 1983 - present, vice president.)

Barfield, Charlie J. Portsmouth, New Hampshire, March 2, 1983. (United States Navy, 1942 - 1946, 1948 - 1965, radioman, *USS Picuda, USS Pomodon, USS Grampus, USS Gudgeon, USS Sea Robin*: Portsmouth Naval Shipyard, 1982 - present.)

Beane, Benjamin. Rochester, New Hampshire, March 24, 1983. (Portsmouth Navy Yard, 1918-1949, machinist, shop planner, supervisor.)

Burke, George. Portsmouth, New Hampshire, September 19, 1983. (Portsmouth Naval Shipyard, 1943-1946, 1951-1956, 1973-present, sheet metal worker, hull inspector.)

Burtner, Evers. Kingston, New Hampshire, May 13, 1983. (Massachusetts Institute of Technology, Class of 1915; M.I.T., 1916-1958, Associate Professor of Naval Architecture and Marine Engineering; Portsmouth Navy Yard, 1917-1918, draftsman, engineer.)

Castelazo, Arthur H. Portsmouth, New Hampshire, February 7, 1983. (United States Navy, 1938-1967; Portsmouth Naval Shipyard, 1964-1967, Public Works Officer.)

Dalla Mura, Bart. New Castle, New Hampshire, May 11, 1983. (United States Navy, 1921 - 1925, radioman; Portsmouth Navy Yard, 1927 - 1961, general foreman or quarterman, Shop #31, Inside Machine Shop.)

Enright, Joseph F. Portsmouth Naval Shipyard, Portsmouth, New Hampshire, April 9, 1983. (United States Naval Academy, Class of 1933; United States Navy, 1933 - 1963; Commanding Officer, *USS Dace*, 1943; *USS Archerfish*, 1944-1945.) Delivered as a speech at the 83rd Submarine Anniversary Ball.

Evans, Robert L. Bow Lake, Strafford, New Hampshire, March 26, 1983. (United States Naval Academy, Class of 1932; United States Navy, 1932 - 1957; Massachusetts Institute of Technology, M.S., 1937; Portsmouth Navy Yard, 1937- 1940, ship superintendent.)

Ford, Curt J. Portsmouth, New Hampshire, February 10, 1983. (Portsmouth Navy Yard, 1936-1969, Public Works laborer, shop stores, welder, bookkeeper, comptroller.)

Francis, Samuel. Rye, New Hampshire, April 24, 1983. (United States Naval Academy, Class of 1946; United States Navy, 1946 - 1971; Officer on *USS Bugara, USS Clamagore, USS Burrfish, USS Blenny, USS Cavalla*; Commanding Officer, *USS Lapon, USS Corsair, USS Piper*.)

Gray, William H. Kittery, Maine, June 9, 1983. (United States Navy, 1935-1958; *USS Sailfish, USS Finback, USS Batfish, USS Tusk*, Third Class Torpedoman; Chief of the Boat on *USS Sailfish, USS Batfish*.)

Harford, Robert, Portsmouth, New Hampshire, September 19, 1983. (Portsmouth Naval Shipyard, 1941-1942, private contractor; 1943 off and on to 1981, machinist.)

Hermenau, Waldemar "Chuck." Newington, New Hampshire, February 11, 1983. (United States Navy, 1935-1957; *USS Dolphin* 1937-1942, Electrician's Mate Third and First Class.)

Hoyt, Philip. Rye, New Hampshire, January 6, 1983. (Portsmouth Navy Yard, 1934-1973; Chief Design Engineer, 1967-1973.)

Johnston, Robert. Portsmouth Naval Shipyard, Portsmouth, New Hampshire, January 19, 1983. (Portsmouth Naval Shipyard, 1967-present; Public Affairs Assistant, 1977-1983.)

Jones, Ray P. Rye, New Hampshire, February 21, 1983. (United States Navy, 1951-1981; *USS Irex, USS Robert E. Lee*, Officer; *USS Barbel*, Executive Officer; *USS Blueback*, Commanding Officer; 1977-1981, Portsmouth Naval Shipyard, Administrative Officer.)

Keefe, William F. "Bill." Portsmouth, New Hampshire, April 29, 1984. (Bring Back the *Albacore* Committee organizer; Portsmouth Submarine Memorial Association, member, 1982-present, former City Council member and Vice Mayor, Portsmouth, New Hampshire.) Delivered as a speech at the Return of the *Albacore* reception.

Lawrence, Helen. Rye, New Hampshire, February 21, 1983. (Portsmouth Navy Yard, 1943-1945, 1958-1982, Electrician's helper.)

Legare, Armand F.F. "Legs." New Castle, New Hampshire, March 11, 1983. (United States Naval Academy, Class of 1946; United States Navy, 1941-1963; *USS Sennet, USS Cobia, USS Batfish*, Officer; *USS Flying Fish*, Commanding Officer.)

Letch, Wilma "Bill." Portsmouth, New Hampshire, January 10, 1983. (Portsmouth Navy Yard, 1918-1970; "Best job," Group Superintendent, Mechanical.)

MacIsaac, Daniel R. Kittery, Maine, October 19,1983. (United States Navy, 1940-1961; *USS Bonita, R-2, USS Redfish, USS Blenny, USS Spadefish*, Torpedoman; Portsmouth Naval Shipyard, 1971-present, Electronic Technician.)

Marion, Donald J. Manchester, New Hampshire, January 20, 1984. (Portsmouth Naval Shipyard, 1951-1971, Radio Mechanic, Electronics Technician, Electronics and Sonar Equipment Installer. Tiger Team supervisor at Holy Loch, Scotland, Electronics advisor in Mutual Defense Assistance Program to Spain and Turkey.)

McConnell, Robert F. Hampton, New Hampshire, December 1, 1983. (United States Navy, 1942-1964, navigator and journalist, *USS Seal, USS Conger, USS Albacore*, 1956-1960, *USS Nautilus, USS Haddock, USS Sea Lion, USS Crevalle*. Chief of the Boat on the *Crevalle*; Portsmouth Naval Shipyard, 1961-1964, Assistant Public Information Officer and Aide to the Shipyard Commander.)

McLees, Gerald C. Portsmouth, New Hampshire, February 23, 1983. (United States Navy, 1934-1956, Electrician's Mate Second Class, *USS Squalus, USS Sailfish, USS Crevalle, USS Sea Leopard*; Portsmouth Naval Shipyard, 1957-1972, Electrician, Quality Assurance Control.)

Palfrey, Kennard. Portsmouth, New Hampshire, March 10, 1983. (Portsmouth Navy Yard, 1928-1963, Mechanic, Foundry Pattern Maker, Planning and Estimating Shop.)

Pitts, George. New Castle, New Hampshire, February 24, 1983. (Portsmouth Navy Yard, 1940-1970, Draftsman, Designer, Design Department.)

Poss, Edgar L. Eliot, Maine, October 21, 1983. (United States Army, 1934-1938; United States Navy, 1938 - 1954, *USS Grenadier, USS Grayling, USS Threadfin, USS Spikefish, USS Grouper, USS Tusk, USS Tigrone, USS Sea Robin, USS Pomodon,* Radioman.)

Rowe, John F. Newington, New Hampshire, February 3, 1984. (United States Naval Reserve, 1937-1946, 1940 war duty volunteer; *USS Lark,* minelayer; Portsmouth Naval Shipyard, United States Naval Reserve Center, 1946-1949, Naval Reserve Center Officer.)

Russell, Howell. Portsmouth, New Hampshire, January 26, 1984. (Portsmouth Navy Yard, 1943, apprentice machinist; David W. Taylor Model Basin, Carderock, Maryland, 1946-1974, apprentice model maker, Acoustics Laboratory engineer, Plastic Technologist, Project Manager; Supervisor and Branch Manager, 1974.)

Shea, John. Rye, New Hampshire, February 21, 1984. (Portsmouth Naval Shipyard, 1954 - present, Electronics Technician, Noise Sound Reduction Specialist.)

Smith, Frederick H. "Pete," Jr. Newington, New Hampshire, February 23, 1984. (United States Navy, 1948-1971, tender *USS Sperry, USS Sea Lion, USS Irex, USS Dogfish, USS Sailfish (SS572), USS Barbel, USS Sablefish;* Portsmouth Naval Shipyard, 1962 - 1964, Assistant Planning and Estimating Superintendent on Type Desk; *USS Albacore,* 1964-1966, Engineering Officer; *USS Croaker,* 1966-1968, Executive Officer; Portsmouth Naval Shipyard, 1968-1971, Ship Superintendent. Production Department; Assistant Planning and Estimating Superintendent, Planning Department.)

Sousae, Jack F. Gonic, New Hampshire, March 24, 1983. (United States Navy, 1942-1972; *USS Seal; USS Swordfish,* 1958-1961, Senior Superintendent of Nuclear Construction.)

Van Billiard, Russell. Portsmouth, New Hampshire, February 5, 1984.(Portsmouth Naval Shipyard, 1951 - present except three years (1953 - 1957) as Naval Ordnance Officer. Design of Submarine Ordnance; Engineer Supervisor, Design Division; Fleet Support Type Desk.)

White, Frederick. New Castle, New Hampshire, February 23, 1983. (Portsmouth Navy Yard, 1935-1969; 1940-1944, Quarterman; 1944-1959, Master, Rigger Shop; 1959 - 1969, Service Group Superintendent, Woodworking, Paint, Riggings and Temporary Services.)

Whitney, Percy. Kittery, Maine, March 23, 1983. (Portsmouth Navy Yard, 1941-1972, Apprentice rising to Superintendent of the Foundry and Patterns.)

Woods, Eldredge B. "Bud." Kittery, Maine, April 18, 1983. (Portsmouth Naval Shipyard, 1948 - 1971, Naval Architect; Supervisor, Hydrodynamics and Launching Division.)

Index

About the Author

Walking up the gangplank with *The Piscataqua Gundalow: Workhorse for a Tidal Basin Empire* stuffed in his duffel bag, Richard E. Winslow III is a familiar shipmate to Portsmouth Marine Society readers.

Turning his attention to Portsmouth submarines has been a happy choice for his second Society endeavor. Winslow's association with the Portsmouth Naval Shipyard began almost forty years ago. As a youngster he accompanied his father on a tour of a captured German U-boat docked at the Shipyard.

In addition to his books on the gundalow and the American Civil War, Winslow is the Associate Editor of *The Papers of Henry Clay, Volume 7, Secretary of State, January 1, 1828–March 4, 1829* (1982).

Winslow is also a researcher and librarian at the Portsmouth Public Library and the Portsmouth Historical Society. The latter is located in the historic John Paul Jones House, where Winslow and the hostesses can almost hear Jones's footsteps on the creaking floors in the adjoining rooms.